D0555087

Battered Woman Syndrome as a Legal Defense

History, Effectiveness and Implications

BRENDA L. RUSSELL

McFarland & Company, Inc., Publishers

Jefferson, North Carolina, and London

LIBRARY OF CONGRESS CATALOGUING-IN-PUBLICATION DATA

Russell, Brenda L.
    Battered woman syndrome as a legal defense : history,
effectiveness and implications / Brenda L. Russell
        p.   cm.
    Includes bibliographical references and index.

    ISBN 978-0-7864-5883-7
    softcover : 50# alkaline paper ∞

    1. Self-defense (Law)—United States. 2. Battered woman
syndrome—United States. 3. Abused women—Legal status, laws,
etc.—United States. 4. Evidence (Law)—United States.
5. Law—Psychological aspects—United States. 6. Sex
discrimination in crimal justice administration—United States.
I. Title.
KF9246.R87   2010
345.73'04—dc22   2010024750

British Library cataloguing data are available

Cover images ©2010 Photodisc and Shutterstock

Manufactured in the United States of America

McFarland & Company, Inc., Publishers
  Box 611, Jefferson, North Carolina 28640
    www.mcfarlandpub.com

For my parents,
CARL AND JANICE RUSSELL,
and for my son,
DILLON.

Acknowledgments

I would like to express my appreciation to the reviewers that provided substantial insight and suggested improvements for this text. In particular, I would like to thank James Fuller for his editorial assistance on a much earlier draft of this book and Mark E. Zimmer, Esquire, and shareholder with Mogel, Speidel, Bobb & Kershner, P.C., law firm located in Reading, Pennsylvania, who evaluated the legal points in this book. Similarly, I would like to thank Cheryl Terrance for her review and comments of an earlier draft and Jason Tremblay for his editorial expertise. I would like to thank my student assistants from Penn State Berks, Amro Fadel, Abby Hafer, Heather Stapleton and Emily Fitzpatrick, for their assistance in collecting resources and offering helpful ideas, and my research colleagues Shane Kraus and Laurie Ragatz. I would also like to thank my family and friends for all their support during this process. Without their support and encouragement this would not be possible. I'd like to give a huge heartfelt thank you to my son, Dillon Russell-Kenniston, and Rick Balian for their unwavering support.

Table of Contents

Preface

When you think of a victim of domestic violence, what comes to mind? Most people picture a heterosexual female being abused by her male partner. This is not surprising as the work of feminist scholars over the last 30 years has led to an increased awareness of the topic of violence against women. Once considered a private matter and largely ignored by neighbors and the legal system, domestic violence is now a widely recognized phenomenon where prevention and services are abundant for female victims of abuse. As a result of earlier feminist movements, society has largely acknowledged abuse toward women and continues to work successfully toward condemning violence. Yet, as society has grown more familiar with understanding and condemning victimization toward women, recent scholarly debates on the topic of intimate partner violence argue that though their motives may differ, women can be just as abusive as men. Such gender symmetry is the crux of much scholarly debate in sociological and psychological circles. A growing amount of research has demonstrated that both men and women suffer from intimate partner violence. Researchers and scholars are only just beginning to recognize issues associated with intimate partner violence against heterosexual men and individuals in same-sex relationships. While society has come to associate females with victimization, it has been slow to accept the possibility that females can also be responsible for violence against an intimate partner. The reluctance to believe that females can also be perpetrators of abuse is controversial in nature and has its origins in gender roles and gender stereotyping as well as the historical vestiges that fall on the heels of the battered woman syndrome.

The battered woman syndrome was originally believed to aid women in their struggle for equality in the legal system, and while it has aided in the quest for equality (primarily in self-defense law), use of the syndrome has also led to some unexpected backlash effects. Since it began to gain momentum in the courts, many scholars were afraid that the syndrome had created a standard to which all battered women would be compared. The word *syndrome* suggests that individuals suffering from the syndrome would experience similar symptomology. However, while there may be some commonalities among victims of battering, all victims look and respond differently. If a self-proclaimed victim's actions do not correspond to a stereotype of what a victim of battering is supposed to be, then how are they evaluated?

This book examines the controversy over the use of the battered woman syndrome (or more recently, the battered person syndrome) in the courts, primarily relating its effectiveness in legal decision making when victims of battering turn to homicide in response to a partner's aggression or threat. The book also addresses the evolution of the syndrome and contributions made by psychologists and legal scholars that aid the understanding of the use of the syndrome as evidence in trials of battered women who kill. In particular, issues of potential bias in the courtroom are explored.

I have studied this phenomenon for over 15 years and conducted research on the use of the syndrome and found that individuals do have stereotypes of victims of battering and these stereotypes can negatively affect decisions of culpability in criminal trials. In fact, my research explores the extent to which individuals held stereotypes about battered women and how these stereotypes influenced judgments of culpability in cases of self-defense. This research found that the more "typical" the defendant was compared to an "atypical" battered woman defendant, the more lenient the verdict. This led to additional studies on how heterosexual men and individuals in same-sex relationships would be evaluated if they were to use evidence of the syndrome in a criminal case. Courts have generously extended admission of expert testimony about battered woman syndrome into cases where women commit contract killings, child neglect, or murder and allege their actions were the product of coercion or duress. But what if a heterosexual man or a homosexual man or woman were to ask for such testimony in these cases? Would it be allowed? If so, would their cases be evaluated differently because of the nature of their relationship or gender?

This book explores the potential backlash effects that may occur as the result of our own stereotypes of what victims of battering are supposed to be. These backlash effects are, to some extent, rooted in stereotypes and latent discrimination toward gender, sexual orientation, color, ethnicity, and age. Stereotypes are used as a basis for many decisions. This is a normal process and, indeed, practical. However, such stereotypes may cloud judgments, particularly when evaluating whether someone who kills their partner is justified.

Since research on the impact of the battered woman syndrome and the process of juror decision making is in its infancy, many important questions remain as to the interaction between juror decision making and evidence of the syndrome. The resulting conclusions of the examination of the legal, empirical, and theoretical foundations of the syndrome invite the reader to question whether battered woman syndrome actually exists, and consequently, whether testimony in the courtroom is appropriate. I speak to the fact that regardless of the syndrome's existence, a shared schema of a battered woman does exist, which can ultimately affect all who use the syndrome. By using empirical research and social psychological theory, I argue that it is to this standard that victims of battering who fatally strike back against their abusers are compared. Hence, juror decisions of culpability may then rest upon how well a battered woman (or battered partner) "fits the syndrome" in accordance with the juror's own stereotypes and as described by the defense.

This book has been written to provide readers with the most recent information regarding the topic of domestic violence and the use of the syndrome in the courts. It is not intended to persuade, but rather to offer a domain in which to think critically about the issues surrounding the topic of the battered woman's syndrome and its use in the courtroom today. In essence, I write to enlighten the general public, with the hope society will eventually change to incorporate more gender-neutral perspectives and promote sociological equality for all.

Introduction

I want to remind us that we have won what we now have because we, or others before us, struggled for it. It was not given to us. We had to be responded to because we publicly declared that women could not continue to be beaten. If we lose the political meaning of what we have worked for, the spirit of our work places, and our view of women's oppression, then although we still have won victories and still have protected women, we will have also lost something essential—our part in a struggle for human liberation [Schechter, 1982, p. 257].

Written almost 30 years ago, these words continue to ring true, yet the struggle for human liberation goes on. The evolution of the battered women's movement has made substantial strides over the years. Domestic violence is no longer a taboo topic hidden under a shroud of embarrassment or behind closed doors. Thanks to the feminist political movement, society now has sincere public concern and awareness for violence against women; yet with this shift have come complexities in the ways in which battered women are—and should be—treated within the legal system.

As the battered woman syndrome developed in social science literature and within the general public, legislative changes followed. Previously, if a woman committed homicide against a partner who was battering her, the typical defense was insanity. Since 1983, courts increasingly have included the battered woman syndrome as a component of expert testimony in the courtroom, and self-proclaimed battered woman who kill their partners now typically use the law of self-defense to explain their actions. While the battered woman syndrome is not an official legal defense of its own, most states allow expert testimony regarding the syndrome to aid judges and jurors in their decision-making processes concerning claims of self-defense. Furthermore, the battered woman syndrome is not considered a psychiatric diagnosis, nor does it exist in the *Diagnostic and Statistical Manual* (DSM IV, 1994) used by psychologists and psychiatrists to diagnose psychiatric illnesses. While it should also be noted that some battered women actually are afflicted with psychiatric disorders as a result of domestic violence, such as Post Traumatic Stress Disorder (PTSD) or major depressive disorder (MDD), not all battered women exhibit psychiatric symptomology or diagnoses. This does not negate the fact that victims of domestic violence experience trauma or abuse.

This book is intended to introduce readers to the battered woman syndrome, one of the foremost theories used to capture the plight of an estimated two to four million women assaulted by male partners each year. It provides an overview of the development of the battered woman syndrome, particularly as it is used to support a plea of self-defense by women who kill their batterers, as well as the controversies and difficulties which have arisen as the syndrome has become more accepted and expanded in its scope. In particular, it explores the ramifications for the defense if the defendant in question does not fit the stereotype of the battered woman in the minds of the judge or jury. In this regard, this text provides a comprehensive look at the evolution of the battered woman syndrome and its role in the court system.

Over the past decade, three important issues have surfaced regarding the use of the syndrome as evidence in the courts that call for examination. First, courts around the world have expanded the use of the syndrome as evidence in an increasingly wide range of cases without reviewing or calling into question the methodological rigor on which the syndrome is based. This broad acceptance of the syndrome comes despite new requirements set forth by the U.S. Supreme Court (*Daubert v. Merrell Dow Pharmaceuticals, Inc*, 1993) that call for more stringent methodological review, rigor, and acceptance of scientific research before it can be admitted as evidence in a case. As courts continue to expand the use of the syndrome as evidence in cases, they have neglected to re-evaluate the methodological context within which the syndrome was defined. In the wake of Daubert and subsequent legal decisions known as the Daubert Trilogy (*General Electric Company v. Joiner*, 1997; *Kumho Tire Co. v. Carmichael*, 1999), it is likely that if such re-evaluations were to be conducted, the admissibility of expert testimony about the battered woman syndrome in the courtroom would be called into question.

Second, there is an increasing amount of empirical and theoretical analysis regarding the battered woman syndrome and a shift away from wholehearted acceptance of the syndrome as a form of evidence in the courtroom. Yet despite the fact that many scholars now avoid "syndrome" terminology in favor of discussing "battering and its effects," which emphasizes the context of the situation and circumstances of the abused (lack of resources, risks associated with leaving the batterer, inadequate response from law enforcement) as opposed to focusing on the victim's pathology, legal precedent in many jurisdictions continues to rely upon the term "battered woman syndrome." Scholars (Biggers, 2005; Douglas, 1987; Dutton, 1996) have consistently noted that the use of the syndrome as evidence often leads to the perception that the defendant in question is mentally unstable. This can cause significant difficulties, because in order to claim self-defense, the defense counsel must demonstrate that the defendant's actions were reasonable given the circumstances, and mental instability is often at odds with acting in a rational or reasonable manner. Moreover, the mere suggestion that a woman is mentally unstable or irrational can be counteractive in ensuing civil cases such as child custody, as she may have difficulty demonstrating that she is a "fit" parent (Follingstad, 2003). Many contemporary scholars and theorists believe the use of social framework evidence, which relies on the state-of-the-art research to provide a context for a particular situation, can address a victim's responses in the context of their circumstances and social structure without focusing on the defendant's reaction as a pathological response to their environment (Plumm & Terrance, 2009) and can be used in cases where women kill their abusers to help provide a context for the event instead of focusing on the mental state of the defendant. However, research on this topic is not yet substantiated.

Lastly, and a central argument of this book, is that the introduction of the battered woman syndrome, as presented to the public and legal system, has inadvertently created a standard to which battered women are compared (Blackman, 1990; Crocker, 1985; Dowd, 1992; Ferraro, 2003; Russell & Melillo, 2006; Sheehy, Stubbs & Tolmie, 1992). This brings forth a related argument that while the use of expert testimony relating to the syndrome is clearly helpful for some defendants, battered women who are atypical with regard to the characteristics and experiences associated with the syndrome are unlikely to see such benefits, as jurors may judge them more harshly if they do not fit their perceptions of what a battered woman should be.

There is a surprising lack of empirical research on the effects of the use of expert evidence of the battered woman syndrome by the defense in cases where defendants do not fit the stereotypical characteristics of the syndrome. Since the term "battered woman syndrome" was first coined, scholars have cautioned that the syndrome would lead to a stereotype all battered women would be expected to fit, such as being passive or socially isolated. In fact, 30 years after its introduction into the courtroom, very few studies have empirically examined the existence and content of stereotypes of battered women and their effects. While courts around the world are accepting the use of the syndrome as evidence in an increasing variety of cases, it is unclear whether the admission of such evidence actually assists jurors in making more informed decisions, or whether it may activate jurors' stereotypes and affect their legal decisions in ways which may negatively affect the defendant's case. Many scholars had asserted that the syndrome produced a standard to which defendants would be compared, but research on the topic was severely lacking. Over the past ten years or so, preliminary research suggests that stereotypes of battered women do exist and when mock jurors are provided with expert evidence regarding the battered woman syndrome, defendants who do not fit the stereotype associated with it end up faring worse in our legal system than do those who match the stereotype associated with the syndrome. However, research on this topic continues to be scarce, and most studies on the effectiveness of evidence of the battered woman syndrome or battering and its effects had only been explored when the defendant was a woman claiming she fatally retaliated against her abuser in self-defense. The battered woman syndrome, and related social framework evidence of battering and its effects, is commonly used by women in criminal cases including murder, child neglect and abuse, duress (coercion by the batterer to commit a crime), and civil cases (divorce, child custody, contracts, and orders of protection). More recently, evidence of the syndrome is also being injected into cases where the defendant is not a heterosexual woman. For instance, Carl Colberg shot and killed his son, a New York State trooper, after claiming that he was a battered parent who suffered years of abuse at the hands of his son (*People v. Colberg*, 1999). In this case, the courts agreed that the battered woman syndrome should be gender neutral, and Carl Colberg was the first man to use the battered person syndrome in New York State. Now adopted by many states, the battered person syndrome is beginning to be used in situations including same-sex relationships, heterosexual men battered by women, and familial disputes. So what happens in these cases? Does changing the battered woman syndrome to the battered person syndrome or battered spouse syndrome affect legal decisions? What are the implications of these cases, particularly when the defendant does not fit the stereotype of what many perceive to be the typical victim of battering?

Battering can happen to anyone, and each individual should have the right to use the battered person syndrome as a vehicle to aid in legal decision making. However, perceptions about traditional gender roles, attitudes, prejudices, and biases inherent in most individuals make it difficult for many people to understand situations that don't seem to fit into their preconceived beliefs about who can and cannot be a victim of abuse. If the syndrome is used as an explanation for a person's behavior, the syndrome itself creates a typology from which the actual situation is compared to existing stereotypes.

When the circumstances do not fit into the rendition of the story (i.e., schema or stereotype) that has been created, then using the syndrome can actually work against individuals who use it to bolster their defense.

This book has been written to provide the most recent information regarding the use of the battered woman syndrome. It is intended to offer a platform for thinking critically about the issues surrounding the topic of the battered woman syndrome and its use in the courtroom today. While many researchers and scholars (Dutton, 1996; Ferraro, 2003; Schneider, 1986; Schuller, 2002; Terrance & Matheson, 2003) have questioned the efficacy of the syndrome evidence in the courtroom and in society, the syndrome's proponents also have strong arguments as to why it is still needed for individual and societal purposes. In essence, this book is intended to enlighten students, scholars, legal practitioners, and the general public, with the hope that society will eventually change to incorporate more gender and race neutral perspectives and promote equality for all. Within this context, readers will notice that a recurrent theme within the book is that anyone can be a victim or perpetrator of domestic violence. Yet, most people assume that victims of domestic violence are women. This is a key premise of this book. Gender is attached to the term "battered woman syndrome." For this reason many people may have difficulty understanding that intimate partner violence can be initiated by anyone. The majority of research on this topic relates specifically to women, and for this reason the book focuses primarily on domestic violence against women. However, in order to incorporate more gender and race neutral perspectives, individuals have to become receptive to the fact that intimate partner violence is wrong no matter who initiates it.

In order to provide a platform that can address all of these issues, this book has been divided into three parts. The first part provides a general description of the problem associated with the use of the syndrome in the courts. Then a historical analysis of society's attitude toward domestic violence is necessary to better understand the problem of battering and helps to provide the framework for understanding how societal views toward gender are tied to perceptions of abuse. Keeping within the historical framework, a general overview of theoretical views and academic interest of victims and perpetrators of abuse is introduced to demonstrate how the various theoretical perspectives of violence have helped to shape academic and public views, as well as understanding how individuals respond to abuse. This section tries to tease out mythical perceptions of victims of battering from reality. In this regard, social perceptions of battered women are examined as victims but also as aggressors in relationships. To extend this even further, incidence and prevalence of heterosexual men and individuals in same-sex relationships who experience domestic violence are also addressed. Lastly, this section attempts to further distinguish reality from myth and recognize how culture and diversity plays a pivotal role in understanding abuse. Issues associated with diversity such as ethnicity, culture, and socio-economic status have been found to be related to the reality of abuse. Some individuals are more likely to become victims or remain in abusive situations than others. It is also crucial that the diversity of abuse be recognized, particularly when it may be related to individuals who kill their abusers.

The second part of this book provides information on the legal aspects of domestic abuse, primarily when women kill their abusers. This section begins with an analysis of the battered woman syndrome with all its glory and shortcomings. Emphasis on the evolution of the theory is provided as well as more contemporary alternatives used in courtrooms today. Oftentimes, when women fatally strike back at their abusers, they use the law of self-defense to describe how their actions were justified given the circumstances. For this reason, a brief introduction to the law of self-defense is provided. Once the battered woman syndrome was allowed into the courts, experts were needed to explain characteristics associated with the syndrome to judges and jurors in order to help them make more informed decisions about the case. The evolution of expert testimony in the court system and the process by which experts have been allowed to testify in self-defense cases and the content of such testimony is explored. This book is primarily concerned with exploring two questions: whether or not expert testimony on the battered woman syndrome (or alternative forms of testimony such as on battering and its effects) actually helps the defendant, and whether testimony should be allowed in the courtroom based on the laws of admissibility of expert testimony. A discussion of the legal issues that pertain to interjecting expert testimony into a case provides the groundwork for inquiry into these questions.

The last part of the book introduces some of the psychological theories that explain how individuals make judgments about others and how these judgments underlie legal decision making. As these theories are introduced, they should enlighten readers about how stereotypes are created and the gendered nature of how domestic violence is perceived. The chapters lay a foundation for a critical analysis of determining whether the syndrome actually exists and how sociopsychological theories impact the ability to objectively evaluate defendants in domestic violence cases. The last chapter discusses some of the ways the future of the syndrome can be redefined.

It is hoped that this book will provide opportunities for readers to explore the role of domestic violence and the way gender issues impact personal and legal perceptions of abuse. Over the past thirty years society has struggled to accept the fact that women are primarily the victims of abuse. Now that violence against women is recognized, our minds must be open to the fact that abuse is abuse, no matter who is involved. Once domestic violence is understood beyond the context of gender roles and identified as abuse that should not be tolerated by anyone, only then can the human struggle for liberation continue.

A Note on Terminology

There are a variety of ways one can address the terminology associated with the syndrome. For instance, the battered woman syndrome, the battered woman's syndrome, and the battered women's syndrome are terms commonly cited by scholars and laypersons. An analysis of frequently used databases (e.g., PsychInfo, Sociological Abstract, Criminal Justice Abstracts, Proquest, and LexisNexis) found the term "battered woman syndrome" was used most frequently. Therefore, for the sake of consistency, the term "battered woman syndrome" will be used in this text.

CHAPTER 1

A General Description of the Problem

What comes to mind when you think of a victim of battering? Stereotypes are often used as a basis for many decisions. This is a normal process and is indeed practical. However, as the research shows, stereotypes may also cloud judgments. Certain stereotypes may have some basis in reality while others may not. Some battered women are passive, some are financially dependent, some have children and some do not. Battered persons can be anyone: male or female, heterosexual or homosexual, and from any background, ethnicity, or socioeconomic status; yet when many of us hear about a victim of battering, we have preconceived notions of what characteristics victims should or should not have.

Consider some of the following hypothetical scenarios:

SCENARIO A

Angela is a 27-year-old Caucasian woman who has been in an abusive relationship since she was 18 years old. She and her husband John live in Alabama, where John started to assault her about a year into their relationship. The beatings got increasingly severe. One day, Angela was making dinner for her four children and for John when he came home drunk and began verbally abusing her about her inability to make a decent dinner. She got up to go to the bedroom and he followed her. Angela knew that he was coming after her to beat her. A shotgun was sitting by the wall in the bedroom. Angela picked it up and aimed it at him. She told him to back off so she could leave with the children. He continued to come toward her and she shot him. She was charged with second-degree murder, and claimed her acts were in self-defense. A jury of her peers found her not guilty by reason of self-defense.

SCENARIO B

Jessica, 35, was a principal at the local elementary school in Connecticut. She was fairly well-known in town and respected by many. She was financially independent and had no children. What most people did not know, however, was that Jessica was repeatedly abused both verbally and physically by her boyfriend of three years, Scott. She had been hospitalized just two months before with a broken nose. However, she told the doctor that she had bumped into a door. Jessica had tried to leave her boyfriend before, but each time he would woo her back. Things would be better for a while, then Scott would become abusive again. Jessica was actually seeing another man and trying to get out of the relationship with Scott. On the night Scott died, he had come over to Jessica's house to discuss their relationship. Jessica could tell that Scott was already agitated before Jessica could begin to discuss a break-up. Scott yelled at her, saying, "I know you've got a new boyfriend!" Jessica told him there was no need to yell, and this agitated him further. Scott started shouting and coming toward her with his fist clenched. She ordered him out of the house and Scott refused to leave. Instead, Scott yelled even louder and began coming after her in the kitchen. A knife was on the kitchen counter from dinner. Jessica picked it up and as Scott came toward her, she fatally stabbed him. Jessica was charged with second-degree murder. She claimed her behavior was self-defense. A jury of her peers, knowing Jessica was involved with another man, found her guilty of manslaughter. She was sentenced to seven years in prison.

SCENARIO C

David and Joe lived in New York where they had been lovers for over a year. However, David had become verbally and physically abusive toward Joe almost immediately after they had started seeing each other. Joe's friends could see that David was abusive and encouraged Joe to leave David, but Joe wanted to try to save the relationship. Despite the abuse, he loved David. David was home when Joe came back from his friends' house. David became angry that Joe was with "those jerks" again, saying Joe could not see them again because they didn't like David. Joe said he couldn't do that. In anger, David hit Joe on the side of the head. Joe fell to the floor. David came at Joe on the floor and began kicking him. Joe found a heavy statue on the floor and aimed it at David. He knocked David down, and they fought. Joe struck David repeatedly in the head with the statue and David died. Joe was charged with second-degree murder, but claimed his actions were in self-defense. A jury found him guilty of manslaughter. He was sentenced to six years in prison.

Scenario D

Peter had been married to Danielle for two years. Their marriage was fraught with difficulties. Danielle was a heavy-set woman who stood almost six feet tall, while Peter's average body made him approximately three inches shorter than Danielle. The difference in height and weight had never bothered Peter, but a year into their marriage Danielle started physically abusing him. Danielle always hit Peter with her fists, saying she was "just kidding," but it was often painful. In fits of anger, Danielle would strike Peter over and over again. Peter was brought up never to hit women, but sometimes he would hit her back to defend himself. Peter felt like he couldn't tell anyone about Danielle's behavior for fear he would be laughed at. On the night Danielle was killed, Peter had come home from work late. Danielle was angry that he had not phoned to say he would be late. Danielle began punching him in the head and chest the moment he walked through the door. She actually grabbed a frying pan and hit him over the head. At this point, Peter was trying to hold her back, but she kept punching. Peter fell to the ground and wept. While he was on the floor, Danielle started to kick Peter. Peter grabbed Danielle's leg and she flipped over. Peter then pinned her on the floor and tried to stop her attack. Danielle seemed to calm down. Peter proceeded to get off of Danielle. Once Peter got off of Danielle, she told Peter she was not through with him and that he "was going to die tonight." Danielle then went into the bedroom and retired for the evening. While she was sleeping, Peter walked upstairs and picked up a gun that was in the closet. He proceeded to shoot Danielle three times while she slept. Peter then called the authorities and described what happened. Danielle was later pronounced dead from gunshot wounds. Peter was charged with second-degree murder. He claimed his actions were in self-defense. A jury of his peers found Peter guilty of second-degree murder. He was sentenced to 15 years in prison.

These scenarios illustrate both direct confrontational and non-confrontational situations. Expert evidence on violence in intimate relationships is often accepted in these cases. While a battered woman is typically the defendant, aspects of a battered person's psychology apply to battered men as well, and may be introduced at trial. The primary difference among these scenarios is the defendants. Scenario A is probably the most common perception of what constitutes a battered woman. In scenario B, the defendant experiences a direct confrontation but has characteristics not typically associated with a battered woman (i.e., she was independent and involved in another relationship). Scenario C also depicts a case of direct confrontation, though the defendant is male and homosexual. Scenario D portrays the defendant as a heterosexual male, much less likely to be characteristic of a battered person.

All of these scenarios end with the same result—the killing of the abuser. However, juries of their peers evaluated the cases differently. For instance, in the most typical situation (scenario A), the defendant received a verdict of not guilty by reason of self-defense. Defendants in scenarios B and C were convicted of manslaughter and sentenced to six and seven years, respectively. Finally, the heterosexual male defendant in scenario D was convicted of second-degree murder and sentenced to 15 years. While fictitious, these scenarios illustrate how different kinds of abusers and victims are perceived differently because they are filtered through stereotypes and biases. Simply, some of these cases feel more typical than others both with regard to our perception of who gets battered in intimate relationships and with regard to what constitutes self-defense. Furthermore, such scenarios can become even more complex when other people are involved, such as situations in which the victim is forced to allow an injured child to die rather than seek medical attention, or is coerced into becoming a drug mule by the threat of violence to herself and others.

In this book, the role of the battered woman syndrome (and battering and its effects) in society and the court system will be examined, primarily in cases of self-defense. The preceding scenarios were presented for two reasons: first, it should be recognized that when most people think of victims of battering, they think of heterosexual women. Battered women are primarily the victims of intimate partner violence, but male spouses, cohabitating partners, and individuals in same-sex relationships can all be victims of abuse as well. The latter groups are less likely to be recognized as victims of abuse, and certainly the body of resources available for these groups and general research knowledge on the subject is severely limited. Second, individuals tend to evaluate scenarios (or cases) through a lens of expectation based on our experience. Even though all cases of domestic violence differ, most people have created a mental script of what they believe constitutes a victim of battering. Thirty years ago, battering was considered a private matter and evidence suggested the public believed victims of battering were masochistic, passive, had low self-esteem, and could willingly leave their abuser if they chose. While the battered woman syndrome was effective in bringing much needed attention to the matter, it also helped to create a standard to which all battered women are compared. This standard guides general beliefs about who may or may not be likely to be battered. This, in turn, can affect legal decision making, particularly when the defendant does not fit into these general beliefs.

When Women Kill Their Abusers

Each year, thousands of American women—and some men—are regularly abused, both physically and psychologically by their partners (Straus & Gelles, 1990). At some point in the relationships, some women respond by killing their abusers. In fact, women are responsible for approximately 11 to 15 percent of all homicides in the United States (Uniform Crime Reports, 1997; Roberts, 2003). Of course, women murder for reasons other than abuse. They murder non-relatives or acquaintances, but are much more likely to murder someone they know: children, parents, other relatives, and intimate partners (Mann, 1996).

Research shows that when women kill, they are more likely to kill an intimate partner than are men (Straus, 2005), which strongly suggests that when violence is severe enough in the home to result in death, women are the primary perpetrators (Straus, 2005). In other words, males are responsible for a larger percentage of homicides overall compared to females, but if the percentage of women who commit homicide is only considered, these women are more likely to kill an intimate partner. Many researchers have found evidence suggesting that such high rates of women murdering their male partners can be attributed to self-defense, retaliation, or acts of desperation after years of victimization (Browne, 1987; Browne & Williams, 1989; Grant, 1995; Jurik & Gregware, 1989; Jurik & Winn, 1990; Maguigan, 1991; Mann, 1996). While the consequences of the woman's actions will vary, women who fatally strike back at their abusers are often charged with second-degree murder or manslaughter. In order to find the defendant guilty of second-degree murder, jurors must believe she intentionally committed murder or blatantly disregarded the fact that her behavior would cause death or harm. What distinguishes murder from manslaughter is the state of mind of the defendant. Courts rely upon malice as the distinguishing factor between murder and manslaughter. Second-degree murder and voluntary manslaughter are intentional killings, while involuntary manslaughter is considered unintentional homicide (Brody, Acker, & Logan, 2008).

When the issues of murder and self-defense are examined in particular, the focus is primarily on the mental state of the defendant at the time of the crime. Often in cases of manslaughter the defendant is prompted to kill by a sudden passion or great provocation, and defendants use diminished capacity to mitigate charges. Diminished capacity is frequently used when the defendant is not insane, but rather suffers from emotional distress, a physical condition, or some other factor that led them to commit the crime because they did not appreciate the true nature of the crime. In essence, what distinguishes murder from manslaughter are mitigating circumstances that would partially excuse an intentional killing. In contrast, self-defense is a legal defense used when a defendant reasonably believed it was necessary to defend him- or herself against another person's use of unlawful force. When defendants' actions are deemed necessary for self-defense, their actions are justified according to law; however, if their actions are not perceived as reasonable (that their belief that defending themselves from imminent harm by using lethal force was really not a reasonable perception), then the defense may attempt to classify the defendant's actions as imperfect self-defense.

The most common plea of defense involving murder or manslaughter of an abusive husband or boyfriend is self-defense (Faigman, 1987; Jurik & Winn, 1990; Maguigan, 1991; Pagelow, 1992). A verdict of not guilty by reason of self-defense would suggest that jurors believed that the defendant's behavior was justified given the circumstances. However, attempts to use the law of self-defense in such cases have been fraught with legal difficulties. Battered women's claims of self-defense are often complex and fail to fit neatly into the classical self-defense paradigm. In order to ascertain the defendants' situational and psychological realities and assist jurors in understanding them, the courts have embraced evidence of battered woman syndrome theory in the form of expert testimony in many cases of abusive partner homicide.

The Battered Woman Syndrome

The battered woman syndrome theory was first introduced to the public in 1979 by Lenore Walker in a book entitled *The Battered Woman*. Walker had conducted research on self-proclaimed battered women and found that many of the women shared similar experiences and personality characteristics. In 1984, Walker coined the term "battered woman syndrome" (Walker, 1984), in which she identified two key factors which she argued were associated with all battered women. The first is "learned helplessness." Walker first adopted this term (Seligman, 1975) to describe the lack of control women felt in an abusive relationship and to provide an explanation as to why women would not simply leave an abuser. The second factor is a "cycle of violence." Walker noted a three-phase pattern of abuse that described a mounting tension building up to abusive incidents, leading to acute battering and escalation of abuse, followed by the abuser's remorse and promises to stop the abuse. She further described additional personality characteristics, which she argued were shared by all battered women, including: belief that the abuse was their fault, passivity associated with learned helplessness, traditionalist views of gender roles within the home, and low self-esteem. Walker asserted that these patterns associated with battered women could be recognized as a syndrome (a cluster of identifiable features). Walker (1993) described the battered woman syndrome as "part of a recognized pattern of psychological symptoms called post-traumatic stress disorder (PTSD), reported in the psychological literature as produced by repeated exposure to trauma" (Walker, 1993, p. 133) and as a "group of usually transient psychological symptoms that are frequently observed in a particular recognizable pattern in women who report being abused" (Walker, 1993, p. 135).

Controversy and Debate About the Battered Woman Syndrome

Many legal scholars and social scientists have argued that the introduction of an overly singular battered woman syndrome to the legal system following Walker's theory has inadvertently created a standard against which all battered women are compared (Blackman, 1990; Crocker, 1985; Dowd, 1992; Ferraro, 2003; Russell & Melillo, 2006; Sheehy, Stubbs, & Tolmie, 1992). Defendants who claim to be battered may be at a disadvantage when their experiences or behaviors deviate from the standard. Each individual embraces stereotypes or misperceptions about battered women. What happens when a defendant does not fit the concept, or stereotype, of what a battered woman should be?

Research has investigated whether laypersons actually embrace "stereotypes" of battered women and how those stereotypes influence legal decision making (see Russell & Melillo, 2006, for an in-depth review). Russell and Mellilo (2006) argued that while researchers assume that passivity or lack of social networks (helpful friends and family) are a piece of what some might consider a stereotype associated with battered women, it is still unknown whether people actually embrace stereotypes of battered women, the content of such stereotypes, and if such stereotypes exist, whether they affect legal decision making.

Previous research on the topic had only investigated one characteristic assumed to be "atypical" (i.e., passivity v. aggression or social support v. no social support) with regard to battered women homicide defendants. Most of these studies found that when one characteristic of the defendant was manipulated, it had virtually no effect on legal decision making (Schuller & Hasting, 1996; Terrance & Matheson, 2003). Although these studies offer insight, it was evident that research was still needed to understand what information is used for juror decision making. Other scholars (Farrell & Holmes, 1991) have noted that cases that deviate only slightly from the stereotyped category are readily filled in with stereotypical imagery, and often pose little problem for decision makers. This may explain the lack of significant findings in studies that manipulated only one (typical or atypical) characteristic of the defendant. In other words, because each of these studies manipulated only one or two exceptional features, perhaps it was easier to fill in these features with stereotypical imagery. Based on a social psychological phenomenon called prototype theory, which describes how individuals categorize knowledge and process information using stereotypes, it was likely that the additive effects of portraying multiple attributes would better reflect mock jurors' prototypes of a battered woman and influence verdict decisions.

In order to examine whether stereotypes would affect legal decision making, Russell and Melillo (2006) conducted a series of research studies. The first phase assessed whether individuals actually held stereotypes of battered women. The second phase analyzed the degree to which participants believed some of the characteristics were associated with the stereotype. Lastly, the extent to which stereotypes (i.e., passive v. aggressive history; type of case, confrontational v. non-confrontational; and gender of participant affected judgments of culpability. Researchers expected that participants would be least likely to convict when the characteristics of the defendant closely matched people's stereotypes of battered women, or when scenarios most closely matched the typical battered woman. In contrast, when the defendant was depicted as atypical, this would lead to harsher verdicts.

First, in order to determine whether people held stereotypes about battered women, the researchers conducted a preliminary study that consisted of a thought listing task where participants were asked to list all features they believed to be typical of a battered woman (social, psychological, physical, and behavioral). The results of this study found the most common features mentioned in the physical attribute category included having bruises, small in stature, thin or overweight, young or middle-aged, fragile and weary. Psychological attributes most often mentioned included fearful, anxious, guilt-ridden, angry and untrusting. Social attributes most often mentioned were a lack of social interaction, dependence on partner, poor, and little or no friends or social network. Lastly, attributes most often mentioned in the behavioral category included appeasing her partner, drug/alcohol addiction, hiding signs of abuse, and making excuses for her partner's behavior.

In phase two of the study, participants were asked to rate the extent to which they believed each attribute was representative of typical attributes of a battered woman. Those attributes that were rated the highest with regard to typical of a battered woman were included in the third phase of the study. Three attributes from each category (social, behavioral, physical and psychological) were included in a scenario that was designed to depict either a typical or atypical (using antonyms of typical attributes) female defendant accused of murdering her husband in either a confrontational or non-confrontational case as typical or atypical, and who had an aggressive or passive response history (i.e., a history of aggression or passivity toward their partner).

This research (Russell & Melillo, 2006) revealed that stereotypes of victims of battering are plentiful. Some of these commonly held beliefs (i.e., victims of abuse are passive, have children, and are dependent upon their partner) are consistent with research findings, but many are not, suggesting that many individuals' stereotypes or perceptions are simply wrong. Researchers also found that verdicts were directly influenced by the typicality and response history (passive v. aggressive) of the defendant. Defendants portrayed as atypical with an aggressive response history received the highest amounts of guilty verdicts and were perceived as less credible. Atypical defendants were less likely to be believed by mock jurors and perceived to have more options available to them compared to typical battered women. Conversely, typical defendants with passive response histories were most likely to receive verdicts of not guilty based on self-defense and found to be more credible.

The results of this study demonstrated three important issues. First, laypersons do, in fact, embrace stereotypes about battered women (i.e., battered women are passive, have children, have low socio-economic status [SES], etc). Second, this study provided strong support for the contention that defendants are more likely to have multiple attributes relating to the syndrome, and the more typical (or atypical) attributes defendants have, the more likely these attributes can influence judgments of culpability. Third, the importance of gender in evaluating judgments of culpability was evident. Although women were less likely to assign verdicts of second-degree murder, an equivalent number of men and women rendered verdicts of manslaughter. Women, however, rendered a verdict of not-guilty by self-defense significantly more often than men.

This research provides persuasive evidence that judgments of guilt and general culpability are influenced by the extent to which the defendant fits or does not fit the typology of a battered woman. It sheds light on the fact that battered women who do not fit the stereotype of a battered woman may be at a disadvantage in the courtroom.

Similarly, Ferraro (2003) provided excellent examples of how the legal system responds to women who "don't fit the standard of a woman or a battered woman" in situations where she was called as an expert to testify in self-defense homicide cases. In one case, the defendant was depicted by the prosecution as a "working class woman with no children; as a tough woman who could defend herself physically; and as an 'outrageous flirt' who did not fit the so-called typical image of a battered woman" (p. 116). The prosecution used witnesses to attest to the defendant's personality as "tough" to advance the notion that she could defend herself. Ferraro goes on to supply a host of additional cases and situations that demonstrate the criminal justice system's inclination to demonstrate how a woman fits or does not fit the syndrome.

Controversy swirls around exactly which cases should include evidence of the syndrome and which should not. In 2001, the battered wife defense came into question in Queensland, Australia. The case described a tumultuous 33-year marriage filled with verbal and emotional abuse. One evening, after another night of particularly nasty verbal assault, the defendant walked out to the shed in the family's backyard, grabbed a large piece of wood, and proceeded to hit his spouse in the back of the head three times. The battered spouse in this situation was Terry Goodfellow, a 58-year-old male and retired police detective who claimed his wife Beverly was an aggressor who made him feel as though he were trapped in the relationship. Terry claimed diminished capacity because he was not in control of his actions at the time of the killing. The court agreed, acquitting Terry of murder, and convicting him of the lesser charge of manslaughter, and he was sentenced to seven and a half years in jail.

This case sparked much debate about the use of the battered woman defense for men, with many advocates of the battered woman syndrome afraid that this case would open the door to men getting away with violence toward their spouses. A central tenet of the battered woman syndrome in Australia is that a woman has endured sustained abuse over a period of time. It is also assumed that she has become emotionally and financially dependent upon her male partner and ultimately feels trapped in the relationship. Critics of the use of the battered woman syndrome in cases such as Goodfellow's claim it is inappropriate because men are less likely to find themselves emotionally trapped and financially dependent in a relationship (Watt, 2004).

Would the presentation of evidence of the battered spouse syndrome be more appropriate if the defendant in this case were a female, claiming years of emotional abuse by her spouse? What if the same situation occurred with a same-sex couple? Would the battered spouse syndrome be appropriate as evidence? Most likely, Terry Goodfellow does not fit most people's perceptions of a victim of battering, but does that mean that men cannot become emotionally trapped or financially dependent in a relationship or use the same evidence in court as women who claim to be battered? These issues will be explored throughout this book.

Using the Syndrome to Dispel Myths About Battered Women: Is It Still Needed or Does It Deflect Responsibility?

One of the beneficial aspects of introducing the syndrome to the public and the courtroom is to educate people and to address misperceptions and myths. A number of empirical studies have found that laypersons, and even legal professionals such as judges and attorneys, embrace stereotypes and misconceptions about battered women and the nature of abusive relationships (Aubrey & Ewing, 1989; Dodge & Greene, 1991; Eaton & Hyman, 1992). One of the most common misperceptions is that battered women could leave the batterer at any time (Aubrey & Ewing, 1989; Dutton, 1993; Ewing, 1987; Walker, 1979). More recent research, however, has found that over time, perceptions of battered women may have changed, as community members from New York and Australia did not believe that battered women were responsible for the domestic violence, nor did they believe that violence is not legitimate at any time or that victims could leave an abusive relationship easily (Reddy, Knowles, Mulvany, McMahon & Freckelton, 1997). Community members also believed that physical violence constituted domestic violence (Carlson & Worden, 2005; Worden & Carlson, 2005). Evidence provided via expert testimony of the battered woman syndrome is designed to dispel any existing myths about battered women which may be held within the general public, as well as to offer an explanation of why the defendant perceived no other alternatives but to protect his or her life.

Another crucial argument made by scholars concerns the language associated with the syndrome. Scholars have noted their apprehensions about the use of "syndrome" language in the context of testimony. Critics of the battered woman syndrome believe the syndrome is an "abuse excuse" and that we live in a "syndrome" society that takes the focus off of the defendant and onto the victim (Dershowitz, 1994). In other words, if the defendant can show how abused they were, it is easy to believe the victim deserved what she (or he) got. In this view, the "syndromization of criminal law" has led to a negation of personal responsibility for crime. The syndrome is seen as providing a justification in which a history of abuse is used to explain the defendant's actions, potentially leading to increased empathy for the defendant (Downs & Fisher, 2005), and encouraging vigilantism (Downs, 1996), where women can get away with murder. Others (Osthoff & Maguigan, 2005) maintain that these fears relate only to unusual cases of non-confrontational homicide, where the defendants ultimately pled guilty or were found guilty after trial, and should not be of widespread concern.

Feminist legal scholars have often noted that battered women are convicted because they kill in circumstances that do not include a traditionally defined imminent threat of death or serious bodily harm. This has led to the assumption and dominant portrayal of the typical battered woman homicide defendant as a vigilante who strikes back at the only available moment, often during breaks in the attack (Maguigan, 1991). Nowhere is this better depicted than in the television movie *The Burning Bed*, based on the case of Francine Hughes, who burned her abusive husband while he was sleeping. However, Maguigan (1991) suggests these assumptions are prevalent because most cases reviewed by legal scholars are appellate decisions (appellate courts review decisions made by lower courts) involving battered women. A systematic survey of those decisions found that the appellate decisions did not support the commonly held assumption that most battered women kill in non-confrontational situations (Maguigan, 1991). In other words, when the bigger picture of all cases involving battered women is considered, the majority of cases actually involve direct confrontation. Furthermore, the most common impediment to a "fair trial" for battered women was not the structure or content of existing law, but the way it was applied by trial judges (Maguigan, 1991). Maguigan's (1991) argument that unfair trials were more likely to be the result of how the law was applied by trial judges suggests that it was more often the inclusion or exclusion of expert testimony in a case that was at issue. For example, in the case of *Commonwealth v. Jones* (1993) an indictment against Jones was dismissed by an appellate court because there was support and expert statements suggesting that Jones "fits into a battered wife syndrome." Further, in *Commonwealth v. Rodriguez* (1994) a defendant who was accused and convicted of manslaughter for stabbing her abusive husband as they were fighting appealed to the high court because testimony of the battered woman syndrome was not allowed into the court. Her conviction was later reversed.

Dispelling Myths of Mental Instability

Language associated with the syndrome may also lead to perceptions of the defendant's mental instability rather than raising consciousness about the reasonable survival strategies battered women may use in abusive situations. The language associated with the battered woman syndrome is also inherently associated with traditional feminine characteristics such as passivity and helplessness, which reinforces conventional ideas of femininity (Ferraro, 2003). Women who violate traditional constructs associated with femininity, including working women, homosexual women, and African American women, are often considered "less feminine" (Ferraro, 2003, p. 113). Those who deviate from the traditional idea of femininity tend to be penalized more harshly than those who do not deviate from the standard. For instance, battered African American women may be less likely to fit the

stereotype of a battered woman; they are six times more likely to be imprisoned for domestic violence incidents than battered Caucasian women (Richie,
2001, cited in Ferraro, 2003).

One of the most significant arguments against the use of the syndrome
is that it may be suggestive of an illness or psychological disorder (Crocker,
1985; Schneider, 1986; Stubbs, 1992). In fact, Schneider (1986) has noted that
there is "an implicit but powerful view that battered women are all the same,
that they are suffering from a psychological disability and that this disability prevents them from acting normally" (p. 207). Studies on mock jurors'
attitudes toward battered women in homicide cases suggest this might be true
(e.g., Finkel et al., 1991; Kasian, Spanos, Terrance & Peebles, 1993; Russell
& Melillo, 2006; Schuller & Hastings, 1996; Terrance & Matheson, 2003).

Concerns have been voiced in a report sponsored by the Violence Against
Women Act that suggested that when syndrome terminology was used, it
would lead to comparing women to a laundry list of symptoms and pathology typically associated with the syndrome (Dutton, 1996). Dutton addressed
these concerns with judges, attorneys, and other experts and concluded that
"the concept of the battered woman's syndrome is not adequate to portray
the necessary information to assist the fact-finder to understand the evidence
or to determine a fact in issue" (p. 4). Thus, while legal actors and experts
agree that the syndrome does not quite capture the plight of the battered
woman, many states continue to refer to the syndrome in their statutes and
laypersons continue to compare battered women to a stereotype ultimately
created by the syndrome.

As a result of this research and scholarly debate on the topic, there has
been a significant shift in thought in the last ten years with regard to the content of expert testimony. Some theorists and scholars (Biggers, 2005; Crocker,
1985; Ferraro, 2003; Schneider, 2000; Sheehy et al., 1992) have consistently
argued that the battered woman syndrome should be removed as evidence
completely, shifting the focus from generalized psychological reactions such
as learned helplessness to emphasizing the individual situation and circumstances of the event. Others believe that expert testimony on the syndrome
is here to stay and there is a need to shift the focus of the content (Biggers,
2005; Douglas, 1987; Dutton, 1996) to eliminate references to pathology and
to minimize attention to the pathological aspects of the individual. A compromise of these two perspectives can include providing testimony of battering and its effects. Much of the recent research on the battered woman
syndrome has examined the effects of such alternative forms of testimony
(i.e., social framework evidence of battering and its effects), and all have
met with mixed results (Schuller & Hastings, 1996; Schuller & Rzepa, 2002;
Schuller, Wells, Rzepa & Klippenstine, 2004; Terrance & Matheson, 2003).

However, one common denominator of these studies is that while expert testimony—of any kind—tends to lead to more lenient verdict decisions, most forms of expert testimony can also lead to more perceptions of mental instability of the defendant.

While theorists and scholars have been engrossed in this controversy regarding the content and use of the battered woman syndrome, it has yet to become an important issue with legal actors. Legislators, judges, and lawyers seem unimpressed and/or uninformed about the scholarly debate. They believe it is merely a matter of "semantics" (Ferraro, 2003). On the one hand, there is scholarship that suggests that the use of the battered woman syndrome is outdated and carries with it a host of stereotypes to which battered women are compared. On the other hand, there is legal precedent that continues to allow testimony on the syndrome to continue. Once legal precedent had been made and set, it is difficult to deny its admissibility in court. Instead of re-evaluating the syndrome as evidence, courts are actually expanding its use, and in some cases, state legislation virtually guarantees its use. While activists and scholars call for a re-examination of admissibility of the syndrome in the court system, many legal actors tend to dismiss this controversy, leaving reform of the use of the syndrome with a questionable future.

In conclusion, this chapter has provided a general overview of the problems associated with the syndrome that will be addressed in greater depth in later chapters. Individuals tend to evaluate information based on how it fits their stereotypes. While this is a natural and necessary process, seeing through the lens of a stereotype can affect legal decision making when battered women kill their abusers. The battered woman syndrome was developed to assist legal actors in understanding the plight of the battered woman and dispelling myths associated with victimization. However, scholars have argued that the syndrome has led to a standard to which all battered women are compared. The language associated with the syndrome reflects pathology which can conflict with assessing the reasonableness of the defendant's actions. While some people argue that use of the syndrome actually deflects responsibility of the defendant to the victim, others believe that the syndrome provides an important context to understand the dynamics within an abusive relationship. Providing a historical context should help to understand the origins of these stereotypes and the evolution of the battered woman syndrome.

DISCUSSION QUESTIONS

1. When you think of a victim of battering, what do you think of? Do you think your own beliefs could affect how you evaluate a male heterosexual defendant who claims to be a victim of battering?

2. Think of at least two ways the battered woman syndrome can help defendants and two ways in which the syndrome might damage a defendant's claim of self-defense?

3. The battered woman syndrome was originally allowed in the courts as evidence to help dispel myths associated with battered women. Do you think these myths still exist? If so, which myths continue to exist?

4. When scholars suggest Walker's theory of the battered woman syndrome has "become a standard to which all battered women are compared," what do they mean?

5. Do you believe expert testimony of the syndrome deflects responsibility of the defendant and places the blame on the victim?

CHAPTER 2

A Historical Analysis
of Legal Responses to Battering

> *From the earliest twilight of human society, every woman [...] was found in a state of bondage to some man.... How vast is the number of men, in any great country, who are little higher than brutes, and [...] this never prevents them from being able through the laws of marriage, to obtain a victim.... The vilest malefactor has some wretched woman tied to him, against whom he can commit any atrocity except killing her [...] and even that he can do without too much danger of legal penalty* [J.S. Mills 1869; cited in McCue, 1995, p. 69].

John Stuart Mills, a well known philosopher of his time, made it clear that women were regarded as little more than the property of their husbands. Mills was ahead of his time in voicing his opinion about the inequality between men and women. It was this voice, along with many other like-minded individuals, that would come to change the way women were perceived and treated. However, this change has been slow in coming, and equality continues to remain elusive.

Close examination of the history, laws, and practices of early Western civilization leaves little question that women's inferior status within and outside of the family excluded her from the rights of liberty and legal process. For example, in Roman times, husbands were considered "legal guardians" of their wives and were permitted to use reasonable physical force in disciplining them, such as breaking their noses or blackening their eyes (Buzawa & Buzawa, 2003; Dowd, 1992). Christianity then provided ideological justification for patriarchal marriages, and the state codified these relations into law (Buzawa & Buzawa, 2003; Dobash & Dobash, 1979). Marriage laws explicitly recognized the family as the domain of the husband (Schechter, 1982).

In the context of English common law, a woman could not own property without her husband's authorization or control. A woman's status excluded her from the legal process and placed her within the category reserved for children and servants. A woman's status as property is underscored in cases of rape as described in English common law. English rape laws considered rape as a crime against the husband, father, or fiancé of the victim (Dowd, 1992). Rape cases were considered settled if the male "owner" of the victim was compensated for the damage to his "property" (Dowd, 1992).

In many parts of Europe, a man could kill his wife without legal punishment well into the 1600s (Dowd, 1992). In contrast, a wife who killed her husband was penalized as if she had committed treason because her act of homicide was considered analogous to murdering the king (Dowd, 1992). According to Dobash and Dobash's (1979) historical overview of wife beating, "Throughout the seventeenth, eighteenth and nineteenth centuries, there was little objection within the community to a man's using force against his wife as long as he did not exceed certain tacit limits" (p. 56). English common law endorsed wife beating under the "rule of thumb." The tenets underlying the rule of thumb date back to 1800 BCE, as the code of Hammurabi declared women's subservient status, allowing a husband to inflict punishment on any member of his household for any transgression (Federal Law Enforcement Training Center, 1999). In the 1700s, English common law adopted the code of Hammurabi and decreed that a husband had the right to chasten his wife with a whip or rattan no larger than his thumb in order to reinforce discipline. This restriction was meant to be a means of protection from overzealous husbands (Dowd, 1992), but it also reflected that courts were beginning to ponder the extent to which physical punishment should be religiously sanctioned or state sanctioned (Buzawa & Buzawa, 2003). Courts then began to consider the justification for physical punishment against women, but justifications ranged from adultery to nagging. Just before the colonial era, wife battering became associated with the lower classes. Upper and middle class women continued to suffer from battering but kept their experiences quiet (Lentz, 1999).

A historical analysis of the colonial United States suggests that the Pilgrims of Plymouth Colony in Massachusetts actually enacted the first laws in the world that denounced domestic violence and made battering illegal (Pleck, 1987). However, these laws were more symbolic in nature as the Puritans were not completely opposed to domestic violence. In fact, their religious beliefs permitted moderate forms of battering, particularly when related to enforcing family rules. Between the years 1633 and 1802 there were only 12 cases of domestic violence that were even brought to the courts in Plymouth

(Pleck, 1989). This tacit acceptance of domestic violence despite laws that forbade it suggests that the new colonial societies were torn between their religion and social reform. Religious ideology was the underlying foundation of what was considered acceptable and the boundaries of what constituted domestic violence were soon broadened to include what was "suitable in the Eyes of the Lord" (Buzawa & Buzawa, 2003), leaving the definition of domestic violence subjective and open to interpretation.

America was greatly influenced by English common law and implicitly adopted the "rule of thumb" until the early nineteenth century, recognizing a husband's right to beat his wife (Mather, 1988). The husband's right to discipline his wife was upheld in the Supreme Court of Mississippi in 1824 (Dowd, 1992). In 1864, a North Carolina court ruled that the state should not interfere in cases of domestic abuse, because the family was a private institution. Thus, parties were left to resolve their own disputes. For instance, it was believed that charges against a husband for assault and battery against a partner would "open the doors of the courts to accusations of all sorts of one spouse against the other and bring into public notice complaints for assault, slander, and libel" (1910 Supreme Court Decision, cited in Federal Law Enforcement Training Center, 1999, Chap. 5, p. 2).

Expanding Rights for Women and Legal Reform

Privatization of family violence and historical attitudes toward women has contributed to the somewhat slow evolution of accepting criminal justice procedures for battered women. By 1910, only 35 out of 46 states had begun reform legislation that would classify wife-beating assault as a crime (Dowd, 1992). These changes in America occurred when women began demanding rights to divorce, to separation, to obtain control of their property, and to obtain custody of their children (Schechter, 1992). Around the same time, women who were opposed to domestic violence associated with alcohol abuse were effective in aiding alcohol prohibition. Over time, the expanding rights of women slowly combined to loosen the legal and moral authority that husbands held over their wives. However, the historical legacy of the legalized injustices of pre-modern times documents a societal ideology that is not easily erased. In spite of more recent liberations, violence has persisted.

It wasn't until 1954 (*Easterling v. U.S.*, 1954) that the courts recognized that the physical attributes of an individual defendant might justify the use of a dangerous weapon to ward off an unarmed attacker. In this case the defendant, a battered woman, had used a pocketknife to repel her common-law husband after he had grabbed her by the hair, beat her about the head, choked her, and threatened to kill her. In addition, after 1962, civil tort actions (assault and battery, intentional infliction of emotional injury, etc.) by one spouse against another were permitted and spousal immunity has now been abolished in most states (McCue, 1995).

The most significant changes in the legal system began in the 1970s. These changes can be attributed to the evolution of the women's movement and mounting political pressure over perceived inadequacies of criminal justice responses to the issues of women (Buzawa & Buzawa, 1990, 2003). The women's rights and feminist movements of the late 1960s and early 1970s raised public consciousness about societal neglect toward the unique problems experienced by women. While the initial focus of the women's movement was on rape and stranger assault, eventually women's rights activists began to recognize the severity of the problem of domestic violence.

The official beginning of the battered women's movement was considered to take place in 1971 in the English town of Chiswick, when 500 women and children marched in protest to a reduction of monies originally allocated for schoolchildren. This protest led to the establishment of Chiswick's Women's Aid, a women's forum where community issues and domestic concerns could be addressed (Barnett & Laviollette, 1993; McCue, 1995). Erin Pizzey, founder of Chiswick's Women's Aid, found it evident from these community meetings that domestic violence was a serious problem.

Pizzey recognized the need for a refuge for battered women and their children, and soon Chiswick Women's Aid became the first Battered Women's Center. Pizzey's experience with battered women provided the basis for a book about wife abuse, *Scream Quietly or the Neighbors Will Hear* (Pizzey, 1974), which drew media attention and attention from scholars, propelling a movement which would create refuges for many women around the world.

Feminists from the United States interested in the issues of battered women soon flocked to England, where they studied the dynamics of abuse and the development of women's shelters (McCue, 1995). United States feminists then used English ideas and basic plans and replicated them in a few areas in the United States. In 1974, the first shelter in the U.S. opened in St. Paul, Minnesota. Since then the number of shelters has grown to exceed 2,000 throughout the United States (Saathoff & Stoffel, 1999; Schrager, 2008). Since 1974, the battered women's movement has struggled from grassroots organizations to government-funded programs.

The late 1970s also witnessed an increasing use of self-defense when battered women were charged with murder or manslaughter of an abuser. This presented a problem for the justice system as elements of traditional laws of self-defense were crafted to address disputes between men (for reviews, see

Castel, 1990; Faigman, 1987; Gillespie, 1989; Schneider, 1980). The traditional standards and requirements were designed to apply to conflicts between male strangers who were relatively equal in physical size and strength (Castel, 1990). With the increase of self-defense cases involving female defendants in partner homicides, most courts have had to expand the rules of self-defense to accommodate situations where women kill their intimate partners in self-defense.

This was also a pivotal period for enacting state laws that established more effective criminal court proceedings for dealing with domestic violence, particularly in the context of a self-defense case decided by the Supreme Court of the State of Washington in 1977 (*Washington v. Wanrow*, 1977). In the case of Yvonne Wanrow, a murder conviction was appealed on the basis that the trial court had instructed the jury on the issue of self-defense using the masculine gender to explain the circumstances justifying the use of force. Wanrow and her lawyers felt that the use of masculine gender implicitly advised the jury to use a male standard in assessing the reasonableness of the woman's conduct. Due to Wanrow's appeal, gendered terminology was removed, resulting in a woman's right to have "she" and "her" substituted for "he" and "him" when a jury considered the circumstances in which a battered woman used force to defend herself.

In the wake of the *Washington v. Wanrow* decision, state laws and legislative responses continued to grow. In 1977, Oregon became the first state to adopt the Family Abuse Prevention Act, which mandated arrests in domestic violence cases and served as a model for the nation (McCue, 1995). State laws continued to be enacted concerning domestic violence, providing for shelters, improving reporting procedures, and establishing criminal procedures. By 1980, all but six states had passed laws levying a surcharge on marriage licenses for the benefit of funding battered women's shelters and allowing probable cause (warrantless arrests) in cases of domestic violence.

This process, however, soon came to a halt in the financial recession between 1980 and 1982. Curtailed funding led to the closing of many shelters and counseling offices (McCue, 1995). Federal funding was restored in 1983, as federal monies were allocated to begin a task force on family violence to examine the scope of the problem of domestic violence under the auspices of the Child Abuse and Prevention Treatment Act. With this additional funding, some shelters and counseling centers were restored (McCue, 1995).

While legislative and legal reform resumed with renewed vigor, problems persisted. The law, with a fundamental obligation to its citizens to protect them from harm, was still at times improperly applied. In February of 1982, Jena Balistreri was severely beaten by her husband. Mrs. Balistreri was allegedly treated rudely by police responding to the call and told she "deserved the beating" (Archer, 1989). She was offered no medical treatment and police refused to arrest her assailant. Over the next five years, Mrs. Balistreri suffered numerous episodes of battering, and her requests for assistance from police were ignored (*Balistreri v. Pacifica Police Dept.*, 1988). Similar cases (e.g., *Thurman v. City of Torrington*, 1984) illuminating the potential seriousness of abuse have led to more aggressive responses from police departments, mandatory arrests of assailants, and additional training and policy to address potential lawsuits that accompany failure to protect and enforce laws (Dowd, 1992; Buzawa & Buzawa, 2003).

The Rise of Empirical Research and Battering

Initially, academic interest in battered women increased indirectly through concerns about child abuse. The fundamental article propelling the issue of family violence to the academic forefront was "The Battered Child Syndrome" in the *Journal of the American Medical Association* (Kemp, Silverman, Steele, Druegenmuller & Silver, 1962, cited in Buzawa & Buzawa, 2003). This article called for physicians and other caregivers to recognize and intervene in such cases. According to Buzawa and Buzawa (1990, 2003), this article and subsequent publications focused particularly on the etiology of the problem and treatment of the victim and offender.

Eventually, the issue of battering became of interest to many scholars. One author (Roy, 1977) stated that research associated with marital violence had gone through two significant periods. The first can be characterized as blaming the victim, where causes of domestic violence were believed to originate from personal or internal factors; the second focused on evaluating available evidence and putting an end to myths surrounding domestic violence. Myths were replaced by theoretical models that have shifted from one-sided views of dysfunction on the part of the victim or abuser, to more multifaceted beliefs associated with the nature of domestic violence, which include the dynamic interaction of psychology and wider social variables. Many researchers would argue that they are still trying to understand exactly what is myth and what is reality, but research has come closer to understanding many more of the psychosocial variables involved in domestic violence. A significant period of research has occurred over the last 10 to 15 years that examines how changes in the legal system and society interact to affect victims and perpetrators of abuse as well as societal attributions of responsibility.

Legal and legislative growth has continued into more recent decades.

Much of the response to the issue of battering from the legal system in the past 25 years coincides with an influx of empirical research and theoretical views provided by social scientists. In order to be objective in cases when battered women claim self-defense, legal actors and social scientists first had to tease out social myth from empirical fact. Many of the legal accommodations enacted for battered women victims and defendants were derived from careful review of empirical evidence regarding the prevalence of domestic abuse and characteristics associated with battered women.

In 1990, after reviewing over 100 cases of women serving time in state prisons for killing or assaulting their abusive husbands or partners, Democratic Ohio Governor Richard F. Celeste granted clemency to 25 women, the first mass release of women prisoners in this country (McCue, 1995). In addition, as of 1993, marital rape was a crime in all 50 states; however, 30 states continued to have exceptions from prosecution if only "simple" force is used; in other words, the degree of violence used can define whether a man is prosecuted for a rape or not (Dowd, 1992; McCue, 1995; National Clearinghouse for Marital and Date Rape, 2005). Furthermore, the Violence Against Women Act (VAWA), signed by President Clinton in 1994 and expanded in 2000, makes sex-based violence a civil rights violation and allows for compensatory damages and attorney's fees. Within the VAWA, a federal claim can be brought for any act that would be considered a felony, including rape and spousal abuse, regardless of whether any criminal charges have been brought. The act includes funds for a National Domestic Violence Hotline, an increase in funds for the Family Violence Protection Services Act, funds for shelters, interstate enforcement of protective orders, training for state and federal judges, and funding for school-based rape education programs. According to McCue (1995), on May 24, 1995, a jury in West Virginia was the first to find a man guilty under the new federal laws in the Violence Against Women Act that made crossing the state line to assault a spouse or domestic partner a federal offense. Baily, the defendant, severely beat his wife and then drove around two states with her locked in the trunk. In this case, there was no history of violence prior to the offense, and while his wife survived the event, she was left with permanent brain damage. The defendant was sentenced to life plus 20 years in prison (opinion unpublished, *United States v. Bailey*, 1995).

The Role of Social Stereotypes in the Evolution of Domestic Violence Law

Bound up within societal ideology and legal processes are traditional sex role stereotypes. For example, our social system previously defined the husband's role as one of dominance, authority, and provider of the family, while the wife's role consisted of dependence, nurturing the children, passivity, and submissiveness (Dowd, 1992; Schneider, 1980; Yllo, 2005). It was assumed that women were passive and submissive to men, and therefore would quietly absorb the physical harm visited upon them by their husbands. If women were passive victims of violent husbands, then given these traditional views of women, their very natures seem askew when women use deadly force against men. These women's actions contradict social stereotypes and threaten the basic conception of traditional society (Dowd, 1992; Schneider, 1980). For instance, social scientists and legal scholars (Dowd, 1992; Schneider, 1980; Yllo, 1993, 2005) have argued that when a woman is charged with homicide and attempts to explain her use of force as a reasonable response to abuse in the home, this approach ultimately threatens the jurors' image of the family as an institution of love, nourishment, and protection (Schneider, 1980). Given such attitudes, it is not surprising that insanity was the traditional defense of women who killed their husbands (Schneider, 1980; Walker, 1984).

Reforms in the law of self-defense include using the battered woman syndrome as evidence in cases where a woman kills her partner. Despite the fact that while the battered woman syndrome is not an official legal defense of its own, most states use the syndrome to aid judges and jurors in their decision-making process. According to the National Clearinghouse for the Defense of Battered Women (NCDBW, 1997), the battered woman syndrome is admissible when relevant. The NCDBW reported that as of 1997, at least 22 states formally recognized the battered woman syndrome or effects of battering as evidence. Eighteen states plus Washington, D.C., proposed legislation allowing the testimony, with 16 of these states directly referring to the battered woman syndrome. More significant changes include the evolution of terminology from "the battered woman syndrome" to "the battered partner syndrome" or "the battered person syndrome." Still, many opponents remain to such changes in legislation regarding the acceptance of the battered woman syndrome, battered person or partner syndrome (Crocker, 1985; Dutton, 1996; Gelles, 1987; McMahon, 1999; Schneider, 1986; Stubbs, 1992).

In summary, legal and societal response to domestic violence has come a long way, yet there is so much further to go. For instance, as recently as 1997, a judge in Franklin County, New York, was quoted in the courtroom as saying, "Every woman needs a good pounding now and then" (see Federal Law Enforcement Training Center, 1999, Chap. 5, p. 2). The past 30 years have fostered a broad acceptance of the theory of the battered woman syndrome by both legal actors and laypersons. However, it is unclear whether this acceptance actually helps perpetuate a system of inequality or whether it assists in leveling the playing field. There is a great deal left to learn about domestic violence. While there have been great strides in legal responses to domestic violence, perceptions of battered women are a vestige to its history. Theorists and academicians understand this and study these issues to identify societal and individual factors with hopes that by studying its epidemiology, abuse can be eradicated or at least minimized. Their theories and research help to provide insight into the complex interactions between society, individuals, and institutions. There are many different theories and each has a different perspective yet shares a common theme to identify the conditions that create violence and provide ways to prevent it. Such theories and research help to enlighten the general public's views about domestic violence.

DISCUSSION QUESTIONS

1. How did English Common Law affect the slow response to recognize domestic violence as a societal problem?

2. Describe how the privatization of domestic violence slowed the evolution of criminal justice procedures for battered women.

3. In what time period did significant changes take place for battered women? Describe at least three significant historical events responsible for domestic violence reform.

4. What was the role of empirical research on domestic violence in the criminal justice system?

5. Think about how far societal attitudes and the criminal justice system have come towards equality. To what extent do you believe gender equality has been attained?

CHAPTER 3

Theories Related to Domestic Violence: Abusers and Abused

*Is violence a problem of individual people? Is it rather created by charac-
teristics of the social order? If so, which characteristics of the social order
are most important? Conceptualizing violence as a particular type of problem explicitly answers questions about what should be done to eliminate
violence* [Loseke, Gelles, & Cavanaugh, 2005, p.1].

John Stuart Mills (and many other scholars) theorized about domestic
violence almost two centuries ago. Theories of wife beating have been constructed by philosophers, feminists, psychologists, sociologists and criminologists. Current theories offer helpful, but often contradictory, insights
concerning the best way to determine the causes of domestic violence. For
example, sociologists and criminologists often focus on the prevalence of
male violence in general. This outlook leads to postulations of women abuse,
child abuse, war, political assassination, family, marriage, parenting, and gender as having common historical roots and causation (Schechter, 1982). However, it has been argued that such theories explain little about human behavior
in specific contexts such as battering (Dobash & Dobash, 1979). Psychologists
look for causes of violence within the individual perpetrator or victim, leaving some theorists to criticize psychological theories because they ignore the
unique structure of the family as a social institution (Gelles, 1993) as well
as historical traditions condoning familial violence (Buzawa & Buzawa,
2003). Feminist theories focus mainly on the influence of gender and gen-
der-structured relationships within the family structure (Gelles, 1993). Such
theory is not without its critics, who contend that its primary emphasis on

patriarchy fails to account for the lack of variance of patriarchy across time and cultures and ignores non-gendered aspects of social structures and institutions (Felson, 2002; O'Leary, 1993).

While each theory differs on specific points of interest, all share a common goal in identifying conditions that create violence, as well as in offering new insights and directions toward its prevention. More recently, fewer domestic violence theorists are purists who subscribe to only one theory; rather they see each of these theories as providing insight toward a more integrative approach to understanding the causes of battering (McCue, 1995). Social scientific theories of causation of domestic violence can be loosely classified in three general categories: (1) individually focused theories, (2) those that examine family structure, and (3) feminist theories. The following overview of the more prominent theories will aid in understanding the dynamics of domestic violence and its causes.

Individually Oriented Theories

Theories that focus on the individual assailant or victim of domestic violence often look to determine which characteristics may contribute to the likelihood of domestic violence. These theories typically stress the importance of individual stressors created by poverty and unemployment (Shainess, 1977) and investigate the pathological roots of battering.

Initial explanations of family violence had a clear focus on psychological and psychiatric factors. For example, early descriptions of spouse abuse implied that women in abusive situations were masochistic, or the abuse itself was attributed to personality disturbances, drugs or alcohol, or psychopathology of the abuser (Gelles & Loseke, 1993; McCue, 1995; O'Leary, 1993). Disorders often attributed to the batterer have commonly included personality disorders such as asocial or borderline disorder, narcissistic or antisocial disorder, and dependent or compulsive disorder (Hamberger & Hastings, 1986; McCue, 1995). However, over the past two decades, depictions of such disorders have been disputed for a number of reasons. First, it has been argued that the concept of masochism, as it relates to the victim of abuse, has served as a vehicle for victim-blaming. Second, there has been little or no empirical evidence that abused wives were masochistic (Dutton, 1992; Walker, 1987). Third, the use of personality disorders as an explanation for abuse has done little to relieve the problem and actually lessened the responsibility of the abusers because they were seen as having a "medical" condition (O'Leary, 1993).

Individually Oriented Theories and Abusers

Many individual theorists have shifted their focus from these psychiatric disorders to examine alternative personality traits that might be predictive of abuse. This shift in empirical research has found that characteristics of the abuser often include commission of crimes outside of the family (Hotaling, Straus, & Lincoln, 1989), rationalization of their actions by blaming the victim (Dobash & Dobash, 1979), and use of alcohol or illegal drugs (Kantor & Straus, 1989). In addition, Hotaling et al. (1989) found that men who assault their spouses are five times more likely than other men to also assault non-family members. While this same pattern was found with female offenders, the strength of the correlation in female offenders was significantly weaker than in male offenders.

Some of the personality traits associated with abusers include low self-esteem, lack of anger impulse control, deficiency in conflict resolution skills, threats to masculinity, and immaturity (Buzawa & Buzawa, 2003). Researchers have found that males with low self-esteem were more likely to abuse their partners (Hamberger, Lohr, Bonge, & Tolin, 1996). Researchers and theorists suggest that men with low self-esteem feel threatened when there is a perceived disparity of power at home or in the workplace. As women increasingly enter the workforce, men with low self-esteem may batter in order to regain a sense of control in their lives. An abuser's anger and hostility is one of the strongest predictors of potential abuse (Buzawa & Buzawa, 2003; Hamberger et al., 1997). Real or imagined perceptions of rejection (Holtzworth-Munroe & Hutchinson, 1993) or jealousy (Pagelow, 1981) can elicit anger and the potential for abuse. Moffitt, Robins, and Caspi (2001) found that men who batter tend to have greater "negative emotionality" and less effective coping strategies in stressful situations. This lack of effective coping strategies and inability to deal with stress ultimately results in poor conflict resolution strategies (Holtzworth-Munroe & Anglin, 1991). Batterers often display immature personalities that shift the blame to the victim or ultimately diminish the impact of their abuse (O'Leary, 1993).

Many studies have linked alcohol and substance abuse to intimate partner violence. One large scale study of domestic violence in Memphis, Tennessee, found that 92 percent of batterers had used drugs or alcohol at the time of the abuse and 67 percent of batterers were found to have multiple substances (drugs and alcohol) in their system when the assault occurred (Brookoff, 1997). Others continue to find high correlations between substance use and domestic violence (Willson et al., 2000). In fact, research has found that binge drinkers are three to five times more likely to become violent toward a female partner than those who do not binge drink. However, there are researchers who argue that while alcohol and substance abuse are related, there is no research that suggests that alcohol or substance abuse actually causes domestic violence (Johnson, 2000). In fact, some researchers and theorists believe alcohol and substance abuse are only tangentially related to violence and attitudinal factors play a more significant role in explaining intimate partner violence (Kantor & Straus, 1990; Stith & Farley, 1993).

Individually Oriented Theories and Victims of Abuse

One variant of an individual-centered approach holds that battered women can often be distinguished from non-battered women by a number of characteristics. This suggests that certain victim attributes may distinguish victims reporting different levels of abuse (i.e., verbal, physical) from non-abused women. For example, it has been theorized that although most people modify their behavior to avoid future victimization, repeat victims—like offenders—are unable to change behavior patterns (Buzawa & Buzawa, 2003). For this reason, victims of repeated acts of domestic violence were—in earlier individually-oriented theories—termed to be masochistic. While some researchers (Hotaling & Sugarman, 1986) found no risk factors that distinguished female victims of minor violence from female victims of severe violence, other research suggests that some characteristics can be differentiated. One study of a national sample of self-reported battered women and non-battered women found that the more violence experienced by a woman, the more she suffered from psychological distress (Gelles & Harrop, 1989). Women who were exposed to repeated threats and attacks responded with increased levels of isolation and terror and endured more symptoms of Post Traumatic Stress Disorder (PTSD) than non-battered women (Browne, 1987; Dutton, 1992). In addition, another study further differentiated characteristics between battered women who were distressed with their marriages and found that battered women exhibited higher rates of PTSD (58 percent) than women who were distressed with their marriages but not battered (18.9 percent) (Astin, Ogland-Hand, Coleman, & Foy, 1995). However, this distinction is not clear-cut when comparing verbally abused women and physically abused women. Others found that 81 percent of physically abused women and 63 percent of verbally abused women met the diagnostic criteria for PTSD (Kemp, Green, Hovanitz & Rawlings, 1995). When shelter and community samples are examined, rates of women currently experiencing PTSD range from 52 percent to 71 percent (Astin et al., 1995; Kemp et al., 1995; Street & Arias, 2001; Vogel & Marshall, 2001).

Other cognitive reactions have been differentiated between battered and non-battered women. Women exposed to physical violence often view themselves as blameworthy (e.g., have low self-esteem, feel responsible for the violence) (Janoff-Bulman, 1979), perceive the violence to be uncontrollable (Browne, 1987, 1993), develop an increased tolerance for abuse (Browne, 1987), and perceive a lack of alternatives (such as leaving the abuser) available to themselves as compared to others (Blackman, 1989; Browne, 1987; Walker, 1984).

Family-Oriented Theories of Battering

Family-oriented theories and research, most often the domain of sociologists, use many of the "individual" variables to explain why a particular family experiences violence. However, the primary focus is to find out what characteristics within the family system lead to increased levels of domestic violence.

According to these theorists, societal trends and cultural norms affect the family structure in many ways. For example, one researcher suggested that increased social isolation (moving away from family and friends) removes inhibitive and supportive norms that might otherwise counteract violence (Steinmetz, 1980). Similarly, another theory proposed that social values and norms can provide meaning and direction to violent acts (Wolfgang & Feracutti, 1982). From this perspective, cultures that condone the use of violence have the highest rate of domestic violence (Gelles, 1993; McCue, 1995). For example, American culture is seen as encouraging such abuse through accepted practices such as violence in the media and spanking as a form of disciplining a child (Gelles, 1993).

Specific characteristics of a family also have been studied as predictors of future violence. Straus's (1973) general systems approach emphasizes established norms within the family structure. In this approach, violence within the family is dependent upon the established rule of behavior for each individual member; each member's boundaries are defined and patterns of interactions remain stable over time. Therefore, it is theorized that conflicts occur when a family member challenges the established goals of that family's system. This challenge is often followed by a corrective action (violent behavior) taken by the husband with the intention of reestablishing control within the relationship. In relation to this theory, researchers found that high levels of marital conflict over issues of male alcohol use and control in the relationship were the best predictors of several risk factors examined in accounting for male violence toward women (Hotaling & Sugarman, 1986).

It has been suggested that there are two types of violence among intimate partners (Stark, 1992). The first type of violence includes highly coercive aggressive behaviors of men, such as periodic severe beatings accompanied by psychological coercion. The second type of aggression includes behaviors, such as pushing and slapping, which are believed by many couples to be a normal event (Straus, Gelles & Steinmetz, 1980). Normalization of slapping or pushing during family conflicts can have deleterious consequences on the family structure.

In the 1970s, Straus and his colleagues made the unexpected discovery that women—whether married, cohabitating, or dating—physically assaulted their partners as often as men (Steinmetz, 1978; Straus et al., 1980; Straus, 1997), a finding that has been replicated over the years (Straus, 2005). Straus's family conflict studies found the perpetration of violence to be nearly equal between men and women in heterosexual couples. Family conflict studies find that men are the only ones to perpetrate violence in 25.9 percent of domestic violence incidents and women are the perpetrators of violence in 25.5 percent of domestic violence incidents. Men and women are equally violent in 48.6 percent of domestic disputes (Straus, 2005).

Differences between family conflict studies and crime studies should be noted. There has been extensive research done that compares the data of family conflict studies to data from crime studies to obtain a better understanding of violence in intimate relationships (Straus, 1999). Family conflict studies survey random individuals in the general public to assess rates of problems and conflict in their families, while crime studies base their data on police reports or by asking individuals whether they have been the victim of a crime. Researchers and others stress that the underlying problem associated with crime studies is that they only consider events that result in serious injury that needs medical attention or warrants involving the police as a domestic assault (Straus, 1999, 2005). Crime studies overwhelmingly find men as the perpetrator in heterosexual domestic disputes while family conflict studies find much different rates, suggesting that how domestic violence is defined makes a big difference when understanding the true rates of intimate partner violence and no method is without its limitations (DeKeserady & Dragiewicz, 2007). A great deal of research has further validated the claim that women perpetrate violence as often as men in intimate relationships (Archer, 2000; Bookwala, Frieze, Smith, & Ryan, 1992; Das Dasgupta, 2002; Dutton, 1994; Macchietto, 1992), though again, the level of violence may not be as extreme.

Research identifies society's tendency to overlook domestic violence when women abuse men (Adams & Freeman, 2002; Ferguson & Negy, 2004; Gelles, 1999; Straus, 1993, 1994, 2005; Straus, Kaufman Kantor, & Moore, 1997). The sociological perspective explores how society influences and facilitates females as perpetrators. Cultural norms for violence exist in American society; for example, a large percentage of the general public believes it is understandable and culturally acceptable to hit an unfaithful partner (Ptacek, 1988). In particular, the majority of Americans believe that it is acceptable in certain instances for a wife to slap her husband (Ptacek, 1988). A recent research study of 3,769 community members from the state of California found that attitudes toward women who used violence toward an intimate male partner were less harsh than attitudes toward male intimate partners who initiated violence against women (Sorenson & Taylor, 2005). Society's present attitude toward domestic abuse appears to find violence perpetrated by the husband as unacceptable and violence perpetrated by women as more acceptable (Feather, 1996; Ferguson & Negy, 2004; George, 1994; Straus et al, 1997).

Size and strength differences between men and women have also contributed to women being violent toward men. For example, one study (Fiebert & Gonzalez, 1997) of college women found that 29 percent of them had hit a male partner. The majority of these women believed that their actions would not injure their partner and that men are capable of defending themselves. Women are likely to retaliate against their partner because American culture accepts and may encourage aggression from women. The acceptance of retaliation in American culture is apparent by the fact that 40–50 percent of Americans instruct their children "If hit, hit back" (Douglas, 2006). A woman may also become violent toward a man when he withdraws from a discussion of a problem. Research focusing on college women has demonstrated that the majority of women were abusive because their male partner was not listening or they wanted to gain his attention (Fiebert & Gonzalez, 1997).

Women may also become violent as a means to maintain an identity in their family roles. Women's strong need for identity in the family may cause them to become violent when their family roles, like cooking or child care, are insulted (Straus, 1980). Violence perpetrated by women may also stem from the fact that 90 percent of parents hit their toddlers and continue to do so until their children are young teenagers. As the primary caregiver, a large majority of this hitting is done by women (Straus, 1994). Women may carry this violent behavior into their social relationships with their spouses (Straus, 1980).

Many researchers and theorists believe that the criminal justice system tends to overlook violence perpetrated by females. This belief may have some merit, as there has been a significant increase in the number of attempts by men to obtain police protection that have instead resulted in the man being arrested (Cook, 1997). A wife being abusive toward her husband seems largely influenced by her belief that her aggression will not hurt her partner, and the lower the probability of injury the more tolerant society is of assault (Gelles & Straus, 1988; Straus, 1999). Specifically, some police adhere to traditional gender role beliefs that women are victims; therefore, they are reluctant to arrest women for perpetrating domestic violence (Straus, 1999). In some ways, women's violence seems to be facilitated and accepted by American culture.

Is There a Cycle of Violence?

The phenomena of experiencing violence in childhood directly as the victim of physical violence or indirectly (such as by witnessing violence perpetrated against others) have also been explored as factors related to future violence. Some theorists believe that abused children grow up to become batterers or child abusers. Some scholars (Kaufman & Zigler, 1987) contend that many writers perpetuated this myth as fact without offering any substantive evidence. This intergenerational cycle has long been an issue of controversy. Several studies have found that the impact of witnessing parental violence in childhood is a stronger predictor of violence than direct experience of physical child abuse (Pagelow, 1984; Sugarman & Hotaling, 1989). Still, other researchers (Malone, O'Leary, & Tyree, 1989) have found that the strength of this association was fairly low both pre- and post-marriage.

More recent research has examined the histories of violence among male and female perpetrators of domestic violence involved with a batterer intervention program (Kernsmith, 2006). Approximately 75 percent of the sample reported that they had witnessed domestic violence while growing up, almost 70 percent stated that they were victims of child abuse, and 60 percent of the sample had been in one or more previous relationships marred by domestic violence. Interestingly, both men and women in this sample of domestic violence perpetrators reported low levels of fear of their partner, yet females were more fearful of their partner than males. A more recent meta-analysis (Stith et al., 2000) of 39 studies of intergenerational transmission of intimate partner violence revealed a small, but significant, relationship between growing up in a violent home and perpetrating spousal abuse. Similarly, there were small, but significant, relationships between witnessing violence as a child or experiencing child abuse and perpetration of domestic violence. These results found that men growing up in violent homes were more likely to become perpetrators of domestic violence than were females. With regard to victimization, individuals who grew up in a violent home were more likely to become victims of domestic abuse, and being abused as a child was more strongly related to being a victim of abuse than witnessing abuse as a child.

Although researchers have often stated that childhood physical punishment increases the likelihood of future domestic violence (Straus, Gelles, & Steinmetz, 1980), empirical research has found that only 12 percent of women and 13 percent of men who used physical force against their partners had been exposed to violence in their families (Arias & O'Leary, 1984, as cited in O'Leary, 1993); however, results may differ depending on the populations studied. For instance, empirical research done on clinical populations found that 60 percent of a sample of physically abusive men reported that they were victims of child abuse and 44 percent of men witnessed parental violence. These percentages were higher than those for men who were dissatisfied with their marriage, but not physically abusive (Rosenbaum & O'Leary, 1981). While it appears that childhood experiences may influence adult behavior, conclusions about such intergenerational effects of violence remain conflicting and premature.

It should also be noted that over the past three decades psychologists and family therapists have also recognized the interactions between spouses and have placed emphasis on the interactive patterns between the couple. Battering and its relevance in familial therapeutic treatment has become one issue of concern. Few, if any, clinical psychologists have argued that all wife abuse should be treated with couples therapy, but some investigators believe couples treatment can be effective in many cases (O'Leary, 1993; Rosenbaum & Maiuro, 1990).

There has been concern about therapy that includes both the man and the woman in an abusive relationship, as the presence of the abuser can affect the victim. Treatment often centers on the differential impact in aggression between men and women. Because of these differences, some professionals are critical of any theory encouraging couples therapy. Couples therapy, it has been argued, can place the victim in a potentially dangerous situation where physical aggression can actually increase (O'Leary, 1993). Simply feeling as though they have to go to counseling can spark animosity toward the other spouse. In addition, when both parties are in therapy, it may be difficult to share uncomfortable topics (such as abuse) when the aggressor is present. Thus, it has been argued that women in relationships characterized by abuse should receive individual support (O'Leary, 1993).

More recently, many psychologists have recognized the importance of an integrative model when attempting to discover causation of physical violence within the family. Attempts to explain physical violence against family members increasingly stem from a bio-psychosocial account of a wide variety of abnormal behaviors. By ignoring the complex interaction of biological, sociological, and psychological factors within the dynamics of the family, therapists would remain at a disadvantage when treating family members (O'Leary, 1993).

Feminist Theories of Battering

The feminist approach to the causation of battering entails both micro and macro level examinations of "structural violence" pervasive in Western society (Buzawa & Buzawa, 1990; Gelles, 1993; McCue, 1995; Yllo, 1993). According to feminist perspectives, theoretical and empirical understanding of battering cannot be adequately understood unless gender and power are considered. Unifying themes among most feminists are patterns of male dominance and female subservient status when addressing legal disparities in the courtroom (Levit & Verchick, 2006). When intimate partner violence is considered in the context of feminism, it is difficult to tease out the extent to which gender disparities extend from early English common law to traditional laws. For instance, general laws have made substantial changes toward equality. Yet it is still difficult to determine how and to what extent our current laws actually demonstrate the ideal of equality. Interactions between the psychologies of perpetrator and victim, gendered expectations about family relationships, and the patriarchal ideology and structure embedded in traditional and contemporary society all play significant roles in our legal system that cannot be ignored. While there is a wide range of theoretical perspectives within these realms, each is generally shaped by ideas concerning gender and power (Yllo, 1993).

Feminists have continually argued that our traditional heritage works against a family system of equality (Buzawa & Buzawa, 1990, 2003; Dobash & Dobash, 1979; Schechter, 1982). It has been accurately noted that Christianity, Judaism, and other patriarchal religions have helped to perpetuate a male-dominated family structure (Greven, 1996). From this perspective, women have historically been viewed as property and unable to manage their own affairs without a male leader (Dowd, 1992). Under the auspices of religious rite, men were justified in enforcing male standards of accepted "feminine" behavior through whatever means they felt were necessary (Buzawa & Buzawa, 1990, 2003; Dowd, 1992). Some theorists and researchers believe that religious ideology continues to play a prominent role in battering within contemporary society (Bowker, 1993; Greven, 1996). For example, an investigation of clergy beliefs and practices and their relationships with patriarchal practices found that out of all clergy surveyed in Protestant churches in the U.S. and Canada, 26 percent agreed that a wife should submit to her husband and trust that God would honor her action by either stopping the abuse or giving her strength to endure it. The study also revealed that 33 percent of ministers surveyed felt that separation would only be justified by severe abuse, and 21 percent of those clergy felt that no amount of abuse would justify separation (Alsdurf, 1985, cited in Walker, 1987). However, more recently, efforts have been made by religious institutions to help eliminate such perceptions. For instance, in 1992 Roman Catholic bishops in the United States issued the church's first official statement about spouse abuse, saying the Bible does not advocate for women to submit to abusive husbands (McCue, 1995).

In addition to religion, feminist theories have claimed that social and legal systems have historically contributed to the devaluation of women and to the use of violence to control a disobedient wife (Buzawa & Buzawa, 2003; Dowd, 1992; McCue, 1995; Schechter, 1982). Within this model, the institution of marriage and family has encouraged abusive men to use physical force to gain control or power over their wives or intimate partners (McCue, 1995).

Some theorists argue that the interplay between the English common law legal system and patriarchal ideology has served to maintain wife abuse (Buzawa & Buzawa, 2003; Dowd, 1992; Schechter, 1982). From this perspective, patriarchy is fostered within economic and social systems, which has defined the husband's role as one of dominance: the husband is perceived as the authoritarian and provider for the family, while the wife has traditionally been assigned dependent, passive, and submissive roles. Under this model, society has segregated the labor force, leaving women with occupations and contributions often perceived as insignificant. This dynamic has led to a disparity in income between men and women (Buzawa & Buzawa, 1990; Yllo, 1993). Many feminists believe that this disparity often leaves women economically dependent, and therefore less likely to leave an abuser (Schechter, 1982; Walker, 1987). Empirical research has found some support for a connection between economic dependency and failure to leave abusive situations. For example, women with low incomes incur higher rates of victimization (Buzawa & Buzawa, 2003; Tjaden & Thoennes, 2000).

Others have found that the probability of staying in a violent relationship was highest for women whose husbands were the sole breadwinners (Aguirre, 1985). In accordance with this finding, research found both economic independence and a batterer's willingness to participate in counseling were strong predictors of remaining with the batterer (Gondolf, 1988). However, other theorists have pointed out that financially independent women also remain in battering situations for slightly different reasons (Johnson, 1996; McCue, 1995). These women often forfeit their paychecks to the abuser, hold joint bank accounts, or fear losing their reputations and their jobs.

Many feminist theorists also claim that gender-role expectations play a large role in abuse. According to McCue (1995), abusive men often embrace unrealistic sex-role expectations and perceptions of their dominance within the family structure, thus believing in their right to use violence in the home.

In accordance with this theory, a meta-analytic review, which included 29 empirical studies examining the relationship between battering and the maintenance of patriarchal ideology (Sugarman & Frankel, 1996), defined "patriarchal ideology" as consisting of three measures: attitudes toward violence, gender attitudes, and gender schemas. This study found that abusive husbands tended to endorse marital violence, but did not show any difference in masculine or feminine traits compared to non-abusive husbands. However, victims of battering were more likely to embrace more feminine gender roles compared to non-battered women. These results offer partial support for the patriarchal theory. For instance, while measures of violent attitudes were consistent with the theories, violent married men were not found to embrace traditionally masculine traits more often than nonviolent husbands. In the same regard, the feminist perspective would suggest that traditional men abuse their partners because they devalue them, though research data in this area remains mixed; some research suggests that traditional men are, in fact, less likely to be violent in intimate relationships (Bookwala, Frieze, Smith & Ryan, 1992), while in Hotaling & Sugarman's (1986) meta-analysis of eight studies, six of them found that traditional men were more abusive with their partners.

A Feminist Model of Power and Control

Research conducted using the coercive control model of domestic violence suggests that abuse originates from desires for domination rather than from familial conflict (Ptacek, 1988; Shepard & Pence, 1999), as is often suggested by family theorists (Yllo, 1993). These scholars purport that violence is a tactic of entitlement and power and is deeply gender based, rather than a conflict tactic that is personal and gender neutral. This dominance perspective also finds supporting evidence in cross-cultural research conducted on domestic violence. Levinson's (1989) examination of 90 small-scale societies worldwide found that violence between family members was virtually non-existent in 16 societies. Levinson (1989) found that in those societies where violence was virtually non-existent, men and women held equal status.

Still other feminist theories have focused on domination of one class over another (Buzawa & Buzawa, 1990, 2003; Schechter, 1982; Yllo, 1993). From this perspective, men dominate women, Caucasians dominate minorities, and the upper class dominates those with fewer resources. In this context, violence is part of a wider system of male power and control (Yllo, 1993). While these theorists recognize that most men do not use violence, they believe the potential for men to use violence continues to exist, thus men benefit from women's fear of potential violence both within and outside of the home.

Critics of this feminist theory tend to believe the focus of female victimization is exaggerated and only serves to perpetuate fear and distaste for feminism among women (Hoff-Summers, 1994). According to many feminists, the primary motive for harassment, rape, sexual coercion, and battering is the desire for power and control (e.g., Brownmiller, 1975; Dobash & Dobash, 1979; Koss et al., 1994; MacKinnon, 1979). Critics of feminist theory argue that the motivation for violence against women is not necessarily rooted in sexism; therefore, the feminist perspective cannot explain other forms of abuse such as child or elder abuse (Yllo, 2005). Felson (2002) argues that control is a primary motive for most violent disputes, not just those between men and women. He believes that men assault women for the same reasons they assault men. Men have a need to control, but this control is not rooted in sexism. Sociologists such as Felson (2002) and Loseke (2005) suggest that feminists tend to disregard the structural deficits associated with the general social structure and family institution. In fact, Felson states that overall women are less likely to be victims of violence than men. Felson (2002) believes violence against women is not a function of a woman's status or prestige in society, but rather that violent men are simply brutes. Men who batter tend to commit additional crimes, suggesting that the desire to control is individually and culturally-based and not necessarily related to attitudes toward women. All relationships foster the possibility of conflict, and the family structure is particularly suited to be a breeding ground for violence (Felson, 2002; Loseke, 2005). Families have cultural roles that dictate how members act within a gendered environment. Social interaction and general expectations regarding social arrangements of familial duties, such as division of labor, financial dependence, and child care, can cause friction and a sense of inequality, ultimately interacting to create and perpetuate violence (Loseke, 2005).

In essence, many scholars believe that simply because feminists tend to label women as "victims" and men as "perpetrators," society has a difficult time perceiving women as aggressors in relationships and can only perceive women's violence against men as self-defense (Loseke, 2005; Yllo, 2005). Yet, a great deal of sociological research suggests women are aggressors in relationships just as much as men, but perhaps not at the same level of violence.

Currently, there are varying degrees of feminist thought when it comes to accepting the use of the term "battered woman syndrome" within expert testimony in cases of self-defense. Many feminists have critiqued the syndrome because of the stereotypes that result due to its use as evidence in a court of law (McMahon, 1999; Schneider, 1986; Shaffer, 1997; Stubbs, 1994). They have posited an alternative, incorporating dominance theory into a control model of domestic violence, now known as the "power and control wheel" (Pence & Paymar, 1986; Pence, 1993; Yllo, 1993), where violence can be explained by a longing for power and control.

Feminist assessments of the relationship between patriarchal ideology and battering have offered one of two conclusions. Some have argued that abusive husbands accept a patriarchal perception of the family and embrace a traditional gender belief system (Pagelow, 1992). Others have argued that due to the limited research, the formulation of any general conclusion would be hard (Edelson, Eisikovits & Guttman, 1985). The degree to which either a husband's or a wife's patriarchal ideology can predict marital violence remains in dispute.

Communities have a love-hate relationship with domestic violence (Bradfield, 2005). It is difficult to overcome the historical view that males are in power. One study of an Australian community surveyed community members who believed domestic violence was unacceptable and the victim was not to blame (Reddy et al., 1997). However, it was obvious that community members found it difficult to understand the "power dynamics" associated with domestic violence. In particular, they had difficulty understanding why a woman would stay in an abusive situation.

Some feminists believe that the general community doesn't quite recognize the power imbalance often associated with abusive situations (Bradfield, 2005). Various research (Reddy et al., 1997; Dutton, 1992) suggests that laypeople attribute external factors to domestic violence (Dutton, 1992), and not necessarily a man's need to use control. According to the Office of the Status of Women (1995), the most common reason offered for domestic violence by laypeople was financial pressure, followed by substance use, and then a woman's infidelity. Moreover, research conducted by Partners Against Domestic Violence (2000) found that most participants believe external factors played a significant role in domestic violence; participants generally perceived the problem was the marriage, not the abuser. In addition, Reddy et al. (1997) stated that their participants explained domestic violence by concentrating on the relationship and the woman's inability to leave, rather than on the characteristics of the abuser. Some theorists (Bradfield, 2005) contend that if domestic violence is perceived as a product of the situation, it takes the emphasis off the male as the abuser and neglects issues of power and control.

There are many different theoretical perspectives of battering. Psychological theories and research tend to focus on characteristics associated with the individuals (victim or abuser) and how they relate to abuse. Sociology examines the societal and familial structures that can influence and perpetuate abuse. Feminist theorists focus upon gender and power differentials and inequalities. Within each psychological, sociological, or feminist theory lies a continuum of debate and belief. These theories have helped broaden our knowledge of the complex interaction between the social structure and victims and perpetrators of abuse. While there is a great deal of research supporting some theories, there is less research supporting others. Theorists and researchers have brought a great deal of attention to the problem of abuse, for which society should be thankful. However, it is also important to note that history, research, and theory all helped to perpetuate public perceptions of abuse. Within these perceptions of abuse is a basic standard or stereotype of a victim of battering. Some public perceptions of abuse may be accurate and supported by empirical research, and some opinions may not be supported by research. The following chapter will examine some of the more popular opinions embraced by the public and try to tease out which perceptions are true and supported by research and which are not.

DISCUSSION QUESTIONS

1. How do individually oriented theorists study the issue of domestic violence?
2. What are some of the personality characteristics found to be associated with batterers and victims of battering?
3. According to family theorists, how does society perpetuate violence among men and women?
4. After reading about the intergenerational transmission of violence, would you conclude there is a cycle of violence among families who experience abuse?
5. According to feminist theory, what are some of the reasons abuse continues in our society?

CHAPTER 4

Perceptions of Battered Women: Myth v. Reality

The public is asked to condemn as wife abuse only those incidents of violence that are obviously outside of moral boundaries. In constructing wife abuse as a public problem, claims-makers asked the public to morally condemn some types of violence. They also argued that women experiencing this violence should receive public sympathy and we can look at the underlying moral dimension of this claim [Loseke, 1992, p. 45].

Public Perceptions of Battered Women

There is not a great deal of research on public perceptions of domestic violence and battered women, and there is little empirical evidence that either validates or invalidates public perceptions. Some of the common perceptions or stereotypes that are discussed here may actually be accurate. Some are based on empirical evidence, while others are merely theoretical assumptions. It should be noted that while empirical research on publicly held views of battered women and the nature of abusive relationships is fairly recent, social scientists and legal commentators (Crocker, 1985; Dowd, 1992; Yllo, 1993) have suggested that misperceptions held by the general public and legal system have been resistant to change due to the historical impact of the first wave of theoretical views that prevailed in the not too distant past and of the centuries of structural ideology embedded in both traditional and contemporary society (Buzawa & Buzawa, 1990, 2003; Gelles, 1993; McCue, 1995; Yllo, 1993, 2005). The questions as to why a battered woman would remain in an abusive relationship or why she would commit domestic homicide have been pondered by theorists since the late 1800s (Rasche, 1990). The earliest and most influential scientific reference to the female spouse killer is that of

Cesare Lombroso, an Italian criminologist whose 1895 study of male and female offenders led him to believe "on the whole, homicidal actions by women could be attributed to passion, or to the monstrous qualities of murderesses who were born criminals" (Lombroso & Ferrero, 1895; cited in Rasche, 1990, p. 36). In the late 1920s, as the popularity of modern psychology increased, it was believed that only women of low intelligence remained in abusive relationships (McCue, 1995; Rasche, 1990). In the 1930s and 1940s, it was believed that battered women were masochistic, while since the mid–1970s experts have asserted that women remain in abusive relationships because they are isolated, have few economic or educational resources, fear retaliation, and have been continually terrorized by repeated battering into a condition of learned helplessness (Rasche, 1990). Undoubtedly, many of these theoretical perspectives continue to influence public perceptions of battered women.

While empirical research regarding characteristics specifically associated with battered women did not occur until the late 1970s, it was evident in the early 1970s that the historical impact of the first wave of theoretical views influenced, and continues to influence, public and professional perceptions. Recently, there has been an increased amount of research examining the knowledge of laypersons in relation to battered women who kill their abusers and the utility of expert evidence in the courtroom in such cases (Bradfield, 2002). These studies have found evidence that the general public embraces myths and misperceptions of battered women.

By the early 1970s, laypersons and professionals had already formed attitudes and beliefs about the issue of domestic violence and associated characteristics of both victims and abusers (i.e., LaViollette & Barnette, 1993). Some predominant beliefs held by the public and by professionals at the time included: battering was not a widespread occurrence, victims of violence enjoyed the battering, and battering only happened to poor, passive women with lots of children and little education. In the past 30 years, laypersons have formed further general depictions of battered women that may or may not be accurate (Browne, 1987; Carlson & Worden, 2005; Dutton, 1992; Follingstad et al., 1989; Finkel et al., 1991; Greene, Raitz & Linblad, 1989; Walker, 1979, 1984; Worden & Carlson, 2005). Until recently, researchers and theorists did not have a strong empirical background to support the prevalence of these misperceptions. Recent studies, however, have found that the public does indeed embrace such perceptions, as well as many others (Reddy et al., 1997; Russell & Melillo, 2006; Terrance & Matheson, 2003).

The term "battered woman" is merely a descriptive construct, but just as many feminist scholars feared, it seems to have produced public views that are contrary to conclusions drawn by experts in the field (Aubrey & Ewing,

1989; Dodge & Greene, 1991; Ewing & Aubrey, 1987; Greene, Raitz & Linblad, 1989). For example, Dodge and Greene compared the opinions of laypersons to those of experts in the field of abuse. They found that compared to experts, laypersons are less likely to believe that the battered woman could be persuaded to stay in the relationship by an abuser's promises to reform, that she would believe she had no other alternative than to use deadly force to protect herself, and that she would believe her husband could kill her. Furthermore, laypersons were more likely to believe the women were dependent, passive, probably abused because they provoked their own beatings, or remained in an abusive relationship because of emotional instability and/or masochism (Downs & Fisher, 2005; Ewing & Aubrey, 1987; Shaffer, 1997).

One of the most consistent findings of public perceptions toward battered women is the public impression that a battered woman is free to leave the relationship if she really wanted to (Aubrey & Ewing, 1989; Browne, 1987; Dodge & Greene, 1991; Ewing & Aubrey, 1987; Walker, Thyfault & Browne, 1982). Such public perceptions have great ramifications for accepting the general reality of the plight of the battered woman, as well as in legal decision making. These attitudes may have changed over the years. In order to investigate possible attitudinal shifts, Reddy et al. (1997) surveyed community members in Australia to assess their perceptions of battered women. They found that participants believed that a battered woman was not responsible for the abuse and that she could not remove herself from the abusive situation. Reddy et al. (1997) also found that laypeople believed that domestic violence was not justifiable and that men were responsible for their own behavior. The researchers believe their study provides evidence that the community they studied is well-informed, and therefore, testimony by expert witnesses about battered woman syndrome meant to dispel myths and misperceptions is not necessary. This study suggests that individuals in Australia are quite knowledgeable about battered women, yet it remains unclear exactly what individuals think of when they think of a battered woman. The extent to which laypersons embrace misperceptions of battered women or battered persons is still not clearly understood. Additional research must be conducted before it can be concluded that there is no need to dispel myths regarding victims of battering.

In a series of studies (Carlson & Worden, 2005; Worden & Carlson, 2005), researchers surveyed public opinions in New York State about domestic violence. They, too, found that, overall, the public believed that physical aggression constituted domestic violence and was not condoned. However, respondents were unsure about the legal issues associated with domestic violence. Participants in this study were more likely to think the cause of domestic violence was rooted in relationships and individual problems and less likely to be a function of society or culture. The survey found most believed domestic violence was common in their communities and that it affected a significant minority of couples. The majority of respondents also believed that a man's aggression was more likely to be defined as domestic violence compared to women's aggressive behaviors. Moreover, respondents were more likely to believe women were not the cause of their own abuse; however, almost one-quarter of respondents believed women want to be abused, and most people believed a battered woman could end an abusive relationship. While this study extends some of the research to public opinions of Americans, scholars still don't know exactly what people think of when they think of a victim of battering. Victims of battering can occur more often in particular age groups, ethnic groups, and socioeconomic status. However, it is important to realize that battering can happen to anyone. Yet, scholars understand few of the implications of what happens to a victim of battering when they do not fit the profile of the "typical" victim of battering. The results of this study also showed that a man's aggression toward women was considered domestic violence, while women's aggression toward men was generally classified as something else. This finding suggests that perhaps laypersons continue to hold misperceptions about who can be battered and how. Given that battering or abuse is increasingly being used as an explanation for illegal activities in a myriad of situations and victim-batterer relationships (i.e., same-sex couples, cohabiting couples, elder abuse, heterosexual male victims), it is necessary for laypersons and legal officials to understand the dynamics of battering, particularly in situations that may not necessarily include physical battering and/or heterosexual females as victims.

Research has found that individuals who are less informed about the dynamics of abuse often assign harsher sentences than their informed counterparts (Schuller, Smith & Olson, 1994) to battered women homicide defendants. Education, age, and gender also play a role in legal decisions regarding battered women. In general, women and men who have egalitarian sex-role attitudes, who are more educated, or who are younger, seem to hold less negative attitudes toward battered women (Aubrey & Ewing, 1989; Schuller & Vidmar, 1992).

While these studies have aided in uncovering public perceptions, such research is still in its infancy. Many assumptions have yet to be examined, though more recent research has demonstrated that public perceptions are often in line with research findings. For example, it is widely assumed that the public believes that battering occurs more often with poor, undereducated, younger adults, and research has begun to find that many of these perceptions are empirically supported. It is clear that domestic violence can cut across all demographic populations, yet recent research has found that over half of the women receiving welfare have experienced battering, many of whom reported physical and mental health problems (Meier, 1997; Raphael & Tolman, 1997). Women with lower incomes have higher rates of victimization (Tjaden & Thoennes, 2000), and while domestic violence affects individuals of all ages, recent data (Tjaden & Thoennes, 2000) shows that rates of domestic violence among women of various races are comparable for all age groups with the exception of ages 20–24; African American women were found to experience greater domestic violence during this age group compared to White women.

Researchers still have much to learn regarding the extent to which public opinions are accurately represented by empirical evidence. This is important as public perceptions may affect legal decision making in misinformed ways. In addition, the research itself often uses methodologies which themselves may reinforce stereotypes or which do not work to illuminate lay persons' understandings of battering scenarios which do not fit such stereotypes. The research typically utilizes vignettes depicting battered women in various situations that lead to fatal injury to their abuser. These vignettes often depict the battered woman in a stereotyped representation of a "good wife," while the husband was clearly "bad." Researchers often depict the abused female as "a caring mother and long suffering wife, perhaps a Cinderella-type character" (Reddy et al., 1997, p. 143). Often the victim is represented as passive, walking on eggshells to appease the abuser, taking care of household chores and dinner, and taking care of the children. There is frequently evidence of previous abuse, and the victim typically kills during a direct confrontation. Reddy and colleagues caution that using these types of vignettes provides important information, but it is not clear whether and how respondents would change their answers if the woman or victim did not fit the stereotype of a battered woman depicted in such stories.

There is a great need to empirically investigate issues such as sexual orientation, race, ethnicity, and victim attributes that may appear atypical to the stereotype often associated with battered women. The application of these standards may leave battered women defendants who attempt to explain their behaviors based on the battered woman syndrome at a disadvantage if their characteristics or experiences deviate from the stereotypes (Blackman, 1990; Kasian et al., 1993; Terrance & Matheson, 2003). A recent study found that the further the defendant moved away from jurors' beliefs about what a battered woman should be, the harsher their verdicts became (Terrance & Matheson, 2003).

Still, the syndrome is indeed helpful for many women defendants who do not deviate much from the standard. The battered woman syndrome has been helpful in counteracting myths about battered women, yet recent research suggests that (to some extent) public attitudes have changed, and some people are more knowledgeable about abuse. If attitudes have changed, is expert testimony really needed? Research has consistently found that the use of expert testimony regarding the battered woman syndrome leads mock jurors to render more lenient verdicts and find women who kill their abusers generally more credible (Schuller & Rzepa, 2002; Schuller, Wells, Rzepa, & Klippenstine, 2004).

Legal Perceptions of Battered Women

Just as the general public holds common beliefs about battered women, empirical evidence suggests that the legal system and legal actors hold similar perceptions. Many states have recently created task forces to explore the pervasiveness of gender bias in aspects of court functioning and to use the findings as the basis for judicial education (Riger, Foster-Fishman, Nelson-Kuna & Curran, 1995). To the author's knowledge, there have been 44 State and 11 Federal task forces who had completed reports on gender bias in state courts (National Judicial Education Program, 2008). Federal courts are now following suit. The consistent conclusion across states is that gender bias is a major problem in the courts, particularly with respect to issues of domestic violence, divorce proceedings, child custody, and courtroom dynamics, and that female legal actors perceive more bias against women than do male legal actors (Riger et al., 1995).

Despite the importance of objectivity in the legal process, misperceptions generally associated with battered women may ultimately affect all aspects of jurisprudence. Research shows that even legal actors in the justice system hold stereotypes of battered women. Within a sample of Canadian police officers and justice officials, many believed that battered women were unreliable and manipulative liars (Rigakos, 1995), and many U.S. police officers also felt uncomfortable with domestic violence issues, believed some of the abuse may be justified, and thought some battered women remain in abusive situations because they enjoy the abuse (Saunders, 1995). Allard (2005) believes these attitudes tend to strengthen negative feelings about battered women.

That domestic violence is perceived as a lesser crime by legal actors has been consistently documented (Eaton & Hyman, 1992; Maryland Special Joint Committee, 1989). For example, it has been noted that family judges are often more attuned to the issue of battering than criminal judges; criminal court judges often think of domestic violence cases as family matters, and therefore focus on other more high-status offenses which they perceive as more serious (Buzawa & Buzawa, 2003; Eaton & Hyman, 1992). In addition, general task force research on gender bias in the courts (Eaton & Hyman, 1992; Maryland Special Joint Committee, 1989; Resnik, 1991) has found that many victims and legal actors believe that crimes involving domestic violence are not treated in the same way as crimes in which the complaining party and the defendant are strangers. Many advocates for victims of domestic violence believe that general court systems continue to have difficulty understanding the psychological and social contexts of victims of domestic violence, which ultimately leads to less punitive processing of batterers (Buzawa & Buzawa, 2003). It is important to note, however, that law enforcement officials and legal actors are taking steps toward changing the legal response to battering (Buzawa & Buzawa, 2003). For instance, specialized domestic violence courts have been implemented and are steadily rising. Furthermore, many prosecutorial departments have added victim advocates to their staff and added "no drop" policies that disallow victims to drop charges against their batterer, and law enforcement officials have added protocols that require the arrest of the primary offender.

One empirical research study that demonstrates that domestic violence continues to be handled differently from other crimes was conducted by McCormick, Maric, Seto, and Barbaree (1998). Their research found that the relationship of the perpetrator and victim played a large role in sentencing decisions. The study investigated 204 incarcerated rapists from a sexual behavior clinic. Participants were classified into groups according to their relationship to the victim. Of the 204 participants, 103 were classified as stranger rapists, 36 as acquaintance rapists, and 65 as partner rapists. The study used archival data such as police reports, criminal records, and case notes. In addition, the degree of force used when committing the rape was explored, as well as degree of injury, excessiveness, and victim resistance. The study found a direct inverse relationship that showed rates of sentencing (as measured in months) decreased significantly when there was a prior relationship with the victim.

One committee found that courts tend to fail to grant victims of abuse credibility. When victims delay reporting abuse or withdraw a protection from abuse (PFA), judges may assume the violence is not that bad, or else the victim would leave the abuser. This suggests that many legal actors do not take into consideration external and internal influences that may keep victims of domestic violence with their abusers (*Melior Group v. Kramer & Associates*, 2001).

Moreover, some scholars believe that judges and legal actors have a difficult time with women who commit violent acts, as this often runs counter to their prescribed gender role (Crocker, 1985; Jenkins & Davidson, 1990; McCue, 1995). In the past, women who committed spousal homicide were traditionally advised to plead temporary insanity or diminished capacity (Castel, 1990). One of the most important reasons for this is that the female homicide offender is somewhat of an anomaly. For instance, an average of three to five children are killed by their parents daily in the U.S. When Andrea Yates drowned her five children in the bathtub, the media focused on the supposed anomaly of a mother who would kill her own children. At the same time that Yates was drowning her children, however, a man in California purposely left his barbeque grill on in his home knowing it would asphyxiate his sleeping children. In the midst of depression because his wife left him, Garcia attempted to kill himself and his six children. Garcia and only one of his six children survived. But this case did not receive the media explosion Yates did. The disparity of attention to these cases demonstrates how society reacts when women kill. Because of societal expectations of male attributes (e.g., aggression) and female attributes (e.g., gentle, passive, nurturers), violence by women is rarely seen as acceptable and it is still often perceived as surprising. Women who fail to conform to gender expectations are often typecast as abnormal, dangerous, or mentally ill (Castel, 1990). Castel (1990) opined that a battered woman's killing of her batterer is still not acknowledged as justified, even if it was in an attempt to save either her own life or the lives of her children (Castel, 1990). Yet there are many recent cases, such as that of Mary Winkler, a preacher's wife from Tennessee, who shot her husband and used the battered spouse syndrome as a part of her defense, which show the utility of testimony about the syndrome for some. Charged with first degree murder, Winker was convicted of voluntary manslaughter by a panel of jurors that included ten women and received a sentence of 210 days and 3 years probation. Obviously, Winker's jury felt some form of empathy for her and believed the evidence presented that Winkler had been abused by her husband on a regular basis.

Gender-bias task forces have documented many incidents of gender bias in the courts. Some task forces have found that women have been denied credibility in the courts and often face a legal system that is generally uninformed about matters regarding domestic violence (Eaton & Hyman, 1992; Maryland Special Joint Committee, 1989; Ninth Circuit Gender Bias Task Force, 1993). While the majority of gender and racial bias task forces were incorporated in the late 1980s and 1990s, follow-up research continues to report that racial and gender bias continues at disproportionately high levels in many states (*Melior Group v. Kramer & Associates*, 2001; Report of the Oregon Supreme Court, 1998; Report of the Third Circuit Task Force on Equal Treatment in the Courts, 1997, 2000; Washington State Minority and Justice

Commission, 2001). Many participants within the legal system believe judges do not understand the causes and consequences of domestic violence, and some participants of the court feel as though their experience was demeaning (*Melior Group v. Kramer & Associates*, 2001). In addition, while some scholars believe women receive more lenient sentences than men for lesser crimes (Armstrong, 1977; Winn, Haugen, & Jurik, 1988, as cited in Mann, 1996), others have found that women receive harsher sentences for homicide than men (Browne, 1987; McCue, 1995). The debate of whether women receive similar sentences as men continues. For instance, while there is research that suggests that gender differences in sentencing are diminishing, some researchers find that women who kill men receive more harsh sentences than women who kill women (Mann, 1996). In contrast, however, more recent research has shown that offenders who victimize women and particularly men who victimize women received the longest sentences (Curry, Lee, & Rodriguez, 2004). Needless to say the debate concerning gender differences in sentencing continues on. There are so many factors to consider when assessing sentencing it is difficult to attribute differences in sentencing specifically to gender.

Task forces have found that legal actors discredit victims of battering whom they presume may have provoked attacks against themselves, or generally mistrust their accounts because of conflicts with documented characteristics of the case, such as the tendency to minimize the seriousness of abuse, and sometimes feel distrust caused by frustrations associated with women who fail to carry through with their charges (Buzawa & Buzawa, 2003; Eaton & Hyman, 1992; *Melior Group v. Kramer & Associates*, 2001). Research on this topic is lacking and it is difficult to tease out whether differences in the legal system truly exist and, if so, in which direction they may lean. For instance, the results cited in the report by the Federal Task Force (*Melior Group v. Kramer & Associates*, 2001) were based on surveys provided to criminal judges regarding issues of domestic violence. It is possible that judges' replies to this survey reflect a heightened response toward being indiscriminant toward race and gender. Furthermore, generally speaking, there is more that is known about violence and legal outcomes for men than is known about women. Even less is known about legal outcomes pertaining to domestic violence cases when women are arrested and convicted of domestic assaults. Scholars have only just begun to investigate women who are arrested for domestic abuse, and even less is known about the characteristics of female aggressors. Perhaps coming to the realization that these issues should be researched in greater depth has helped us to understand and change societal beliefs about the dynamics associated of abuse in all relationships. Despite some legal progress over the years, changing general societal beliefs has been, and continues to be, extremely difficult.

Battering Is Not a Widespread Problem:
Empirical Evidence of the Prevalence of Battering

Recent estimates of the number of women who are severely assaulted each year by male partners have varied considerably from two million to more than eight million (McCue, 1995). Estimates of prevalence of physical abuse by a husband against a wife continue to be based primarily on the use of the Conflict Tactics Scales (Straus, Gelles & Steinmetz, 1980). When estimates of violence are limited to more serious levels (use of a weapon) as measured on the Conflict Tactics Scales, abuse appears to occur at a lower rate of about 4 percent of the population. This is roughly equal to 2 to 3 million couples in the U.S. (The Jacob's Institute of Women's Health, 1996).

Obtaining accurate statistics of rape and assault is difficult because studies of prevalence are difficult to design and are always flawed to some extent. Measuring domestic violence is also difficult. The Department of Justice's National Crime Victimization Survey (NCVS) assesses large representative populations in the U.S. and their experiences with victimization. While the NCVS has its shortcomings, it is considered one of the best sources of information on violence in the U.S. (Felson, 2002). Other agencies examine medical records and doctors' reports of physical injury; the Uniform Crime Reporting (UCR) Program examines incidents reported to law enforcement. The UCR (2006) showed approximately one-third of female victims of murder or non-negligent manslaughter were killed by their husbands, ex-partners, or boyfriends. This percentage was again verified in the Supplemental Homicide Report (SHR) data in 2000, which showed that about one-third of female homicide victims were killed by their husbands, former husbands, or boyfriends. When crime studies such as the UCR or SHR are considered, it is clear that women are the victims of intimate partner violence more often than men. Yet, some researchers (Belknap et al., 2001; Kruttschnitt, 2001) have reported that gender differences among men and women who kill intimate partners are quite similar, while others have found that women kill their partners more often than men kill their female partners (Straus, 2005). With all of these conflicting research findings it is difficult to understand how this could be. Felson (2002) has argued that when victims of violence are examined in general, statistics show that men are overwhelmingly more likely to be the victims of all forms of violence, with the exceptions of rape and sexual assault (Felson, 2002). For instance, the UCR (2006) found that approximately 70 percent of victims of murder and non-negligent homicides were men. When statistics are limited to assaults not related to sex, men are still more likely to be assaulted than women; however, women suffer more injury than men in these assaults (Felson, 2002). It is easy to misinterpret statistics suggesting that women are overwhelmingly the victims of violence, when in fact men are more likely to be the victims of all forms of violence (with the exception of sexual assault and rape) compared to women (Felson, 2002). Another reason why statistical interpretations differ is because of the difference in the type of information collected by family and crime studies.

While considerable research efforts have been directed at identifying specific demographic factors associated with battered women, accurate data are difficult to obtain. Typically, statistics may be hindered by under-reporting of battering incidents (Browne, 1993; Johnson, 1996; Mather, 1988), lack of systematic compilation of domestic violence statistics by local and state police departments (Buzawa & Buzawa, 1990; Johnson, 1996), and methodological approaches which often exclude the poor, immigrants, military families living on base, and individuals who are hospitalized, homeless, institutionalized or incarcerated (Browne, 1988). However, on the basis of the last 20 years of empirical research, experts now suggest that a more accurate estimate may be as high as four million women in the U.S. who are severely assaulted by male partners in an average 12-month period (Straus & Gelles, 1990).

Simply measuring the number of aggressive acts between a couple may not necessarily be indicative of domestic violence for men and women. Not all violence may be classified as domestic violence. There are relative differences between men and women's use of relationship violence, including the severity of aggressive acts used, consequences, and motives of violence. Johnson and Ferraro's (2000) review of the literature in the 1990s led them to declare the importance of making distinctions when describing intimate partner violence. Johnson (1995, 2000) argued that when considering the gender symmetry of intimate partner violence, the types of violence and corresponding motives should be considered. For instance, he distinguished between *common couple violence* (mutual violence most often found among couples that does not escalate over time, and is less likely to be severe), *intimate terrorism* (based on the need for control of another, this type of violence often involves emotional abuse, is less likely to be mutual, and is more likely to involve more serious violence), *violent resistance* (a form of self-defense most likely used by women), and *mutual violent control* (both partners vie for control in the relationship and are violent toward one another). Johnson and Ferraro (2000) suggest that when we reflect on statistics of victimization and perpetration of intimate partner violence, these typologies should be considered, yet critics (DeKesaredy & Dragiewicz, 2007) warn that the social context and motives of abuse cannot be determined by such typologies.

Women as Victims

Women tend to experience substantially more psychological and physical injury during a domestic assault than men; therefore, they are in need of a greater amount of resources to deal with the effects of the abuse. Women are most likely to be stalked and killed by their abusive partner after leaving the abusive situation (Saunders, 2002). In recent years, although many states have enacted mandatory arrest laws to counteract the problem of domestic violence against women, after the enactment of these mandatory arrest laws, women's arrest rates for domestic violence soared (see Mallory et al., 2003; Martin, 1997), primarily because police often arrest both individuals (dual arrest) when a domestic dispute occurs.

Tjaden & Thoennes (2000) conducted a large scale survey to assess intimate partner violence using a random digit dialing system within the 50 contiguous states and District of Columbia. Researchers surveyed 8,000 men and 8,000 women. The researchers found that almost 8 percent of women reported being raped by their intimate partner in their life time. Intimate partners in this study included current and former cohabitants. The National Organization of Women (NOW) estimates two to six times that many women are raped but do not report it. NOW adds that every year 1.2 million women are forcibly raped by their current or former male partners, some multiple times (Violence Against Women in the United States, NOW, 2001). The Bureau of Justice Statistics further states that about seven in ten female rape or sexual assault victims indicated they knew the offender. It is important to note that less than half of reported rapes or sexual assaults end with an arrest (Catalano, 2005), and statistics indicate the relationship of the victim to the offender is a factor in actual reporting of a rape or sexual assault. The closer the relationship, the less likely law enforcement would be informed. When the offender is a current or former husband or boyfriend, approximately three-fourths of victims do not report the crime to police. As the relationship between the victim and the offender becomes more distant, it is more likely the crime will be reported to police (USDOJ, OJP, 2002).

In 1998, it was estimated that almost half of the women involved in domestic assaults were injured (Rennison & Welchans, 2000). Researchers found that during the time period of 1992 to 1998 women were almost 40 percent more likely to become a victim of assault in domestic violence compared to other types of assault (Simon & Perkins, 2001). Furthermore, in 1998, 53 percent of homicide victims were women (Rennison & Welchans, 2000). Finally, women are also more likely to experience stalking. Results from the NVAWS suggested that women are four times more likely to be stalked during their lifetime compared to men, and it is more likely that their stalker is a current or former intimate (Tjaden & Thoennes, 1998). Stalking has been found to be related to threats of violence and injury (Tjaden & Thoennes, 1998).

The Great Debate: Are Women Equally Violent? Male Victims of Domestic Abuse

According to the NVAWS, 8 percent of men reported that they had been the victim of rape or had been physically assaulted by an intimate partner during their lifetime (Tjaden & Thoennes, 2000). Tjaden and Thoennes (2000) also found that almost three million men are physically assaulted by an intimate partner annually, of which 580,000 resulted in injury.

The debate about "gender symmetry" of violence among partners (Frieze, 2005; Straus, 2005) has been going strong for over 20 years. The debate pertaining to gender symmetry of domestic violence can be explained by considering the differences between intimate terrorism and common couple violence (Johnson, 1995; Johnson & Ferraro, 2005). While Johnson and Ferraro (2000) suggested that men make up the majority of the intimate terrorist group and violent resistance is most often used by women (Johnson & Ferraro, 2000), more recent research has found comparable rates of intimate terrorism among men and women in a large Canadian sample (LaRoche, 2005), while other studies (Graham-Kevan & Archer, 2003) have found women are more likely to be intimate terrorists than men. When we consider this new research, we begin to believe that perhaps gender symmetry in intimate partner violence does exist.

One study (Williams & Frieze, 2005) examined over 3,500 individuals and found that 18 percent of couples reported experiencing some type of violence within their relationships. Almost 30 percent of those reported mild-mutual violence and another 20 percent reported mutual-severe violence. Men were found to be the targets of violence initiated by women and women were also more likely to claim to be the aggressor when violence was one-sided. Studies on aggression in dating relationships are also consistent with intimate partner abuse (Follingstad, Bradley, Helff, & Laughlin, 2002; Ehrensaft, Moffitt & Caspi, 2004; Russell & Oswald, 2002). For instance, in a national study of over 11,000 respondents between the ages of 18 and 28, researchers found that of those individuals who reported domestic violence, almost 50 percent was reciprocal and women were the sole perpetrators in 70 percent of non-reciprocal violent responses (Whitaker, Haileyesus, Swahn, & Saltzman, 2007). Similarly, more recent studies are finding that women are more likely to initiate domestic violence disputes than men (Kwong, Bartholomew, Dutton, 1999; Fergusson, Horwood & Ridder, 2005; Prospero, 2008; Straus, 2006). While some scholars (Stark, 2006) continue to believe that women are still more likely to be the victims of intimate terrorism than males, more recent research tends to lean toward showing that women are just as likely (if not more likely) to initiate violence or be intimate terrorists than men (Felson & Outlaw, 2007).

It should be noted that much of what is reported may actually reflect what Johnson (1995, 2000) termed "common couple violence." Aggression can be defined differently by many researchers; however, many studies use the conflict tactics scale, which is a survey that is designed to measure levels of physical force and aggression among men and women. For instance, the conflict tactics scale measures all forms of aggression from a slap to more serious behaviors such as kicking and choking. Yet there are serious limitations noted with the use of CTS, including under-reporting by female victims and the survey's inability to consider motive and context of abusive behaviors (DeKeseradly & Dragiewicz, 2007).

Studies using the CTS have repeatedly shown equal or higher rates of assault by women and more recently by adolescent girls. The National Family Violence Survey published in 1980 (Straus et al., 1980) and a follow-up conducted in 1990 (Straus & Gelles, 1990) consistently showed the number of assaults committed by women was slightly higher than those committed by men. For instance, the number of assaults perpetrated by women was 124 per 1,000 couples, as compared to 122 per 1,000 assaults by men as reported by their female counterparts. When examining minor and severe assaults, minor assaults by women constituted 78 per 1,000 couples compared with 72 per 1,000 for men. In other words, women had initiated more minor assaults than men. The number of severe assaults committed by women was 46 per 1,000 couples compared to 50 per 1,000 severe assaults committed by men (Straus, 2005). Even though men committed more severe assaults, none of these differences were statistically significant. On the other hand, studies on the prevalence of intimate partner violence have shown that women are the primary targets of domestic violence from male partners (Tjaden & Thoennes, 2000).

Characteristics of Abusive Women

We are just beginning to learn about the characteristics of females who batter men or men who remain with abusive partners. Some research is beginning to examine the motives and tactics used by women who batter their partners. A recent study (Hamel, Graham-Kevan, & Prospero, 2008) examined 208 men and 174 women from 22 sites that represented 12 counties in California and found no significant differences among men and women batterers in jealous behaviors (i.e., preoccupation, threats, intimidation, economic abuse, and stalking), use of manipulative tactics (coercion and threats to self-esteem), and use of children and the legal system. Another study examined 43 incident reports of women processed for domestic violence offenses and attending battering intervention programs (Ward & Muldoon, 2007). The authors found that the most frequent physical strategy used by women was pushing and the most frequently cited psychological strategy was intimidation. Ward and Muldoon (2007) found that women tended to aggress toward men because of anger precipitated by dissatisfaction with the relationship or fear of victimization. Similarly, Swan and her colleagues (2005) investigated 108 women who had admitted using violence toward their partners and found anger, aggression, victimization, PTSD, and childhood abuse contributed to aggressive behavior toward intimates. Women were more likely to aggress toward their partners when they themselves had been victimized and experienced child abuse. Women who were victimized were more likely to suffer from symptoms of PTSD and depression and likely to aggress against others. For instance, the quote below suggests that anger plays a significant role in abuse and aggression may not be aimed specifically at her husband, but rather anyone who would cross her.

> *"I'm either a really good drunk or I'm an out-and-out s**t, horrible, violent, abusive, emotional drunk. I'll beat up Blake when I'm drunk, I don't think I have ever bruised him, but I do have my way. If he says one thing I don't like then I'll chin him. I'm not a fighter, but if I am backed against the wall I'll kick the s**t out of anyone. I don't think your ability to fight has anything to do with how big you are. It's to do with how much anger is in you"* [Soul singer Amy Winehouse, World Entertainment News Network, http://www.starpulse.com].

While recent research has found that men and women are just as likely to initiate assaults in intimate partner relationships, it is unclear just how many women may be considered batterers or how many men consider themselves to be battered. Society trains men to be macho and women to fear potential violence from men (Holtzworth-Munroe, 2005), so while women may indeed fear the potential of violence from men, men often do not consider women as intimidating and may actually find their aggression humorous (Holtzworth-Munroe, 2005). If a man is the target of a woman's aggression, he may decide to remain in the relationship for some of the same reasons women remain with their abusers. Love and promises to change may keep many men from leaving. Emotional or financial dependency, cultural factors, or children may also be significant factors when considering leaving the abuser. Research has yet to examine these factors, as well as the psychological factors associated with the consequence of abuse. Men may not recognize the behavior as abuse, or if they do recognize it as abuse, they may be reluctant to share this information with others for fear they may not be believed or supported. Battered men do not have the same opportunities as battered women with regard to resources. Shelters are not available for men, and other support systems traditionally used by women (family, friends, social agencies) may be less accepting of male victims of intimate partner violence. Despite the recent research that suggests men and women are equally responsible for abuse in relationships, many members of society remain in a state of denial that women can actually abuse men. Over the last 30 years, society has been hypervigilant about recognizing women as victims of domestic abuse and identifying violence against women as the function of patriarchal power differentials. This process of recognition took hundreds of years before battering women was deemed unacceptable in contemporary social circles. Unfortunately, at this point in time, society is not ready to realize that just as men abuse women, women also abuse men. The thought of women abusing men remains a foreign concept that is (to many people) laughable or unbelievable. But it is no laughing matter when women kill their abusers.

What About Women Who Kill?

For every 100 female partners that men kill, women kill approximately 60–70 male partners (Gauthier & Brankston, 2004; Wilson & Daley, 1992) with more than 1,000 women killing their intimate partner each year (Huss et al., 2006). A large proportion of female precipitated homicides are believed to be the product of self-defense. Women commit fewer than 10 percent of all homicides in the U.S. (Uniform Crime Reports, 2004), and researchers have estimated that homicides committed by women are seven times more likely to be in self-defense to a partner's aggression and threat as compared to male-perpetrated homicide (Campbell, 1986). Yet, some researchers (Felson & Messner, 1998) conclude that women actually kill in self-defense much less then is estimated, though women are more likely to be motivated by self-defense compared to males who kill their partners. In other words, when women kill their partners, they are more likely to do so in the act of self-defense. In contrast, when men kill their intimate partners, it is very unlikely that they are motivated by self-defense. Snell (1991) found that women serving sentences for violent offenses were twice as likely to have committed a crime against someone close to them (36 percent) compared to males incarcerated for violent offenses (16 percent). One researcher (Richey-Mann, 1989,

1996) examined 296 cases of female-perpetrated homicides representing six cities in a four-year period and found that almost 76 percent of homicides were committed in the home. Rates of African American women and non–African American women who killed family members were similar, while African American women were more likely to kill an intimate partner.

There is much debate among those who believe that women who commit violent acts toward their partners do so in self-defense and others (Felson, 2002; Jurik & Gregware, 1989) who argue that women who commit violent acts toward a partner often initiate the violence and are aggressive. Jurik and Gregware (1989) evaluated 24 homicide cases in which women had killed their husbands and found that women initiated the violence in less than half (40 percent) of the cases and less than one-quarter of these (21 percent) homicides were committed by women because of prior abuse or threat of abuse or death. Furthermore, more than half the sample (60 percent) of women who killed their partners had a previous criminal record (Jurik & Gregware, 1989). A similar study by Mann (1989) investigating African American homicide offenders found that women who killed their male partners were often found to be impulsive, violent, and had violent criminal records. Statistically, women committed more partner homicides in heterosexual relationships. These results give some credence to the idea that individuals who are committing homicide are simply aggressive brutes (Felson, 2002), and it is less likely that intimate partner violence is primarily a sex-based crime. However, when one considers domestic violence in general, women are more likely to be the victim of attacks severe enough to cause injury and need for medical attention (Cantos et al., 1994; Malloy et al., 2003; Stets & Straus, 1990; Tjaden & Thoennes, 2000; Zlotnick et al., 1998). The contrast among research findings can be overwhelming and difficult to interpret, mainly because of research methods chosen to collect data.

Prevalence of Domestic Assault and Homosexual Relationships

Most state statutes refer to domestic violence as domestic assault under criminal law. Domestic assault is typically defined as attempting to cause, or willfully or recklessly causing, bodily injury to a family or household member, or willfully causing a family or household member to fear imminent serious bodily injury. As stated previously, domestic violence has been considered a crime against heterosexual women. Research is beginning to illustrate heterosexual men and individuals in homosexual relationships also represent a significant number of victims in domestic violence incidents (Cantos, Neidig, & O'Leary, 1994; Malloy, McCloskey, Grigsby, & Gardner, 2003; Stets & Straus, 1990; Tjaden & Thoennes, 2000; Turell, 2000; Zlotnick, Kohn, Peterson, & Pearlstein, 1998). Rates of intimate partner violence are estimated to range between 25 to 50 percent of lesbian couples (McClennen, Summers, & Vaughan, 2002). For instance, results from NVAWS (Tjaden & Thoennes, 2000) found that 11.4 percent of women in lesbian relationships experienced rape or physical assault and 15 percent of males in same-sex relationships experienced partner violence. Additional research by Balsam and Szymanski (2005) found that of the 272 participants recruited from a Gay Pride event, 44 percent reported being the victim of violence at the hands of their partner.

The question remains as to whether heterosexual male victims and homosexual male victims of domestic violence can receive equivalent treatment to heterosexual female victims within the criminal justice system. Less is known about homosexual domestic violence, but similarities have been found to exist between homosexual and opposite sex domestic violence in the reasons behind the perpetrator's use of abuse (Potoczniak, Mourot, Crosbie-Burnett, & Potoczniak, 2003). Lesbian perpetrators, like heterosexual perpetrators, sometimes desire control in the family situation and use violence to maintain this control (Dalton & Schneider, 2001). An additional similarity between heterosexual and homosexual domestic violence can be the presence of the abusive cycle and the tendency of violence within the cycle to become more persistent and severe (Merrill & Wolfe, 2000; Walker, 1984, p. 52). Emotional, physical, sexual, and financial abuse, common in heterosexual domestic violence, was also found in violent homosexual relationships, although gay men were less likely to experience financial abuse (Merrill & Wolfe, 2000; Renzetti, 1992). One research study (Turell, 2000) investigated rates of abuse among gay men, bisexuals, transsexuals, gay women, and lesbians. The author provided two different self-report classifications for lesbians and gay women but did not disclose why they did so other than perceived political differences among the terms. The author found that 44 percent of gay men, 58 percent of gay women, and 55 percent of lesbians reported being victims of domestic violence. The prevalence of homosexual domestic violence is questionable because it is difficult to recruit a representative sample of gay men, gay women, and lesbians, and domestic violence may go largely unreported to the criminal justice system. Gay men and lesbian victims of domestic violence may avoid reporting to police for fear of a homophobic response and the possibility that they are not protected under domestic violence laws (Dalton & Schneider, 2001).

One of the most profound differences between homosexual domestic violence and heterosexual domestic violence is that there are greater external influences, such as threats of "outing" a partner to friends, family, or place of employment (Johnson & Ferrero, 2000). Same sex couples, particularly lesbians, are less likely to be believed by friends, law enforcement, and social workers that they are abused because battering is considered a male domain. Research has found that the greatest difference between homosexual and heterosexual couples is in the way police, medical professionals, and helping programs respond to victims (Potoczniak, 2003). Heterosexual males and homosexual victims may not realize they are being abused because of the lack of responses by professionals (McClennen, Summers, & Vaughan, 2002; Merrill & Wolfe, 2000; Renzetti, 1992). Society tends to believe that violence between two men or two women is mutually initiated and less severe because the parties are generally equal in strength (Dalton & Schneider, 2001). A study on jurors' perceptions of rape found that rape committed against a gay, lesbian, or bisexual individual (GLB) by another GLB individual was considered less serious than a heterosexual rape and resulted in less stern punishment for the GLB perpetrator (Hill, 2000).

Battering Is a Private Family Problem: An Empirical Examination of Societal Cost

What was once thought to be a private family matter is now recognized as having a societal impact that exhausts financial and protective resources. For example, in 1995 societal costs were estimated at $5.8 billion in medical care, mental health services, and loss of productivity, and estimates based on inflation for 2003 increased to $8.3 billion (Center for Disease Control [CDC], 2006). The costs increase to an estimated $67 billion when one considers medical and additional costs related to quality of life losses in one year in the United States (Miller, Cohen, & Wienrsema, 1996). Surveys conducted by the National Crime Victimization Survey (NCVS) (1996) indicated that the financial losses to women victims of non-lethal intimate violence exceeded $150 million per year. This included medical costs (40 percent), property loss (44 percent), and the remaining amount consisted of lost pay. Female victims of domestic violence are more likely to require medical attention, take time off from work, and spend more time in bed (Rand, 1997). Additional research by the NVAW showed approximately one-third of women reporting rape or physical assault received medical attention (Tjaden & Thoennes, 2000).

More recent research estimates that 35 percent of women who visit hospital emergency rooms are there for symptoms of ongoing abuse. The Bureau of Justice Statistics (1991) found that approximately one in five women victimized by their partners or ex-partners reported they had been a victim of many similar crimes and sustained at least three assaults within six months of being surveyed. Stark & Flintcraft (1983) also noted that 47 percent of the husbands who battered their partners did so at least three times or more each year. Furthermore, because repeated beatings frequently result in hospitalization or surgery, many insurance companies have become wary of providing insurance for battered women. In fact, many insurance companies have denied coverage for battered women (McCue, 1995), leaving them to obtain state assistance (Parsons, 1996). While the Violence Against Women Act (2000) required the attorney general to study and identify states laws that address insurance discrimination toward victims of intimate partner violence, these reports have been slow in coming and there is little protection for women who are beaten by their husbands from being victimized again by insurance companies that deny victims health, disability, or life insurance (Parsons, 1996).

The financial impact of resources lost to the consequences of battering in America is staggering. For example, some researchers have argued that because a batterer tends to isolate his mate and frequently refuses to allow her to work, potentially valuable workers are kept out of the employment market (Archer, 1989). However, when battered women are allowed to work, their job performance is severely impaired by the abuse they receive (Johnson, 1996; Meier, 1997; Walker, 1984). In fact, national levels of domestic violence cost employees an estimated three to five billion dollars annually (Johnson, 1996; McCue, 1995) due to worker absenteeism, harassment, or impaired effectiveness on the job due to pain or depression (Walker, 1984). Intimate partner violence has indirect organizational costs associated with worker production, as over half of victims of abuse miss three or more days of work monthly (Zachary, 2000), and abuse affects worker benefit plans because researchers have found almost $2,000 more is spent on victims of violence for health plans compared to employees who are not abused. Lastly, mental health costs were found to be 800 percent higher for victims of domestic violence because of additional psychological and physical problems associated with abuse (Swanberg et al., 1996; Swanberg, Logan, & Macke, 2006; Wisner, Gilmer, Saltzman, & Zink, 1999).

In addition to substantial economic loss, battering not only drains medical resources, but puts a considerable financial strain upon the legal system. According to one study (Pierce, Spaar & Briggs, 1988), statistics from Boston police departments during the time period between 1977 and 1982 found approximately half of the calls received by police were due to family quarrels.

Pease and Laycock (1996) found many of these calls were repeaters, wherein 43 percent of calls for domestic violence involved only 7 percent of households. The number of homicides in Boston as a result of domestic violence was 1,544 in 2004. Of these deaths, 25 percent of victims were men and 75 percent of victims were women (CDC, 2006). From this, it can be inferred that taxpayers incur costs of law enforcement agencies to first arrest and then prosecute the offending spouse. If prosecution is successful, taxpayers pay to keep the convicted person in prison and pay for child support for any children (Archer, 1989). The repercussions to children who have witnessed or have been a victim of abuse also may have a dramatic impact on the future of society (Archer, 1989; O'Leary, 1993; Pagelow, 1984). Research has shown (Wolak & Finkelhor, 1998) that children who witness intimate partner violence can experience adverse behavioral effects, such as increased aggression and delinquency.

In conclusion, scholars have only just begun to examine public perceptions of battered women and victims of battering in general. It is clear that some beliefs and possible misperceptions are held by laypersons and legal actors. As previously mentioned, rates of victimization have been found to range between two to eight million. The discrepancy among research findings pertaining to prevalence of domestic violence among men and women can differ widely based on the way intimate partner violence is measured. The lack of consistencies among methodologies, samples, and definitions of abuse makes it difficult to obtain the true prevalence and incidence of battering. However, some studies suggest that the rate of victimization is more likely to be closer to four million. Despite these discrepancies, the societal cost of abuse is great. Also, while some discrepancies between public opinion and research have been addressed, there are additional characteristics that can play a significant role in abuse such as culture, education, age, and financial status. The diversity of the characteristics of battered women are only recently becoming better understood, and there is little known about the diversity of other victims of battering that should also be considered. The following chapter continues to tease out myth from reality as it addresses the diversity of victims of domestic violence.

DISCUSSION QUESTIONS

1. What were some of the predominant beliefs about battered women held by the public in the 1970's? To what extent you believe society's attitudes have changed?

2. Identify a few of the ways that age, gender, and education might affect perceptions toward battered women.

3. Name and discuss some of the ways misperceptions about battering and victims of battering affect legal decisions.

4. Name at least three reasons why obtaining statistics on the prevalence of battering is difficult to obtain.

5. What is gender symmetry? Describe the debate among scholars. What is your view on the topic, does gender symmetry really exist?

CHAPTER 5

The Diversity of Battered Women: Myth v. Reality

On Tuesday, September 26, 2000, Jose Barajas shot and killed his wife, Maria Luisa Mora Calderon, and then killed himself. Their bodies remained under police tarps where they fell on the shoulder of Highway 101 in San Mateo County, California, until they were removed.

Maria had been beaten and had her life threatened by Jose on numerous occasions. Once she even fled to Mexico, but Jose got her and brought her back. But the abuse was not reported to police, not by Maria, not by their children, and not by neighbors who repeatedly heard Jose's violence and threats. Finally, Maria left, and after 5 months, on Monday, September 25, she told Jose that she was going to take out a restraining order against him. That infuriated him and led him to murder her and kill himself [Healthinmind.com, 2009].

Dysfunctional relationships are not limited to any particular demographic; take, for example, Maria and Jose.

This case is indicative of some of the cultural differences that should be considered regarding domestic violence. In the situation noted above, we see that Maria never reported the violence, nor did her children or neighbors. What is gleaned from this example is the unspoken acceptance of abuse. This story represents just one of the infinite number of differences among victims of abuse—and the importance of culture and demographic factors such as ethnicity, status, age, and education.

The Dynamics of Culture, Ethnicity, and Status

Most empirical research has revealed that domestic violence cuts across racial, ethnic and cultural boundaries, and that no community is immune from

74

its effects (Browne, 1987; Ewing, 1987; McCue, 1995; Pagelow, 1992; Walker, 1979, 1984). Many recent studies have investigated statistical data to determine whether race differentiates battered from non-battered women. Researchers believe that cultural contexts cannot be ignored when identifying intimate partner violence, and various studies have now demonstrated that some races, ethnicities, ages, and cultures experience intimate partner violence at differing rates (Malley-Morrison & Hines, 2004). For example, researchers (Sorenson & Telles, 1991) examined marital violence rates for Caucasian, Mexican American women born in Mexico, and Hispanic women born in this country and found that marital violence occurs in somewhat equal numbers within each racial group — that is, until immigration status is taken into account. Once the researchers controlled for immigration status, they found that Mexican American women born in the United States were almost 2.5 times more likely to experience abuse compared to women born in Mexico. Their results remind us that cultural contexts, including immigrant status, can provide helpful information when determining the etiology of abuse.

Racial differences have been noted by researchers with regard to remaining in or leaving abusive relationships, as well as differences in reporting habits. For example, while Asian American women were less likely to report abuse compared to other races (NVAWS, Tjaden & Thoennes, 2000), one should consider the extent to which culture affects reporting. Some cultures may be resistant when it comes to reporting abuse more than others. For instance, Eng (1995) suggested that abuse is considered shameful to Asian American women. Jewish victims of abuse may be apprehensive to report abuse for fear their children will be shunned by the religious community (Mills, 2003). Further, Gondolf, Fisher, and McFerron's (1991) examination of over 5,000 women in Texas shelters found no differences in abuse among Caucasian, African American, and Hispanic women. However, the researchers did find that Hispanic women in their sample were more economically disadvantaged, remained in abusive relationships longer, and were more likely to return to their abuser. Results such as these reflect the importance of understanding the interaction between socioeconomic status and culture (Johnson & Ferraro, 2000).

One in-depth analysis of abuse within the Latino immigrant population (Coker, 2000) found that Latino women victims of abuse report high levels of fear of police involvement that can lead to deportation of the abuser and to potential separation from their children. In many cases, an abuser may threaten the abused that if she calls the police, the abuser will be deported, thus, removing all forms of financial support. In other situations, if there are children, the abuser may threaten to leave and take the children back to their country of origin. This problem is compounded if the woman or her husband is not a legal U.S. citizen (McCue, 1995).

It is clear that empirical research has found that African American and Caucasian women tend to experience abuse at similar rates, with the exception of ages 20–24, where African American females experience more intimate partner violence. All other races studied in the U.S., including Asian American, Hispanic and Native American, have reported similar rates of victimization as Caucasian and African American women, except that rates for "other" and Hispanics were lower. Hispanic females between the ages of 16 and 34 were less likely to experience abuse from an intimate partner compared to non–Hispanic females the same age (Rennison, 2001).

Reports from the National Crime Victimization Survey (NCVS) between the years of 1992 and 1996 (not controlling for socio-economic status) found that an average of 12 per 1,000 African American women experienced domestic violence at the hands of their partners, compared to an estimated 8 per 1,000 Caucasian women. However, the Bureau of Justice Statistics (1991) found no significant difference between Caucasians and African Americans in the rates of violent victimizations that were committed by intimate partners. More recent research (Tjaden & Thoennes, 2000) has found that Native American women experience the highest rates of domestic violence compared to all other women, while Asian American or Pacific Island American women reported experiencing the least amount of domestic violence. Results of the NVAWS (Tjaden & Thoennes, 2000) found that 37.5 percent of Native American women reported abuse during their lifetimes compared to 29.1 percent of African American women, 24.8 percent of Caucasian women, 23.4 percent of Hispanics, and 15 percent of Asian women. Rates of abuse were significantly lower for Asian American women compared to African American, American Indian, and mixed race groups. When socioeconomic and relationship variables were taken into account, differences in rates of physical assault among racial groups weakened.

It is possible that Native American women are more likely to report intimate partner violence (Tjaden & Thoennes, 2000), and just as possible that cultural shame associated with domestic violence may explain lower report rates of abuse for Asian American women. Previous research has also suggested that African American women are victimized at rates four times higher than Caucasian women (Straus & Gelles, 1986). Data from the National Violence Against Women Survey (NVAWS) also showed rates of intimate violence were higher for African American women, yet when additional socioeconomic variables were controlled, these differences no longer existed.

Racism and economic status are also at issue when battered women enter the courtroom. Task forces have provided evidence that generally suggest poor women and women of color often encounter significant gender bias (Ninth Circuit Gender Bias Task Force, 1993; Resnik, 1991). In contrast, one study conducted by the Joint Task Force on Gender Bias in the state of Pennsylvania, found that Caucasian women were more likely to receive longer sentences than African American defendants. The same study showed that female judges were more likely to find a female defendant's claims of self-defense believable compared to male judges. The Melior Group reported results of a survey of trial court judges (Joint Task Force, 1997, cited in *Melior Group v. Kramer & Associates*, 2001) that found that judges were more likely to find white women defendants who claimed their actions were in self-defense guilty of homicide, while African American defendants under the same circumstances were more likely to receive verdicts of self-defense. The discrepancy between the rates of guilt for white women and African American women might be explained by the possibility that domestic violence may be more consistent with judge's perceptions of African American women than white women. If a judge's perceptions of abuse are more consistent with African American women, then decisions of guilt may be mediated. For example, assault is typically perceived as a crime more frequently committed by men. The Melior Group also found that judges awarded twice as much in damages for assault when the defendant was a man and the victim was a woman compared to if the defendant was a woman and the victim was a man (*Melior Group v. Kramer & Associates*, 2001). Results of this study can be attributed to many different variables. For instance, because judges are elected officials, they may be cognizant of prejudicial bias, and therefore overcompensate for potential prejudice. Moreover, stereotypes might differ according to location or population; therefore, the sample location and selection might play a role in the research findings.

Eaton and Hyman (1992) found that 50 percent of legal actors surveyed believed judges often minimize abuse against women of color. In addition, social scientists (Blackman, 1990) have also argued that the woman's social class and race are important mediators of the criminal justice system response. For instance, one study found that Caucasian women are more than one and a half times more likely to call police for a domestic dispute, and African American women are more likely than Caucasian women to have their children taken away from them because of domestic violence (Bent-Goodley, 2001; Joseph, 1997). Blackman (1990) noted that discrepancies in socio-economic status (SES) are apparent from the level of deciding who is prosecuted; women of higher economic standing, often accompanied by general media coverage, may be less likely to be prosecuted for the same crime than a woman of lower economic standing. Additionally, according to Eaton and Hyman (1992), since domestic violence cases are typically heard in family court, poor individuals are over-represented, and judges and court personnel distance themselves from the problem, dismissing it as indigenous to lower socioeconomic populations. Others suggest that middle-class batterers often get bigger breaks because judges are moved by the batterer's lack of a previous record, that the batterer might be embarrassed at his job, or because they can afford attorneys who may be more persuasive. While there have been major social injustices in the criminal justice system relating to race, much of this injustice has declined in recent years (Spohn, 2000). Yet, despite strides toward eliminating racial differences, one representative study (Bushway & Piehl, 2001) reported that in general, African American defendants are usually given 20 percent longer sentences than are white defendants, while Hispanics and Native Americans also tend to receive harsher sentences than white offenders (Everett & Wojtkiewicz, 2002). Similar research has been found by Willis (1992), in which African American women victims in dating relationships were more often seen as less truthful and more responsible for their own fate in a rape situation than white victims. In addition, white defendants who raped an African American woman, as opposed to a white woman, were considered less likely to commit a similar act in the future, and the defendant's action was often perceived as merely situational (Willis, 1992).

When one considers crime in general and its relation to race, consistent stereotypical behaviors cannot be ignored. For instance, the longer sentences assigned to African American defendants can be attributed to the possibility that race is related to stereotypic perceptions of crime. There are some crimes that have been found to be stereotypically related to race (Sunnafrank & Fontes, 1983). When race and crime are consistent, then decisions of culpability can be harsher. On the other hand, these same stereotypic perceptions can also explain why African American women receive lesser sentences than white women in cases of self-defense where abuse is used to support a defense. If abuse and victimization are more readily connected to African American women, then it is possible that judges use the information of the women's victimization as a mediating factor when evaluating guilt.

While it has been asserted that racial, gender, and socioeconomic differences exist among verdict decisions and sentencing for both victims and perpetrators of intimate partner violence, there is actually little empirical research on this topic. Some research has found no racial differences in decisions to arrest in domestic violence cases (Berk & Loseke, 1980–1981). However, a more recent study (Henning & Feder, 2005) found that minority status and gender played significant roles in the determination of whether to prosecute or drop charges in cases of domestic violence. Two possible reasons can account for the conflicting data between the two studies. First, more recent research may use more rigorous research methodology to identify possible race differences. Second, only recently have researchers begun to investigate women as perpetrators of domestic violence. Since there is little information on this topic, one can only speculate that it is possible that police attitudes may have changed over time to include higher arrest rates for women in domestic violence cases.

Researchers (Henning & Feder, 2005) examined over 4,000 cases of domestic violence arrests and found that women were less likely to be prosecuted and more likely to be released on their own recognizance (ROR) compared to men. Defendant income was also a predictor, as those with lower incomes were more likely to have to pay cash bonds versus being ROR. Lastly, the district attorney's decisions to pursue cases were directly associated with race, as minorities were less likely to get ROR or have their cases dropped compared to Caucasians. The authors could not attribute whether racial differences existed as a function of biased decision making, whether the possibility that minority defendants or those with lower socioeconomic status might use public defenders (as opposed to more effective private attorneys), or whether racial differences are the result of differences in a victim's willingness to cooperate in the investigation (Henning & Feder, 2005).

Additional research (Goetting, 1987) investigating demographic profiles of women arrested for spousal homicide in Detroit between 1982 and 1983 found that the majority of women arrested were of African American descent. An analysis of female homicide cases found that African American women offenders were more likely to kill their intimate partners and to be arrested for murder (Richey-Mann, 1989). Others (Plass, 1993) have found African American rates of family homicide were higher than those of Caucasians. However, it must be noted that the two later studies were based on family homicide rates. Such data on familial homicide do not break down African American homicide rates on the basis of variables such as the relationship between victim and offender. While the general consensus in battered women research appears to be that battering can occur equally within all ages and races, more recent research suggests that racial characteristics and socioeconomic variables play a substantial role in abuse.

How Legal Decision Making Can Be Influenced by Socioeconomic Status

Until only a few years ago, many researchers and legal activists were reluctant to suggest that domestic abuse was a phenomenon that was more representative of poor minority women (Meier, 1997). Meier believed conflicting ideologies of feminism and the anti-poverty movement led to a lack of acknowledgement and synthesis of the social causes of poverty and abuse. She believes that the effort made by the battered woman's movement to emphasize male domination is at odds with anti-poverty activists who are reluctant to associate battered women as having character flaws (i.e., lazy, uneducated) that are often associated with poverty. Only recently have researchers and legal activists begun to recognize that differences do exist and to call for a more in-depth analysis of how victimization is inherently related to social structures. For example, studies have shown us that intimate partner violence is higher among women with lower incomes (Tjaden & Thoennes, 2000). A series of research studies (Raphael, 1995, 1996; Raphael & Tolman, 1997, as cited in Meier, 1997) found that up to one-third of female welfare recipients reported they were currently in abusive situations, and up to 65 percent of welfare recipients reported experiencing abuse at least once as an adult. Raphael and Tolman (1997, as cited in Meier, 1997) suggest that these findings provide evidence that continued abuse may be directly related to an abused woman's inability to become financially independent.

Decisions of judges and court officials are also influenced by financial status, and judges and court professionals' lack of understanding about the issues of domestic violence affects the quality of justice battered women receive. Eaton and Hyman (1992) reported that it is easiest for judges to understand issues in an economic framework: for instance, battered women who are financially independent have difficulty evoking sympathy and understanding from judges who view them as especially capable of leaving their batterers. However, being financially dependent can work both for and against a battered woman in the court system, particularly in cases of spousal homicide. Legal actors may also pay more attention to non-achievement characteristics of women, as women are often judged based on gender stereotypes, such as passivity and being nurturing (MacCorquodale & Jensen, 1993). Such stereotyping often runs counter to the actions of the defendant on trial for a homicide. Furthermore, this is coupled with the fact that if the defendant was employed and thus financially independent, she may not only be perceived as more capable of leaving the batterer, but may additionally be perceived as neglecting her womanly duty as nurturer to her family.

Why Does She Stay? An Empirical Analysis of the Implications of Race, Ethnicity, and Culture

The overarching question often related to victims of abuse is, why does she stay? The question is based on the general assumption that "leaving will end the violence" (Browne 1987, p. 109). In fact, most women don't stay; over two-thirds of abused women do leave their abusers (Holtzworth-Munroe, Smutzler, & Sandin, 1997). Unfortunately, the situation is far more complex. On average, a woman leaves her abuser up to five times before making a final separation (Mills, 2003). It is unclear exactly how many abused women remain with their abusers (Okun, 1988); however, it is estimated that approximately half will ultimately leave them. Studies vary with regard to how many women leave and how many stay, with rates ranging from 38 percent (Jacobson, Gottman, Gortner, Berns, & Shortt, 1996) to 63 percent (Campbell, Miller, Cardwell, & Belknap, 1994) of battered women leaving their abusers.

Since the abuse occurs in the context of a relationship, there are both practical and emotional reasons why a woman may choose to remain in the situation. For example, the batterer may be someone they love and trust. When the battering begins, the violence is less frequent and less severe, and women initially remain with their batterer out of love and commitment (Browne, 1987, 1993; Strube, 1988). Often, these women are ashamed of letting others know of their situation and frequently dismiss or minimize the significance of each abusive episode, such as by attributing the incident to themselves and doing everything in their power to change their behavior so no further attacks occur (Browne, 1987; Tifft, 1993). In addition, the battering incident may be so discordant with the victim's expectations of what a relationship should be that it is often hard to believe; thus, the victim prefers to deceive herself and quickly places uncharacteristic experiences in the past, returning to positive everyday routines (Tifft, 1993).

Battered women contemplate relationship investment or costs when determining whether to leave their abuser. Costs can be emotional in nature, and children, race, religion, ethnicity, or economic reasons can all be considerations for battered women (Bornstein, 2006; Browne, 1997; Rhatigan & Street, 2005; Rusbult & Martz, 1995). While some researchers have found that investment in the relationship did not play a role in women's intentions to return to an abuser (Gordon, Burton, & Porter, 2004), others (Rhatigan & Street, 2005) have found that abuse was negatively associated with commitment to the relationship and more associated with intentions to leave. Mills (2003) suggests that American culture stresses keeping families intact and placing family above all else. She states that middle or upper class women might be more likely to leave their abusers sooner than those from minority, religious, or racial communities. Female minorities face greater widespread challenges throughout political, clinical, and legal arenas (Mills, 2003).

Some research has found that women are more likely to return to the batterer if they were married, members of longer-term relationships, or affiliated with the Catholic religion (Snyder & Scheer, 1981), and others (Pan-chanadeswaran & McCloskey, 2007) found women who were severely abused and did not seek shelter were exposed to abuse the longest.

Moreover, it should be noted that considerable differences may exist in a battered woman's response to violence depending upon her race (Dutton, 1994; Plass, 1993). A woman's racial, ethnic, and culturally based views may help her to resist domestic violence or may lead her to remain in an abusive relationship. Some (Dutton, 1994; McCue, 1995; Pagelow, 1992) have argued that certain characteristics of domestic violence, such as the denial, isolation, and invisibility of the problem, are intensified in many ethnic communities. In numerous cases, a lack of English language proficiency is an obstacle faced by victims (Dutton, 1994; McCue, 1995). Women who have a poor command of the English language can be limited in their understanding of their rights, legal options, and access to community resources (McCue, 1995).

The belief in the woman's traditional role in the family also plays a major factor in battering. If the woman has a strong desire to fulfill traditional female roles, she can become subservient and obedient to men in the family and put the family's needs first. To reach out for help is often perceived as a violation of the sanctity of the home — or the woman's failure to play her role successfully in the relationship (Dutton, 1994).

Furthermore, some women come from countries where the police are viewed as something to be feared. A woman from a specific racial or ethnic minority group may consider calling the police to be a betrayal not only of her partner, but of her community as well, where police and judicial systems may be perceived as "outsiders." She may view the legal system not as a source of protection, but as a source of racial discrimination and maltreatment for her partner.

Although there has been increasing recognition that women from diverse cultural communities face unique problems, the development of services which provide for their particular problems has been slow in coming (McCue, 1995). In addition, it has often been argued that due to the growing resentment toward immigrants and the prevalence of racism in this country, services for these populations are given increasingly low priority (Dutton, 1994; Pagelow, 1992; McCue, 1995). More importantly, it is difficult to obtain a true picture of racial or ethnic differences in abuse without considering socioeconomic status.

Socioeconomic Status and Abuse

Keep in mind that statistics on socioeconomic status are often misleading (Dutton, 1993; Mather, 1988; Barnett & LaViolette, 1993). For instance, domestic violence studies often utilize samples from shelters and funded community-based programs; it is often the women with the fewest resources who utilize these programs (Barnett & LaViolette, 1993). In other words, depending on her available resources (family, friends, and financial dependence), a middle or upper-class woman may have insurance to obtain therapy or can afford to visit a private physician. The National Women Abuse Prevention Project (NWAPP) reported that domestic violence occurs in people of all socioeconomic and religious groups; for example, police in a mostly white middle-class suburb in Washington, D.C., received as many domestic disturbance calls as were received during the same period in Harlem, New York City. However, low-income battered women were more likely to seek assistance from public agencies, such as shelters and hospital emergency rooms, because they had fewer private resources than middle- and upper-income women. (McCue, 1995; NWAPP, 1989). Thus, while the issues battered women face may be similar, the context may differ, and each woman might experience different barriers to leaving the relationship (Johnson, 1996).

Research (Strube & Barbour, 1983, 1984) has found that economic dependence, employment status, and economic hardship were the most important predictors for a battered woman when deciding whether to remain in an abusive relationship. For example, women who were unemployed were much more likely to seek assistance from a battered woman's shelter than those who were employed (Panchanadeswaran & McCloskey, 2007). Furthermore, some have found an over-representation of unemployed women who were arrested for homicide of a spouse (Goetting, 1987). Yet, one meta-analytic review found socioeconomic status only to be a predictor in cases of severe assault (Hotaling & Sugarman, 1986). In 1996, Richey-Mann examined socioeconomic indicators such as income, occupation, and education in a sample of African American women who killed. Richey-Mann examined random samples of female homicide cases in four major cities and all female homicide cases in two major cities. Her sample consisted of 296 women arrested for murder. She found that the racial composition of her sample was almost 78 percent African American, 12.8 percent Caucasian, and 9.5 percent Hispanic. The African American women in the sample had education lower than the national average, and over 70 percent were unemployed. Of the women who were employed, they typically worked in unskilled occupations. In particular, Richey-Mann (1996) found that African American women arrested for murder overrepresented the lower economic strata.

Research has generally indicated that battered women can come from all socioeconomic backgrounds (Dutton, 1993; Barnett & LaViolette, 1993; Walker, 1979, 1987). Somewhat in accordance with this assumption, Miller's

(1992) investigation of the Orange County probation department in California found the socioeconomic composition of the individuals charged with domestic violence and placed on probation in 1989 was 37 percent white-collar, 46 percent blue-collar, and 8 percent unemployed. In contrast, research investigating large national samples has indicated that battering occurs more often in blue-collar and lower socio-economic status (SES) families.

Research pertaining to the relationship between intimate partner violence and poverty, welfare, and homelessness began in earnest during the 1990s. Researchers (Browne & Bassuk, 1997; Browne, Salomon, & Bassuk, 1999) conducted extensive interviews with 220 homeless women and 216 women living in low-income housing. They found that almost one-third of their sample's previous or current partners inflicted severe physical violence. Further relating such violence to employment prospects, Browne and her colleagues (1999) found that after controlling for a variety of factors that can influence results, the odds for maintaining employment were substantially lower for battered women than for women who had not experienced severe violence.

In addition, Blackman's (1989) investigation of women who had experienced spousal or partner abuse found a median income of approximately $25,000 and a trend which indicated battered women had lower incomes than controls. A study of 6,000 women found more than 50 percent said they had been abused by their spouse, reporting average family incomes of $35,000. Just over 70 percent of their population surveyed was Caucasian, 10.4 percent were African American, and 9.5 percent were Hispanic. Their profile also showed that more than 18 percent had a bachelor's degree or higher (Moewe, 1992). However, when comparing differences in rates of employment and number of children between battered women and non-battered women, Blackman (1989) found victims of abuse were as likely as those who were not victims of abuse to work outside the home, and they had a similar number of children living in the home. More recent research from the NCVS shows that women in households with annual incomes of less than $7,500 were almost ten times more likely to experience violence compared to women with incomes of $75,000 or more (Rennison & Welchans, 2000).

The result of all of these studies suggests that socioeconomic status plays a significant role in the possibility of victimization by an intimate partner. All women who divorce their spouses face economic changes and often hardship. When abuse is added to the equation, women potentially have the added stressors of stalking and threats in addition to economic hardship. When issues of culture and ethnicity are combined with economic status, it is clear that minority women are especially at risk for abuse.

Why Does She Stay?
The Impact of Social Economic Status

Research has found that many abused women's decisions to leave are dependent upon economic factors. When a battered woman leaves her abuser, there is a 50 percent chance that her standard of living will drop below the poverty line (Senate Judiciary Committee, 1990). Research shows that it is clear that there are economic consequences when separating from a partner. Separating from a partner most often decreases the standard of living for women, but has little negative impact, or actually can increase the standard of living for men (Amato, 2000; McKeever & Wolfinger, 2001).

For the most part, recent research relating to income or financial dependence and intentions or actual leaving of abusers suggests that women with larger incomes are more likely to terminate abusive relationships (Lambert & Firestone, 2000; Rusbult & Martz, 1995; Woffordt, Mihalic, & Menard, 1994). One research study found that women who do not leave their abusive partners were less likely to obtain access to food stamps, social security, employee assistance, transportation, or housing compared to women who left their abusers. However, the same study found that income level of the victim was not a significant predictor of remaining with a batterer (Koepsell, Kernic, & Holt, 2006).

The affluent battered woman is often the least likely to report abuse (Johnson, 1996; Barnett & LaViolette, 1993), and she faces a different set of circumstances or problems. For example, if she is married to a successful man at the top of his profession, she may be active in the community, entertain regularly, have children, and manage the home and family activities. Affluent women may feel the same shame and embarrassment all battered women feel, but they may also feel a certain class-based shame, having internalized the belief that domestic violence only happens to "poor and ignorant" women (McCue, 1995). Because the public persona of a successful businessman often carries with it the connotations of "provider" and "loving father," it is often hard to believe such a man is capable of battering (McCue, 1995). This perception makes it difficult for the victim to confide in friends or obtain assistance from law enforcement. The upper-middle-class woman is typically educated, articulate, and affluent; thus, batterers often try to convince the victim that she is overreacting or crazy (Johnson, 1996). A woman who is educated may also be likely to blame herself, asking, "How could I let this happen to me?" (McCue, 1995).

The greatest myth about white-collar domestic violence is the victim should be able to arrange a smooth, bloodless departure, because unlike poor women, they have the financial and social resources (Johnson, 1996). However, the woman who works is usually professionally employed and in constant danger of losing her job due to absenteeism, harassment, and impairment due to abuse received (Swanberg et al., 2006). Some researchers suggest that domestic violence doesn't necessarily prevent employment, but it does negatively affect the victims' ability to sustain their jobs (Tolman & Raphael, 2000). Raphael (1996, as cited in Meier, 1997) found that 55 percent of a sample of 123 women attending support groups for battering missed work. Sixty-two percent were late to work and 24 percent had lost a job because of physical abuse.

When an abusive partner sabotages a woman's efforts to work, it can leave her economically dependent, making it more difficult to leave their batterer. Battered women are more than two times as likely as non-battered women to lose employment because of health issues (Romero et al., 2003), and those health issues can also lead to inability or lack of motivation to work (Raphael & Tolman, 1997). In addition, an estimated 74 percent of battered women who are employed often suffer harassment on the job at the hands of the batterer, either in person or on the telephone, causing 56 percent of them to be late for work, leave early, or miss work (McCue, 1995). Walker, Logan, Jordan, and Campbell (2004) noted that separation or divorce (while ideal in an abusive situation) can cause additional stressors on the victim, and these stressors should be considered in the context of abuse. For instance, Walker et al. (2004) believe that when leaving any relationship (abusive or not abusive), psychological, financial, or social stressors arise, which in turn affects mental and general well-being. The process of separation should not be examined in isolation of these factors.

Does Age Play a Role in Abuse?

Most researchers interested in studying the demographic characteristics associated with battering have revealed that battering occurs across all age groups. However, some studies have indicated that all forms of intimate partner violence occur most frequently among those under age 30. Results from the NCVS (Rennison, 2001) found that younger individuals (between the ages of 16–24) experienced the highest rates of abuse from an intimate partner, yet women between the ages of 35–49 were most likely to be murdered by an intimate partner. It has been documented that the rate of marital violence among those under 30 is more than double rate than those of ages 31 through 50 (McCue, 1995). Research examining women who seek help from agencies or shelters also found that the mean age is 30 or younger (Gelles & Cornell, 1990). In addition, research examining racial differences in homicide found that the mean age of African American female offenders was 31 (Richey Mann, 1990). Similarly, Goetting's (1987) examination of self-proclaimed battered women arrested for spousal homicide found the average age of incarceration to be in early to mid–30s.

Thirteen percent of Pagelow's (1981) sample of 350 battered women were age 40 and above. Walker's original (1984) sample of 403 battered women ranged in age from 18 to 59. Battering does occur with older women, but there is not much research regarding the demographic rates concerning the older battered woman (McCue, 1995). Research has been conducted that suggests that these women have unique needs and issues. For instance, older victims of battering were brought up in a world where domestic violence was considered a private problem and corporal punishment was allowed in schools. They may fear the need to rebuild years of finances and social networks that took years to build, which often plays a role in the decision to stay with the abuser.

Implications of Age and Length of Relationship on Decisions to Stay in Abusive Situation

Despite much research on a battered woman's decisions to leave the relationship, studies often do not examine the aspect of age, but rather focus on the length of the relationship. For instance, it has been suggested that a woman who has invested 30, 40, or 50 years in a relationship has more to lose if she leaves her abuser (Strube, 1988) and may simply be intimidated by the notion of being alone (McCue, 1995). More recent research provides support for this perspective. For instance, research by Koepsell et al. (2006) examined 448 abused women and examined predictors of leaving the relationship. The authors found that of all of the demographic factors examined, age, whether the woman had left the relationship previously, and whether she had sought protection orders were predictive of leaving the abuser. In particular, younger women were more likely to leave their abusers while older women were least likely to leave their abusers. Their research found that overall age was the only demographic factor to play a role. The authors also examined forgiveness, severity of violence, fear of the loss of investments (i.e., emotional investment or physical investments such as real estate, children, etc.), poor quality of alternatives to marriage, beliefs in the morals of divorce, intent of violence, and social pressures to remain in the abusive relationship. Koepsell et al. (2006) found that a woman's forgiveness was a major predictor above all other factors measured. Similarly, researchers (Panchanadeswaran & McClosky, 2007) found that of a sample of 100 abused women, older, Caucasian women and women experiencing moderate forms of physical aggression were more likely to perceive hazards of leaving an abusive situation compared to younger women and women of minority descent. According to researchers, women who are in long-term relationships are often less likely to leave an abuser or more likely to return to a batterer after seeking refuge (Snyder & Scheer, 1981; Strube & Barbour, 1983). Such differences could be attributed to the difference in the traditional psyche of the era. It is believed that battered women who are older are more likely to adhere to traditional sex roles (Walker, 1979) or their career options may be fewer than for younger adults (McCue, 1995). With this in mind, possible interaction effects should be considered, wherein younger women are less likely to be in long-term relationships with their abusers and may actually feel as though they have less invested in the relationship (Koepsell et al., 2006).

Does Education Among Victims of Battering Differ?

Currently, there is little empirical evidence concerning level of educa-tion in relation to vulnerability to battering. To date, only a few studies have addressed this issue (Blackman, 1989; Browne, 1987; Goetting, 1987; Walker, 1979, 1984). Evidence from in-depth interviews of self-proclaimed battered women suggest approximately one-third to one-half are college educated (Browne, 1987; Walker, 1979, 1984). Other research has found comparable results. For example, Blackman (1989) found a slight significant difference in battered women versus non-battered women in levels of education. Accord-ing to Blackman, approximately 40 percent of women victims had college degrees, while almost 50 percent of non-victims held college degrees. Another study conducted by Moewe (1992) found that only 18 percent of the sample of battered women had a bachelor's degree or higher. However, evidence of arrest rates by women who had committed spousal homicide suggest that the under-educated are often over-represented (Goetting, 1987). For instance, Richey-Mann's (1996) in-depth investigation of women who kill used education and employment as a measure of a woman's socioeco-nomic level. She found that her sample had a mean of 10.9 years of educa-tion (lower than the national average) and 63–78 percent of offenders were unemployed at the time of the crime. Furthermore, there has been no evi-dence that level of education differentiates women who leave abusive rela-tionships from those who remain (Gelles, 1976; Koepsell et al., 2006; Panchanadeswaran & McCloskey, 2007). More recent research has found that education does not play a significant role in victimization rates (Renni-son, 2001).

Level of Violence and Leaving the Abuser

Rates of violence and their relation to leaving the abuser have also been investigated. A study by Lawrence (1999) showed that women who had experienced aggression early in a relationship were two times more likely to leave their abusers within 18 to 24 months. The authors found a direct relationship between increased violence and separating from the abuser. For instance, 38 percent of participants reporting no violence separated from their partner, compared to 46 percent of couples experiencing moderate levels of violence, and 93 percent of couples separating after severe violence. Research by Koepsell et al. (2006) found that previous trips to the doctor because of an abusive incident predicted leaving the abuser. Lastly, additional research (Panchanadeswaran & McCloskey, 2007) has found that women who experienced the strongest levels of physical violence but never used shelters remained in abusive situations longer. In fact, women who were poor, unemployed, or received additional support from shelters were more likely to extract themselves from an abusive relationship. While violence in a relationship may be related to separating from an abuser, it should be noted that those who keep going back to their abusers (or do not leave in the first place) may have a more difficult time adapting to the stressors associated with leaving their abusers. Women who remain in abusive relationships may not have access to social support systems and/or shelters or the separation process may be too complex due to additional stressors on the victim (Walker et al., 2004).

In summary, this chapter brings forth the importance of recognizing the diversity of characteristics of victims of battering and the unique roles culture, ethnicity, SES, age, and education play with regard to legal responses and decisions to remain in abusive relationships. Unfortunately, while scholars are still learning about the diversity of battered women and how their diversity affects legal decision making, even less is known about how variables such as race, age, ethnicity, education, and so forth, interact to affect victims of abuse who are not heterosexual females. Now that some general information pertaining to the prevalence and diversity of battered women has been identified and some myth v. reality has been teased out, the battered woman syndrome will be examined in greater depth. The next chapter serves as the beginning of the next section of the book that focuses on the use of the battered woman syndrome in the courts. An in-depth analysis of the syndrome, with all of its glory and limitations, will be examined in the context of its development and use in the courts, particularly when women kill their abusers and claim self-defense.

DISCUSSION QUESTIONS

1. Describe at least three ways in which culture can affect the reporting of domestic violence.

2. Explain how race, gender, and culture might play a role in the legal system's response to domestic violence.

3. After reading this chapter, how would you answer the question, why does she stay?

4. What does recent research suggest regarding victim age, education, and length of relationship and a person's willingness to exit an abusive relationship?

5. Based on what you have learned in this chapter, do you believe that support and shelters actually help women leave abusive partners?

CHAPTER 6

The Battered Woman Syndrome:
The Good, the Bad
and the Alternatives

[The battered woman] has low self-esteem, believes all the myths about battering relationships; is a traditionalist about the home, strongly believes in family unity and the prescribed feminine sex-role stereotype; accepts responsibility for the batterers' actions; suffers from guilt, yet denies the terror and anger she feels; presents a passive face to the world but has the strength to manipulate her environment enough to prevent further violence and being killed; has severe stress reactions, with psycho physiological complaints; uses sex as a way to establish intimacy; believes that no one will be able to help her resolve her predicament except herself [Walker, 1979, p. 31].

To recognize a class of things is to polarize and to exclude. It involves drawing boundaries, a very different activity from grading [Douglas, 1986, as cited in Loseke, 1992].

In the 1960s, federal monies and attention were given to oppressed groups in need of social reformation. During this time, as noted earlier, child abuse was beginning to be recognized as a societal problem through the pioneering work of Henry Kemper (1962) and his book, *The Battered Child Syndrome.* With the emergence of the women's movement, domestic violence and wife abuse would finally become recognized as a societal problem. Lenore Walker (1979) established the battered woman syndrome as a vehicle to explain how and why battered women remain in abusive relationships. It is important to acknowledge that characteristics associated with the syndrome have changed over the years. Walker's own research and those following in her footsteps have led to marked changes in the theory.

91

Walker based the original concept of the battered woman syndrome on a non-random sample of 110 self-proclaimed battered women (predominately White and middle-class) who had contacted social service agencies. Walker (1979, 1982) and her colleagues further developed the theory based on 435 in-depth interviews with self-proclaimed battered women. The majority of Walkers' participants were solicited from community clinics and media advertisements (Walker, Thyfault & Browne, 1982).

On the basis of this data, Walker et al. (1982) identified a set of psychological characteristics exhibited by women whose husbands had physically and psychologically abused them over an extended period of time. In her case studies and observations, Walker (1979, 1982) found that battered women came from diverse economic and educational backgrounds, yet they usually remained economically dependent upon their abusive mates. Walker also found that battered women typically embraced traditional gender-role attitudes and practices, had low self-esteem, were passive, blamed themselves for the batterer's violence toward them, and genuinely believed their batterers would kill them; as a result, battered women would often deny the abuse and keep it hidden from others. The batterer's possessive and controlling behaviors further isolated the women from their families and friends. The women feared that any attempt to leave might result in the batterer's carrying out their threats. Other common characteristics included guilt, denial of the abuse, severe stress reactions, physiological complaints, and a belief that no one could help them out of their predicaments.

Chapter one noted two defining characteristics of the syndrome: a cyclical pattern of violence and learned helplessness. According to Walker's theory, it is the cyclical nature of the victimization and its impact on the woman that psychologically traps her in the relationship. The first phase of this cycle is a tension-building phase in which a build-up of "minor" abusive incidents occur. During this phase, the woman's primary interest is to avoid and prevent escalation of abuse. She becomes placating and passive in an attempt to avoid further violence. The mounting undercurrent of tension characterizing the first phase makes more serious violence inevitable. During the tension phase, Walker (1984) believed battered women develop a keen sense of expectation of violent attacks, and in anticipation of another violent attack may initiate violence in order to get the anticipated abusive event over with. Walker also addressed a term she called "hyper-vigilance," which suggests that women experiencing ongoing trauma, while developing mental incapacities in some regards, develop a unique ability to detect possible danger from their abuser (Downs, 1996, 2005). The tension-building phase is eventually followed by an "acute battering" stage, in which the severity of abuse increases and the woman is subjected to a violent battering incident. Within this cycle, the victim's primary focus is survival, and she often feels fearful and powerless to respond to these attacks. A "contrition stage" soon follows the acute battering stage, wherein the batterer realizes he may have gone too far and attempts to reconcile with the battered woman. This period of relative calm and remorse partly explains why women remain in the relationship. Claims of love and promises of no further violence often persuade the woman to continue living with the abuser in spite of the abuse. In addition, the battered woman typically holds traditional views about a woman's role; her strong sense of family ultimately leaves her vulnerable to her partner's persuasion (Walker, 1979; Walker et al., 1982).

Despite the abuser's "loving contrition," the abuse eventually recurs in the same cyclical fashion until phases of loving contrition decrease and eventually disappear completely. Because the abuse takes on an identifiable pattern, the abused woman can soon predict when battering incidents will occur. As the battering relationship progresses, the frequency and severity of abuse escalates (Browne, 1987; Ewing, 1987; Pagelow, 1992). Furthermore, Walker (1979) stated that in order to be classified as a battered woman, the couple must go through the battering cycle at least two times, stating, "Any woman may find herself in an abusive relationship with a man once. If it occurs a second time, and she remains in the situation she is defined as a battered woman" (p. xv).

In addition to the battering cycle, Walker (1979) utilized Martin Seligman's (1975) theory of "learned helplessness" to help explain why women remain with their batterers. In 1975, Seligman published pivotal research describing the detriments of perceived lack of control. Seligman confined dogs in cages equipped with shocking devices to teach them they could not avoid or control the shocks. When the same dogs were given the opportunity to escape the punishment of the shocks, the dogs cowered passively and took the punishment. Seligman suggested that humans who experience constant oppression or depression could similarly experience learned helplessness when repeated attempts to change or improve their environments are thwarted. Despite her every effort, a battered woman cannot control or stop the beatings. Consequently, she falls into a state of depression and learned helplessness. Once operating from a belief of helplessness, the woman believes there is nothing she can do to alter the situation. Over time, she begins to live in constant fear, perceiving there is no escape from her situation (Walker et al., 1982; Schuller & Vidmar, 1992). This fear is often reinforced by a batterer's threats (or actions) that if she attempts to leave or seek help she will incur greater abuse (Browne, 1987). The cycle of violence along with learned helplessness help to understand how battered women remain with their abusers.

Additional Research and Changes in Theory

In her 1984 book, Walker described learned helplessness in a context not intended to suggest that the woman is helpless, but rather that she may lose the ability to predict whether the actions she takes will lead to a particular outcome. Walker used the theory of learned helplessness in an attempt to describe how battered women become psychologically victimized within the battering relationship, such that they may revert to "survival techniques" rather than "escape skills." Walker (1984) attempted to further her research and gather additional data to investigate why some women would put up with abuse and others would leave their abusers. Walkers' original study found that those who tolerate abuse were more likely to embrace traditional sex roles, to have experienced sexual molestation as a child, and to have experienced childhood violence and "critical or uncontrollable" situations during childhood. However, when she collected additional data and compared responses of battered women to those of college women who were not battered, she found that battered women were no more likely to embrace traditional sex roles than college women who were not abused. Surprisingly, Walker also found that contrary to the idea of learned helplessness, battered women believed they had control over their lives and did not believe they were controlled by others. Furthermore, battered women often showed more positive self-perceptions compared to college women or men and were not pessimistic in nature. In fact, when she compared those women who remained in an abusive situation to those who had left an abusive situation, Walker found that those women who left their abusers displayed more negative symptomology (increased depression, perceived themselves as externally controlled) compared to women remaining in the abusive environment. These issues, and the fact that few women exhibited learned helplessness, were never adequately explained or accounted for in her conclusions (Craven, 2008; McMahon, 1999).

Walker (1984) also investigated 50 battered women homicide defendants. Using the same methodological approach (i.e., observation, in-depth interviews), she found that all 50 women were subjected to repeated—and often brutal—physical attacks by their batterers and frequently endured extreme psychological abuse. In addition, nearly all 50 women claimed they were threatened with weapons, serious injury, disfigurement, and death, especially when they tried to leave their partners. Like the 435 participants in Walkers' original larger study of battered women in general, all of the 50 homicide defendants believed their batterer would or could kill them. Moreover, many felt that leaving the batterer would provide no escape from this danger (Walker, 1984).

Walker's theory of the battered woman syndrome was pivotal in bringing national attention to the problem of battering. Her research and books helped society to understand the seriousness of domestic abuse and transformed intimate partner violence from a private family problem into a social crisis.

Problems Associated with the Syndrome

While Walker's work was instrumental in enlightening the national public and legal system to the plight of the battered woman, there are many unresolved issues associated with her work. Walker noted her own limitations in her empirical research. For example, Walker's own research (1984) showed little evidence for the purported cyclical nature of domestic violence. Only 64 percent of the respondents interviewed reported a tension building stage prior to the battering, and in only 58 percent of the cases did the phase of loving contrition follow an abusive episode. Thus, it appears from the available data that not all couples go through a cycle of violence as proposed in Walker's (1979, 1984; Walker et al., 1982) initial model.

Researchers have also noted the lack of control groups in Walker's work (Faigman, 1986; Follingstad, Neckerman & Vormbrock, 1988). Walker herself stated that due to cost and lack of time, a control group was not feasible (Walker, 1984). Unfortunately, by today's standards, lack of control groups is generally unheard of and is often a premise for peer reviewers not to recommend an article for publication. The sample used by Walker was also not representative (by today's standards) or reliable. Her sample included self-reported professional women experiencing moderate levels of violence. These were women seeking shelter or other assistance ("self-selected survivors," Walker, 1984, p. 229). Walker admitted that her sample over-represented women in professional occupations, acknowledging the bias in her sample. Her sample may not have considered severely battered women or battered women of lower levels of violence. This over-representation of White, middle-class women experiencing moderate amounts of violence begs the question as to whether similar findings would be revealed with different ethnicities, socioeconomic statuses, or levels of violence.

One of the earliest critics of Walker's work found that her theory of the syndrome was not substantiated by her own data, especially battered women who kill, noting that only nine of the several hundred battered women interviewed killed their abusers (Faigman, 1986). Furthermore, Walker did not compare differences between battered women who kill and those who do not kill their abusers, making it virtually impossible to come to any conclusions about battered women who kill. Others (McMahon, 1999) have addressed the discrepancies in data reported in Walker's (1984) book. McMahon (1999) noted that Walker reported that 15 percent of those in abusive relationships were violent themselves. However, inspection of the table Walker provided showed that almost one-quarter of participants in battering relationships reported that they occasionally or frequently used physical force. These findings are similar to conclusions reached by Straus and his colleagues (1980) and suggest that many battered women actually do fight back, and in some circumstances possibly initiate violence. At the least, the data suggests that not all battered women experience learned helplessness.

Moreover, there are obvious issues associated with the interview format used by Walker (1984). Researchers realize that most interviews can be adversely affected by "experimenter effects," "demand characteristics," and "leading questions." While researchers are supposed to be objective and unbiased when conducting a research study, they are often not immune to their own values and expectations. In order to remove these potential biases, researchers often conduct "blind" studies or "double-blind" studies in which the experimenter and the person collecting the data are unaware of the research hypothesis. Using these techniques, experimenter effects are thought to be eliminated and the research is considered valid. When experimenters collect their own data, they may be more likely to interpret behaviors or attitudes in a biased manner, often providing further evidence for their own hypotheses. For example, if a researcher's hypothesis was that young boys would be more physically aggressive than girls at age five, they might, just by human nature, be more likely to observe boys being more physically aggressive than girls on a playground. Demand characteristics, on the other hand, are where participants might be trying to guess what you, the researcher, are looking for, and in an attempt to be more politically correct or socially desirable, provide information that does not necessarily correspond to their true attitudes and behavior. In one example of a demand characteristic, caregivers of children might be less likely to hit or yell at their children if they know that they are being observed through a one-way mirror. Interviews may also be compromised by asking leading questions. In this case, researchers might (unconsciously or consciously) lead participants into answering a question in a particular way. For example, the question, "When he hit you so hard, what did you do?" might evoke a different response from another participant asked, "When he hit you, what did you do?" Research suggests that when leading questions, such as the one above, are used, people tend to exaggerate their answers (Loftus, 1976).

Other critics have questioned the diagnostic accuracy of the syndrome (Dutton, 1993; Faigman, 1986). For example, the cyclical pattern of violence and the development of learned helplessness do not accurately portray all battered women (Downs & Fisher, 2005; Faigman, 1986). Downs and Fisher (2005) point out that almost two thirds of Walker's own sample did not experience the full cycle of violence she proposed. Researchers also raise concerns that the cycle of violence does little to provide contextual information pertaining to perceiving danger from the battered woman's point of view. Dutton (1992) clearly stated that not all battered women experienced the same psychological effects of abuse and that each woman responds differently depending on her situation. Dutton (1992) also raised the importance of recognizing external factors such as social and familial support, personal resources, and institutional responses. These external factors should not be ignored, as they have been found to play significant roles in a battered woman's decision to leave or stay in a relationship.

Others have questioned learned helplessness as it applies to battered women (Browne, 1987; Dobash & Dobash, 1979; Faigman, 1986; Gelles & Straus, 1988; Ewing, 1987; Dutton, 1993). McMahon (1999) found that Walker's definition of learned helplessness changed several times, making it difficult to determine just what characteristics are associated with learned helplessness of victims of abuse. In particular, a woman's perceived passivity is contrary to her fighting back against her abuser. While learned helplessness appears to operate in some battered women, the majority of these women utilize a diverse set of coping responses in an attempt to end the abuse (Dutton, 1993; Ewing, 1987). Some of the responses battered women often take to protect themselves are inconsistent with helplessness. These strategies include efforts to escape, avoid the batterer, and protect themselves and others from violence (Browne, 1987; Dutton, 1993; Ewing, 1987; Gondolf, 1988). For instance, one researcher believed battered victims utilized survival skills to deal with the abuse, and therefore considered them as "survivors," not victims (Gondolf, 1988). Abused women may comply with the demands of the abuser, attempt to escape, hide or disguise their appearance, physically resist abuse, or contact the legal system or domestic violence programs for assistance (Bowker, 1983; Browne, 1987; Dutton, 1993; Ewing, 1987). Interviews with self-proclaimed battered women found that some abused women attempted to retaliate against the violence by hitting or punching the batterer or by using makeshift weapons or household objects to fight against the batterer's actual or threatened violence (Bowker, 1983). In addition, using the Conflict Tactics Scale, a survey technique designed to assess familial violence, Gelles and Straus (1988) found that in many domestic disputes women provoke or fight back against their aggressors. Such theories contradict the portrayal of the demure, passive victim of abuse initially suggested by Walker.

One of the main issues at hand is whether the battered woman syndrome is a legitimate syndrome (Follingstad, 2003). According to Morse (1998), "A syndrome, in medical terminology, is the collection or configuration of objective signs (e.g., fever) and subjective symptoms (e.g., pain) that together constitute the description of a recognizable pathological condition" (p. 364). This definition suggests that a cluster of symptoms should co-occur among those who suffer from the disorder (or event) in order to comprise a syndrome. Interestingly, Walker and most other researchers agree that there actually is no single "profile" that captures the plight of most or all abused women. Most researchers and theorists (Crocker, 1985; Douglas, 1987; Dutton, 1992; Russell & Melillo, 2006; Schneider, 1986; Stubbs, 1992) believe the battered woman syndrome is not a syndrome at all. Even Walker (1984) asserted that each woman can react differently to her environment. Indeed, it is common knowledge that each battered woman reacts differently based on the context of the event and individual history. It is for these reasons that the word "syndrome" has sparked controversy since its initial connection to battered women. The quote by Douglas (1986) at the beginning of this chapter suggests that when a class of things are recognized as similar, individuals tend to polarize or exclude those who do not appear to fit into that class.

Many (Crocker, 1985; Douglas, 1987; Downs & Fisher, 2005; Osthoff & Maguigan, 2005; Schneider, 1986; Shaffer, 1997; Stubbs, 1992) have protested that the battered woman syndrome promotes the perception that women are psychologically unstable. Crocker (1985) clearly stated her apprehension of using the battered woman syndrome, as it is suggestive of a clinical disorder that can make battered women appear emotionally damaged and irrational. From the onset, Schneider cautioned that the battered woman syndrome promotes "an implicit but powerful view that battered women are all the same, that they are suffering from a psychological disability and that this disability prevents them from acting 'normally'" (Schneider, 1986, p. 207). Douglas (1987) agreed and admonished that the battered woman syndrome "clinicalizes battered women, designating them as pathological" (p. 45). In particular, the action of killing or aggressing against an abuser is in direct opposition to the theory of passivity and learned helplessness.

Other more esoteric arguments surround the definition of "abuse" or "battering." In 1979, Walker stated that any physical aggression constitutes battering. According to Walker, in order to be defined as "battered" one must have gone through the battering cycle at least twice. However, the definition becomes murkier, because she also proposes that "a battered woman is a woman who is repeatedly subjected to any forceful physical or psychological behavior by a man in order to coerce her to do something he wants her to do without any concern for her rights" (p. xv). This muddies the water as to whether physical or verbal abuse alone constitutes battering. Furthermore, at what point in a relationship is one a battered woman? For example, if a couple is not married or dating occasionally, can she still be considered a battered woman? What if the batterer was of the same gender as the victim? Could that be considered battering? What if the batterer was another family member such as a son or mother?

Constructs most often used when referring to abuse can include family violence, dating violence, domestic violence, spousal abuse, marital violence, and intimate partner violence. In the late 1990s, the Center for Disease Control (CDC) provided guidelines and adopted the term "intimate partner violence" to ensure greater consistency among researchers. The term consisted of any episodes or threats of physical and sexual violence and psychological and emotional abuse coupled with previous physical or sexual violence among intimate partners (Goodman & Epstein, 2008; Saltzman, Fanslow, McMahon, & Shelley, 1999). This definition helped to clarify abuse between intimate partners (regardless of sexual orientation or marital status) and other family members (McClennon, 2005), yet some believe this definition lacks various types of cultural abuse (acts that represent shame, such as overturning a table or dousing a woman with liquid in Japanese culture) that can be inflicted among intimate partners (Sokoloff & Dupont, 2005b). While there continues to be debate about various terminology associated with battering, intimate partner violence is quickly becoming the standard term when referring to domestic violence.

The use of the battered woman syndrome can be a double-edged sword. As a syndrome, expert testimony of the battered woman syndrome carries with it the medical model, which is a more effective, accepted, and persuasive form of evidence in the courts. However, research has shown that use of the syndrome in court comes with perceptions that women are psychologically damaged in some way (Schuller, 1992; Schuller & Rzepa, 2002; Schuller et al., 2004; Schuller & Hastings, 1996; Terrance et al., 2000, 2003). In response to this, many are calling for testimony that does not include reference to the syndrome or any clinical aspect of psychological instability.

Understanding the Context of the Individual: Case Specific Information

There is a general consensus among many recent researchers and theorists that the term "battered woman syndrome" should not be used as evidence in the courtroom. In particular, ideas about psychological aspects of learned helplessness should be eliminated from all testimony. Instead, testimony should be case-specific and focus on individual reactions (Biggers,

2005). Testimony should shift the focus from learned helplessness and psychological states to circumstances and alternatives, and the reality of the situation (batterers' domination, control, lack of alternatives, risks of leaving) (Schneider, 2000; Sheehy et al., 1992). For instance, a different definition of battered women was proposed that focused on addressing unique characteristics of the individual and effects of abuse (Douglas, 1987). Douglas (1987) believed abused women shared similar experiences such as trauma, learned helplessness, and self-destructive coping responses to violence, but stressed that the unique context of the situation and the individual must be considered. In this regard, Douglas (1987) believed self-destructive coping responses would include putting the abuser on a pedestal, denial, and suppression of danger. In addition, Dutton (1996) stated there is "no single construct or diagnosis" (p. 3) available for battered women. Therefore, if the focus remains on the context of the individual, there are common theories such as PTSD, trauma, and survival that help us to better understand battered women. Alternatives to these theories such as power and control and social framework also help establish the context of the situation and individual.

Post-Traumatic Stress Disorder, Trauma, and Survival

Dutton (1992, 1994) noted that many of the responses of battered women overlap with symptoms of PTSD. PTSD is characterized as a cluster of symptoms following exposure to an extreme traumatic stressor involving direct personal experiences of an event (or witnessing an event) that involves actual or threatened death or serious physical injury, or other threat to one's personal integrity (DSM IV, 1994). The stressor producing the symptoms would be considered distressing to almost any person. It is usually experienced with intense fear, terror, and helplessness. Cluster symptoms can include re-experiencing the traumatic event, avoidance of stimuli associated with the event, a numbing of general responsiveness, increased arousal, anxiety, and depression. Recent studies have emerged in the social scientific literature that use psychological assessments such as the Minnesota Multiphasic Personality Inventory (MMPI or MMPI 2) to measure the prevalence of PTSD in battered women. When levels of violence, social support, and PTSD between women charged with violent crime against their partner were compared to battered women who had not harmed their partner, women charged with a violent crime reported experiencing more severe violence, histories of sexual abuse, less social support, and higher levels of PTSD then women who had not been charged with an offense (Dutton, Hohnecker, Halle & Burghardt (1994). It appears that while the battered woman syndrome falls short in agreement and clinical diagnosis, PTSD is a clinical diagnosis that seems to capture the plight of many battered woman.

Rates of PTSD in the general population range between 10 to 13 percent of women during their lifetime; about 4–5 percent of women report current PTSD (Resnick, Kilpatrick, Dansky, Saunders, & Best, 1993). Studies have shown that rates of PTSD are higher in battered women. For instance, one study found that 84.4 percent of their sample of 77 battered women in a battered women's shelter met the clinical criteria for PTSD (Kemp et al., 1991). Moreover, through interviews and observations of a group of rural battered women, Hilberman and Munson (1977–1978) noted that the symptomology of battered women was analogous to that of rape victims suffering from Rape Trauma Syndrome, a purported cluster of identifiable psychological symptoms associated with rape victims that prosecutors often rely upon to support the testimony of rape victims. However, the same controversy that surrounds the battered woman syndrome is part of the debate regarding the application of rape trauma syndrome in a legal context, as many individuals believe a victim of rape should behave a particular way or exhibit certain characteristics, and those who do not are often judged negatively.

A recent theory that continues to gain momentum is based on the concept of PTSD, equating an environment of abuse to one of combat. The "combatant context" likens the experience of soldiers exposed to combat scenarios to that of victims of repeated abuse. Stark & Flitcraft (1983) compared domestic abuse to a combat battleground. In 1998, Gagne made a similar observation that supported the investigation of a combatant context, drawing comparisons between combatants and battered women. Data on the experiences of soldiers and prisoners of war is very consistent with that of battered women. Symptoms and traumatic events including an ongoing fear of death or serious injury, beatings, witnessing attacks on others, concerns with the length of time under these conditions and an inability to escape, were found in both groups (Barlow & Durand, 1999; Dutton et al., 1994).

The combatant context offers a new approach to expert testimony in these cases. It has been hoped that a combatant context would reduce gender bias and the activation of prototypical thinking by framing homicide in a traditionally male-oriented context—the military. In addition, combat trauma has been heavily researched; therefore, this context could possibly be perceived as more acceptable in the courts as a defense. Previous research has suggested that the portrayal of a defendant as mentally disordered, and having a diagnosed illness of PTSD with a sub-categorization of battered women's syndrome, may lead a jury away from the conclusion that the defendant acted as a "reasonable person" (Kasian et al., 1993; Terrance & Matheson, 2003). This context was developed to address these difficulties by allowing the inclusion of powerful PTSD testimony without creating the stereotypes often attached to the battered woman syndrome concept. One study evaluated whether reference to PTSD would affect how mock jurors perceived the reasonableness of the defendant's actions (Terrance & Matheson, 2003). The authors found that expert testimony with reference to PTSD made the defendant appear more credible, yet pathological, therefore undermining the aspect of reasonableness. Such research calls into question whether the use of PTSD can be effective form of expert testimony.

In relation to PTSD, theorists (Dutton, 1995; Herman, 1997) expanded upon trauma theory to summarize the idea of traumatic bonding that occurs during abuse, yet can also explain why a battered woman's actions can be at odds with learned helplessness. Herman (1997) was one of the first to note that trauma theory could be attributed to battered women. She believed that abused women are reacting as a result of traumatic stress disorder. Dutton (1995) further explained that "traumatic bonding" occurs as a result of intermittent abuse (unpredictable episodes of abuse followed by periods of good behavior) and power imbalance within the relationship, leading victims to identify with their oppressors. Throughout the bonding process, the abuser will influence the victims' behavior and prevent independent decision making (Loseke, 1992). Theorists (Dutton, 1995; Herman, 1997; Loseke,1992) argue that trauma theory offers an explanation for why women remain in abusive relationships and expands upon the concept of learned helplessness, as the theory stipulates that there is no one predictable response to violence (Loseke, 1992). Therefore, this theory allows for greater diversity of abused reactions to violence. Unfortunately, trauma theory continues to pathologize battered women by assuming they remain helpless and unable to make coherent decisions.

One way to recognize the diversity of battered women and refrain from pathologizing them is to focus upon coping mechanisms used by battered women in abusive relationships. Contrary to Walker's theory that battered women were helpless and dependent, authors (Gondolf & Fisher, 1988) believe victims of intimate violence abuse develop survival skills. Gondolf and Fisher refer to this as "survivor theory," which focuses on the assumption that battered women do not just become passive recipients of abuse and develop learned helplessness because of their partner's unpredictable behavior. Instead, the authors believe it is more likely that abused women make repeated attempts to cope with the violence by contacting family, friends, social service agencies, and law enforcement with little or no effect. The authors believe that when women make these repeated attempts to cope with abuse, it is more often traditional family values (i.e., lack of safe havens for women and their children, commitment to the relationship, traditional attitudes, and financial hardship) or a lack of resources that lure the victim back into the abusive relationship. Some researchers and theorists believe that because survivor theory relies on a victim's use of coping strategies in order to survive, this theory is in direct opposition to Walker's theory; it suggests that women are more likely to display symptoms of Stockholm Syndrome, noted as a survival strategy associated with prisoners of war, hostages, and kidnapping victims, in which the captives bond with their captor in response to abuse.

Power and Control and Social Framework as Alternative Contexts

Another alternative theory used in criminal trials of battered women is the Power and Control Wheel (Dutton, 1992) mentioned earlier. This theory provides a context for battered women who kill their abusers. To assist in understanding the etiology of domestic violence, Ellen Pence and the Duluth Abuse Intervention Project (1993) created a theoretical framework to explain the general dynamics of domestic abuse. The power and control wheel is currently used across the county in batterer's groups, support groups, training groups and empirical studies. The control model provides an alternative approach to explain violence and other forms of coercive control within relationships.

The rim of the wheel represents an event of physical or sexual violence. Each spoke of the wheel represents various tactics abusers use to obtain power and control (i.e., isolation, emotional abuse, economic abuse, threats, intimidation, etc.). Once physical or sexual violence occurs, the threat of future abuse is enough to make the victim live in fear of the abuser. In order to maintain power, abusers often use tactics such as intimidation, emotional abuse, isolation, minimization or denial of events, use of children to make the victim feel guilty, or threats to take children away, and use of the women as a servant, with the abuser making all the decisions. This model helps people to understand domestic violence in more contextual terms. If one just considers isolated incidents, it is difficult to understand if a woman has acted in self-defense. Her actions, examined in isolation, will make no sense to a jury. However, when the power and control wheel is used, it is easier to understand the overall context and dynamics of the fear that surrounds the victim's life.

Terminology associated with learned helplessness has led to increased attention to a woman's passivity (Schuller & Rzepa, 2002) and ultimately to the creation of the stereotype of battered women (Schneider, 1986). It is clear that many scholars believe social framework or expert testimony explaining battering and its effects would be more effective than using terminology associated with the syndrome, such as being passive or submissive (Osthoff & Maguigan, 2005). Social framework evidence does not take into consideration the specific individual, but rather addresses the state of the art of the research in order to provide a context for a particular situation. Such testimony takes the focus off pathology and emphasizes the effects of battering (Osthoff & Maguigan, 2005). The combination of case-specific relevant information and social framework evidence of battering and its effects can be helpful for the defendant who claims their actions were in self-defense.

The battered woman syndrome has helped to educate society about the physical and psychological effects of battering. Unfortunately, the efficacy of its use in the courtroom has come into question due to concerns about the methodology used in the research conducted to support Walker's theories. The evolution of the syndrome has led to suggested alternatives that can be used to educate legal actors and laypersons. There have been many alternatives that have been recommended by scholars that describe the potential ways battered women respond to abuse. These alternatives to the syndrome help us to better understand the context of battering and how abuse affects individuals. While many of the suggestions made by scholars appear to have unique theoretical ideas and contributions, they also have many overlapping characteristics that aim to take the emphasis off the pathology of the battered woman. Furthermore, while the intent of these various alternatives is admirable, many of these theories have yet to be empirically tested, and it is difficult to know how each one of these approaches work in the courtroom. The fact that the syndrome, when used in the courtroom to explain a defendant's behavior, has been found to pathologize the defendant can be an important factor when making legal decisions. Does a victim of battering clearly understand the alternatives to killing their partner? Do such alternatives actually exist? The following chapter examines women who kill and evaluates the extent to which these women's behaviors are reasonable or pathological.

DISCUSSION QUESTIONS

1. Describe the cycle of violence associated with the battered woman syndrome.

2. What is learned helplessness and what role does this theory play in explaining the actions of battered women?

3. Critics have argued that there are many problems and limitations to Walker's work. Describe at least three major problems identified by critics of the syndrome.

4. Compare and contrast the three common theories associated with the context of the individual (PTSD, trauma, survival theories).

5. Examine power and control and social framework as evidence. Explain how this form of evidence differs from the battered woman syndrome.

CHAPTER 7

When Women Fight Back and Kill Their Abusers: A Realistic Appraisal of Danger or Pathology?

Dixie Schrieber and Scott Shanahan began dating in 1983. On May 10, 2004, Dixie Schrieber Shanahan was sentenced to fifty years of imprisonment for the murder of Scott Shanahan. In between, there was a marriage, children—and years of horrendous abuse. During the nineteen years that Dixie and Scott Shanahan were together, Scott blackened Dixie's eyes, bruised her, threatened her, dragged her by her hair, pointed guns at her, tied her up and left her for days in the basement, called her vile names, degraded her in front of friends, and generally made her life a living hell. On August 30, 2002, believing that her life and the life of her unborn child were in danger after days of beatings, threats, and the promise, "This day is not over yet. I will kill you," Dixie Shanahan shot her husband while he lay in bed. After less than one day of deliberation, a jury found Dixie Shanahan guilty of second-degree murder. Judge Charles L. Smith III sentenced Dixie Shanahan to fifty years in prison [Goodmark, 2007, p. 1].

While over 1,000 women kill their partners each year (Huss et al., 2006), it should be noted that there is not a great deal of information regarding the motives of women who kill, and the majority of defendants in cases where an abuse victim kills their abuser, both male and female, claim self-defense to avoid punishment (Felson, 2002). Richey-Mann's investigation of homicide motive found that a substantial proportion (41.7 percent) of the offenders stated that their actions were in self-defense, 12.2 percent were considered an accident, and 11.7 percent were the result of emotional reasons (anger, jealousy, and revenge). Furthermore, another study (Haley, 1992) found that more than 57 percent of the female inmates currently serving sentences for homicide in Georgia had a history of domestic violence when the woman killed her intimate partner (Haley, 1992). In addition, in 60 percent of these cases, the woman claimed the victim had assaulted or abused her at the time of the crime. Moreover, one study (Totman, *Encyclopedia of Victimology and Crime Prevention*, 1978) revealed that 93 percent of women serving time for killing their spouses had been physically beaten by their spouses. Within the 93 percent surveyed, 67 percent of these women believed they were defending themselves or a child. Additional research reveals similar findings (i.e., Hansen, 1992; O'Shea, 1993; Rashe, 1993), and suggest that between 40 percent and 60 percent of incarcerated women killed an intimate partner in response to repeated abuse.

Many women incarcerated for killing their intimate partner are first-time offenders such as Dixie. Despite the fact that it appears as though the majority of women incarcerated for killing their partner did so in self-defense, homicide convictions and sentences for these women are often more severe than for men who commit homicide. Researchers (Jacobson, Mizga, & D'Orio, 2007) from the Michigan Women's Justice and Clemency Project examined 82 (68 men and 14 women) homicide convictions between 1986 and 1988. Women were convicted more often than men, and victims of domestic violence were more likely to be convicted and served longer sentences than all other homicide defendants. The authors believed that 75–80 percent of women who killed in self-defense are convicted or encouraged to plead guilty and serve longer prison sentences than men or women who did not have a history of domestic abuse. But before it can be concluded that blatant discrimination is currently at work in the legal system, it should be noted that much has changed, and additional research is necessary to investigate whether results can be replicated with an analysis of more recent cases.

Characteristics of Battered Women Who Kill

When Walker and her colleagues (1982) investigated female homicide defendants in spousal killings, she found that all of the women she interviewed reported that they had been the victims of domestic abuse, almost all had been threatened with physical injury or death, particularly when they attempted to leave their partner, and all believed their partner would kill them. Psychological abuse of the homicide defendants studied by Walker often took the form of social isolation enforced by threats against family and friends, administration of mind-altering drugs, flaunting of extramarital affairs, and sexual abuse of the woman's children. Browne (1987), a former associate of Walker's, composed one of the most comprehensive analyses of battered women to date. Browne (1987) was the first to recognize the importance of a control group in order to discern differences in characteristics of women who killed their abusers and battered women who did not kill their abusers. Browne administered a 200-item questionnaire to 42 women charged with the death or serious injury of a mate and to a control group of 205 battered women who had not killed their batterers. Browne's study revealed few characterological differences within the women in both the homicide and control groups. Although women in the homicide group were somewhat older and from a slightly higher-class background than the women in the control group, their level of education and employment patterns were similar. A comparable number of women in the two groups had been exposed to violence in childhood and had been victims of sexual assault. However, Browne found several significant differences in the behaviors of the male partners who had been killed by their partners compared to women who were abused but had not killed their batterers. Women who killed their partners were more likely to describe their partners as using drugs more frequently than battered women who did not kill. Women who killed also reported their partners used more frequent and severe threats and assaultive behavior, were more likely to threaten to kill someone other than themselves, and abused children compared to reports of women who were battered but did not kill their partners. Some might say that such results suggest that a woman's behavior is primarily a reaction to the level of threat and violence she faces. However, it is also possible that women who killed their partners may have perceived past threats and violence from their partners as significantly more severe in order to justify their response. Browne (1987) also determined that battered women who killed had made more prior attempts to stop the abuse than those who did not kill. The homicide group also reported that they felt more hopelessly trapped in a desperate situation, where staying or leaving meant being killed or beaten, and that helplessness and desperation had escalated along with the assaultive behavior. Browne (1987) also examined the battered women's response to trauma and how these responses ultimately prevented the victims from leaving their batterers. She attributed much of her results to the battered woman's failure to perceive alternatives. Others (Stark, 1990) have agreed, stating that killing is often a woman's safest alternative given the circumstances, and it is often a survival tactic.

Battered Women Homicide Defendants' Perceptions of Alternatives

A battered woman's perception of alternatives is often the crux of her case. The question why didn't she just leave? not only helped to inspire the birth of the battered woman syndrome, but continues to be the most significant piece of information for the defense to convey to the judge and jury. In the Dixie Schrieber case, Dixie had left her batterer many times before, but also chose to return (perhaps under duress, perhaps with hopes he would change, or a host of other possible reasons) to her abuser, ultimately to find herself in an abusive situation she could not escape. Much of the violence endured by the battered woman may be difficult to imagine for the average person; this makes defending battered women who kill a formidable task. However, while the courts continue to contend with these issues, researchers have accumulated much information regarding the victim's response to such trauma, which ultimately reflects the answer as to why these women believe they cannot "just leave."

According to Walker's cycle of violence, escalation of such attacks is virtually inevitable. However, recent research suggests that common couple violence does not necessarily lead to escalation of abuse, while intimate terrorism may be the form of violence most likely to do so (Johnson, 1996). As the severity and frequency of abuse increases, many victims' ability to escape the situation decreases (Dutton & Painter, 1981). Any use of violence in a relationship ultimately affects the balance of power by destroying any sense of openness and trust and replacing it with subordination, threat, and loss (Browne, 1993). Dutton and Painter (1981) suggested that intermittent punishment, with power imbalance, leads to traumatic bonding. Browne (1987) further explained three factors that impact a woman's decision to stay with the batterer: problems in effecting a separation, fear of retaliation, and shock reactions of victims of abuse.

Separating from the Abuser

Some battered women eventually find themselves trapped in situations that may make it difficult, if not impossible, to leave. For instance, they may hope their partners will change, or may concentrate their efforts on keeping the peace within the household (Pagelow, 1992). Often, battered women may feel as though if they only try a little harder, things will improve (Walker, 1979, 1984). In addition, many women attribute battering to external causes such as job pressure and define their situations as normal, blame themselves for the violence, or invoke higher loyalties, such as a commitment to marriage as an institution (Steinman, 1991). They focus on what they need to do to make it through the day, rather than making long-term plans to leave (Browne, 1987; Walker, 1984). During, and even after, an assault, a victim may not resist her attacker; she may become apathetic and withdraw in isolation (Browne, 1987). Assaulted women, post-attack, may become dependent and suggestible and find it hard to undertake long range planning or to make decisions alone (Bard & Sangrey, 1986). They also develop coping strategies based on their evaluation of what method of coping will offer them the least amount of danger (Thyfault, 1984). In spite of these problems, even when a woman does look to her alternatives, they may be more threatening than her existing situation. Many examples for remaining in her existing relationship have already been addressed, including financial dependence, a lack of access to battered women's shelters (Biden, 1993), issues of alternative forms of shelter, and difficulties obtaining legal help (Browne, 1987; Pagelow, 1992; Walker et al., 2004).

Mahoney (1991) coined the term "separation assault" in an attempt to explain why battered women may stay with their abusers. Mahoney (1991) made an analogy between the "Stockholm syndrome" and the battered woman situation. Behaviors associated with the Stockholm syndrome suggest that a unique bonding occurs between the captor and hostage (Mahoney, 1991). The victim, isolated and dependent on her captor, may deny anger directed toward the abuser and focus on their good qualities, feeling grateful to her abuser for having spared her life, and fearing that if the captor is captured, he will return and capture her again. Mahoney cites research that has demonstrated that women who had left their abusive partners, but then returned because he threatened to kill them, showed significantly more partner bonding. Using this analogy avoids a focus on the women's purported pathological or masochistic mental states, shifting it toward a more reasonable response to their situation.

If the woman has children, she must tackle a separate set of issues, including making provisions for them. The battered woman with children often has two choices: either leave her children for her own safety, which may later be cause for desertion in a child custody claim, or pull them out of their school and home environment to face an uncertain future. In addition, if the woman does leave and there are children involved, the batterer may be entitled to visitation rights, and thus she cannot leave the general area. Since the victim is often faced with threats to herself, family, and friends, she cannot turn to what otherwise may be her greatest source of support without risking endangering them. Nevertheless, if the woman does separate from her abuser, she realizes that her partner knows her daily routine, such as her work schedule, and thus may have to give up her employment or constantly be on her guard against further attacks (Browne, 1987; Tifft, 1993; Walker, 1984). Warrants for police protection hardly provide psychological relief to the battered woman, as she knows her abuser and knows his capabilities to harm. A sizeable proportion of battered women are killed because they have made genuine efforts to leave their abusive relationships, thereby providing further anecdotal motivation for women to stay with their abusers.

Fear of Retaliation: A Realistic Appraisal of Threat and Danger

A battered woman's fear of retaliation appears to be a reasonable appraisal. The act of leaving an abusive relationship is often followed by an increase in violence (Browne, 1987; Ewing, 1987; Steinman, 1991; Tjaden & Thoennes, 2000). Researcher's (Fleury, Sullivan, & Bybee, 2000) study of shelter clients showed that one-third of their participants were physically assaulted during a separation, half of those assaults happened in the first 10 weeks of initial separation, and almost two-thirds of those assaults were considered severe (i.e., kicked, raped, choked, stabbed, shot, etc.). According to the Bureau of Justice Statistics (1994), women who left their abusers were victims of violent assaults at rates of 128 per 1,000, and orders of protection did not necessarily change these rates. Women are most likely to be murdered when attempting to leave an abusive relationship or report abuse than at any other time (Tjaden & Thoennes, 2000). In a study of spousal murder in Florida, 57 percent of the men who had killed their wives were living apart from them at the time of the incident (Steinman, 1991). Stark and Flintcraft (1988) found while only 15.6 percent of all assaults among married women were domestic, 55 percent of those assaults occurred when women were separated from their abusers. One study found that women who were separating from their abusers were 6.5 times more likely to experience violence from their partners (Kershner, Long, & Anderson, 1998). Furthermore, Hotton (2001) revealed that 95 percent of women leaving violent relationships experienced psychological abuse during the separation and 39 percent continued to incur physical violence from their partners. Among battered women seeking medical attention for injuries of domestic violence, about 75 percent of these visits to emergency rooms occurred after separation from a batterer (Hart, cited in McCue, 1995). Moreover, an investigation of police reports of homicide found that the most common motivation for the killing of wives by husbands was the husband's feeling of abandonment or fear that he was losing control over his wife (Casanave & Zahn, 1986, cited in McCue, 1995).

It is not surprising that Browne's (1987) study revealed that women in the homicide group reported staying with their abusers because they had attempted escape many times before and been beaten for it or because they thought their partner could retaliate with further violence if they attempted to leave him. Almost all of the women in Browne's study (1987) reported that they felt the abuser could or would kill them, and most in the homicide group were convinced that they could not escape this danger by leaving.

Mental Instability or a Reasonable Response to Abuse?

Researchers have been trying to tease out myth from reality when it comes to deciphering the extent to which a battering victim's behavior is the result of mental instability or a reasonable response to abuse. Scholars such as Follingstad (2003) have attempted to tease out unsubstantiated theoretical characteristics associated with the battered woman syndrome from empirical reality that actually supports such characteristics exist. Follingstad's review provides updated evidence for research supporting or refuting characteristics often associated with abuse, such as PTSD, learned helplessness, low self-esteem, depression, self-blame, psychopathology, interpersonal and cognitive disturbances, traumatic bonding, and others. Separating myth from reality is imperative as these issues can become the basis for arguments used in court.

There is a growing amount of literature regarding the traumatic responses suffered by battered women. The reaction of abused women corresponds closely with reactions of other types of victims. Research has indicated that women who are repeatedly battered report feelings of confusion (Ferraro & Johnson, 1983), anxiety (Dutton et al., 1994), physical complaints, psychological numbness (Ewing, 1987, Walker, 1979), repressed anger, grief, depression and related symptomology such as hopelessness and suicide attempts (Follingstad, Brennan, Polek, Turledge, 1991; Walker, 1979).

While even one assault can have lasting effects, battered women most often go through a severe and repetitious cycle of violence; thus, they are more susceptible to cumulative effects of trauma. A national sample of 366 self-reported battered women and 2,622 non-battered women found the more violence experienced by a woman, the more she suffered from psychological distress (Gelles & Harrop, 1989). When women are exposed to repeated threats and attacks, they often respond with increased levels of isolation and terror (Browne, 1993). Women who are assaulted more frequently, endure physical injury and sexual assault, or receive death threats are much more likely to experience an overwhelming sense of danger, flashbacks, and thoughts of suicide (Browne, 1987, 1993; Dutton, 1992). In addition, battered women have suffered from nightmares, psychological distress when exposed to stimuli associated with the battering, memory loss, affective numbing, sleep disturbances, difficulty concentrating, hypervigilance, and a heightened startle response (Finkelhor & Yllo, 1985; Ogland-Hand et al., 1995).

Many of these responses overlap with the general symptoms of Post Traumatic Stress Disorder (PTSD). Further research regarding stress levels and abuse found that being a victim of assault was related to increased levels of psychosomatic symptoms in both males and females, though these symptoms were more pronounced for female victims of abuse (Stets & Straus, 1990). Female victims of severe assaults were more susceptible to stress and depression compared to male victims of severe assault. Stets and Straus compared men and women who were not assaulted, experienced minor assault, and severe assault. For both men and women, increased amounts of stress were evident with increased assault. However, stress levels were significantly higher for women experiencing assault compared to men.

Stets and Straus (1990) also examined levels of depression and its relationship to assault. Again, similar results were found: as levels of assault increased, so did rates of depression for both men and women. Women experienced significantly more negative effects of depression corresponding to increased levels of abuse. Depression in battered women has been found in many other studies, all suggesting that depression increases with frequency and severity of battering (Dutton & Painter, 1993; Kemp et al., 1991). These studies are correlational in nature, and it is difficult to ascertain whether battering caused depression or whether a host of other explanations (i.e., pre-existing conditions, lack of resources, self-esteem, social support, etc.) may explain this relationship (Follingstad, 2003; Stets & Straus, 1990).

Other Psychopathologies Associated with Abuse

It was often believed that battered women suffered from low self-esteem. Research on this topic is fairly mixed, but some findings suggest there is some legitimacy to this claim (Dutton & Painter, 1993; Cascardi & O'Leary, 1992). Self-blame is another term typically associated with abused women, though research does not support the inclusion of self-blame as a legitimate characteristic of battered women. Overall, studies have found that few women blame themselves for their abusive situation (Cascardi & O'Leary, 1992). In addition, as the violence escalates in frequency and severity, the likelihood that women blame themselves actually decreases (Frieze, 1979).

In the past, studies have found that women experiencing abuse have increased psychopathology (emotional or behavior problems requiring psychiatric intervention). However, the methods traditionally used to measure this phenomenon were obsolete (often having no control group with which to compare battered women with non-battered women). Using modern research protocols, Kemp et al. (1991) and others (Gleason, 1993) have found evidence that battered women have increased psychopathology levels as measured by the Minnesota Multiphasic Personality Inventory (MMPI). However, as with any of the psychopathologies discussed here, it is difficult to determine whether psychopathology was the effect of the battering or if they are the result of pre-existing conditions. McMahon (1999), a proponent of the battered woman syndrome, believes the presence of significant mental disorders found in battered women support the fact that abuse leads to psychological issues and the existence of the "syndrome"; however, most scholars remain skeptical because of the correlational aspect of the data and the inability to tease out extraneous variables that may be causing such a relationship.

Other characteristics associated with battered women include a woman's inability to maintain relationships and interactions with others, as well as cognitive dysfunctions. Research is somewhat mixed with regard to abused women and interpersonal relationships. Some research has found that battered women (even those experiencing severe abuse) have the social support they need (Stao & Heiby, 1992) and battered women did not differ from non-battered women in searching for mental health services (Warren & Lanning, 1992). Further, while some researchers found battered women were more social than non-battered women (Finn, 1985), others found that battered women were significantly more isolative and withdrawn during interactions with others (Star, Clark, Goetz & O'Malia, 1979). Lastly, battered women have also been purported to have some cognitive difficulties such as memory disturbances or overall difficulty in their thinking processes, though there are no studies that suggest that this is true.

What Happens When Battered Women Fight Back?

Battered women who fight back are caught between the perception that battered women are helpless and passive recipients of abuse or that they are the aggressors or initiators of violence. The theory of learned helplessness suggests that a woman becomes a passive recipient of abuse because no matter what actions she takes to avoid abuse, nothing seems to matter. Episodes of abuse come with no rhyme or reason, they just come. If a woman fights back, her actions go against the idea that she is meek, passive, withdrawn, and generally mentally dysfunctional. Furthermore, when women fight back, they may be perceived as bad because "good girls" don't fight.

A woman as an offender goes against the idea of learned helplessness associated with the syndrome. While rates of homicide perpetrated by women are much lower than men, it still remains a major social problem (Straus, 2005). Some scholars (Straus, 2005) believe that 40 percent of all of the injuries found in the NVAW prevalence study could be attributed to women's violence. The main point here is that women do strike back and initiate assaults almost as much as men do. This has particular implications for the battered woman who kills. When using the law of self-defense, the issue of who initiated the violence is important. In addition, the fact that a woman may initiate such violence, and perhaps has a history of such violence, may suggest that she does not demonstrate characteristics associated with learned helplessness or being a female in general.

In conclusion, a battered woman's perceptions of alternatives to killing are at the core of a claim of self-defense. In this regard, getting jurors to understand why the victim didn't just leave the abuser is extremely relevant to the situation. A victim of battering can have a host reasons why they return to their abusers, but women are actually in the most danger of physical injury or death when they attempt to leave or finally separate from the abuser. The cumulative effects of abuse can lead to psychological instability such as depression or PTSD, but the question of whether these pathologies were pre-existing remains unanswered. While additional pathologies have been purported, research is severely lacking to establish the extent to which they exist in victims of battering. Finally, many victims have criminal histories and/or initiate violence against their abuser. Both of these may be influential in determining whether a victim of abuse exhibited characteristics associated with being a female, as well as characteristics typically related to the syndrome (i.e., passivity, learned helplessness). Lastly, the following chapter will address how the issues of provocation and initiation of violence are closely scrutinized when victims claim their actions are in self-defense.

Discussion Questions

1. What did Browne's research find regarding the differences among male partners of battered women who killed versus who did not kill?

2. Note why separating from the abuser is an important topic to consider.

3. Identify some of the psychological effects known to be associated with abuse. Does research suggest all victims of abuse suffer from the same effects?

4. What can be deduced about the potential psychological effects associated with victims of abuse who are not heterosexual females?

5. Describe the conceptual inconsistency among women who fight back and battered women who are to be passive helpless victims of abuse.

CHAPTER 8

The Law of Self-Defense

The evening before Easter Sunday in 2007, Patrick Lancaster repeatedly hit his wife, a highly respected physician in the Cape Cod area of Massachusetts, as she was driving with her grandson in the back seat. The following day, after seeing his mother marked with bruises and black eyes, her 25-year-old son Christopher began to argue with his father about hurting his mother. During the heated exchange, Ann Gryboski shot and killed her husband Patrick Lancaster. She later told police that her husband had physically and verbally abused her for years and the abuse was escalating. *The Boston Globe* reported this story (April 29, 2007) and interviewed Ann's family, who stated that Ann had never mentioned that she had been abused by her husband, but looking back on Patrick's behavior, they could see how he could be demanding and abusive. Ann never called the police regarding previous domestic assaults or took out a restraining order against her husband. The paper claimed that those who knew Ann were struggling to understand what happened. In particular, the article stated, "Why would the highly respected physician stay in an abusive relationship for so long? Why didn't she reveal the abuse to anyone?" (English, 2007). Ann was charged with murder, and her lawyer planned to use the battered woman syndrome to describe why Ann would shoot her husband. Were Ann's actions reasonable? Were her actions in self-defense?

A battered woman's perception of fear, alternatives, and the reasonableness of her actions are at the crux of the question of self-defense. By examining the perceived alternatives of battered women, we may ultimately understand the dynamics leading an abused woman to take lethal action against her mate and assist courts when determining whether evidence of the battered woman syndrome is truly helpful in assessing responsibility in such cases.

Law of Self-Defense: A Review of Criminal Law

Attorneys have mainly used two defenses to obtain acquittals in homicide trials of women who have killed their abusive partners: self-defense and insanity. Self-defense has been the more popular of the two defenses in recent times (Brewer, 1988; Dowd, 1992; Maguigan, 1991; Mather, 1988; Schneider & Jordan, 1981), and a number of women attempt use expert testimony on the battered woman syndrome to support their claims of self-defense (Brewer, 1988; Dowd, 1992; Schuller & Vidmar, 1992). In the scheme of legal history, the battered woman syndrome remains a fairly new psychological phenomenon and the relationship between battering and self-defense is even more novel in criminal law (Brewer, 1988; Mather, 1988).

Scholars have argued that because the traditional elements of self-defense were designed for disputes between males of equal size and stature (Crocker, 1985; Gillespie, 1989), the current claim of self-defense cannot accommodate battered women who kill abusive men. For instance, battered women are often at a disadvantage in size, strength, and economic power. As a result, they may respond by using a deadly weapon such as a knife or gun to ward off an unarmed attacker. Similarly, some women do not retaliate during direct confrontation, but instead respond in non-confrontational situations such as waiting until the husband is asleep or turning to leave (e.g., *State v. Allery*, 1984; *LaVallee v. Regina*, 1988). These aspects of homicide can present problems that don't easily fit into the traditional male-oriented laws of self-defense (Crocker, 1985; Gillespie, 1989). Some feminists have proposed that the law, by definition, does not take into account the social context of the battered woman's act (Dowd, 1992; Schuller, 1994). Unless the woman's actions are understood in the context of the ongoing nature of the violence, the "imminence" of the danger to her may not be apparent to an outside observer, and her use of a deadly weapon to protect herself against an unarmed attacker can cast further doubt on the reasonableness and necessity of the response (Schuller, 1994).

Self-defense, the most widely recognized legal defense used to justify an intentional homicide that was committed as a method of fending off an attacker, rests on the view that a person may take reasonable steps to defend him or herself from physical harm (LaFave & Scott, 1972). The main purpose of the defendant who claims self-defense is to convey to the judge and jury that the homicide was justified (Schneider, 1980), correct or appropriate behavior within the surrounding circumstances (Fletcher, 1975, cited in Schneider, 1980). When determining whether an event is justified, the dilemma in self-defense is to find a middle ground between the objective understanding of a reasonable person and the defendant's subjective understanding of imminent danger. Self-defense is a justification defense where one's behavior is "excused" or "justified" and socially acceptable based on his or her behavior and circumstances.

Questions about justification most often focus upon the actors' moral and/or mental status. Generally speaking, in most state statutes, self-defense is justified when "it is necessary as an emergency measure to avoid an imminent public or private injury which is about to occur by reason of situation occasioned or developed through no fault of the actor, and which is of such gravity that, according to ordinary standards of intelligence and morality, the desirability of avoiding the injury outweighs the desirability of avoiding the injury sought to be prevented" (Section 563.026, Revised Missouri Statutes, 1996).

A justification does not imply that the victim deserved what they got, but rather that the defendant acted "reasonably" based on the situation (Roberts, 2003). The current law of self-defense states that the use of deadly force is justified as self-defense only when the person using such force reasonably believed that he or she was in imminent danger of death or serious bodily injury, and that it was necessary to resort to deadly force to avert that danger (Ewing, 1990; Kinports, 1988; Mather, 1988; Schneider, 1980). Under current law, the traditional elements still exist in their purist forms, but most courts have expanded these elements to allow a more subjective and empathetic view of the defendant who claims her action was justified because she was battered. However, because the doctrine of self-defense paints reality in broad strokes, it leaves the battered woman who claims self-defense wondering how far the pendulum of justice will swing for her.

While, in general, the law of self-defense has essentially the same basic elements in each state, each state law varies to some extent with regard to elements—some may require duty to retreat, others imply no provocation—and jury instructions (subjective versus objective) may differ. Judges' interpretations of cases also differ with regard to what they deem relevant or not relevant to include or exclude from a case. Each case is examined on an individual basis and has varying levels of evidence that make it difficult to compare one to another. Our legal system is a dynamic system, continually changing and evolving. This dynamic system causes changes in legislation and legal precedent. Sometimes this is a quick process, sometimes it is a much slower process than many would like.

While some states differ in their statutes and jury instructions regarding what constitutes self-defense, most statutes and jury instructions have three basic elements: deadly force can be used when the threat of death or serious bodily injury is imminent, the force used must be proportional to the threat, and a reasonable and honest belief of imminent threat must be present.

A judge will decide whether the defendant meets the state requirements for self-defense based on whether these elements are present. Before a juror is allowed to receive instructions to consider a plea of self-defense, the defendant must usually show evidence of all three of these elements. Within these elements are both subjective and objective boundaries from which the judge and jury must assess (1) whether it appeared to the defendant that she honestly believed herself to be in imminent danger, and thus it was necessary to kill the deceased in order to save herself from death or bodily harm, (2) whether the defendant's belief was reasonable in that the circumstances as they appeared to her at the time were sufficient to create such a belief in the mind of a reasonable person, (3) whether the defendant did or did not use more force than was necessary or reasonably appeared to be necessary under the circumstances to protect herself from death or great bodily harm (*State v. Norman*, 1988). In addition, a small minority of jurisdictions require a duty to retreat, wherein the defendant is required to retreat, if she can safely do so, before resorting to deadly force (LaFave & Scott, 1982). Most states also include provisions for the absence of aggression or provocation on the part of the defendant (Brody, 2001). These elements suggest a common underlying theme focusing on the state of mind of the defendant within the self-defense doctrine, and more importantly, on what perceptions judges and jurors hold about the defendant.

Even a classic case of self-defense is ultimately dependent upon the court's perception of the situation and whether or not the defendant acted reasonably. Thus, it is up to the defendant to convey to and convince the jury of their perceptions at the time of the crime. This may be difficult, because it is up to the discretion of the courts as to how the law of self-defense will be interpreted and what evidence will be allowed to assist in conveying the perceptions of the defendant to the judge and jury. It is also a difficult decision for defense lawyers because the only way to convey the defendant's perceptions at the time of the crime are through expert testimony and/or waiving the defendant's Fifth Amendment right and testify in court. In particular, the fundamental issues for the battered woman claiming self-defense are defining when deadly and non-deadly force are necessary, demonstrating imminent danger, and determining reasonableness.

Deadly and Non-Deadly Force

Courts considering a claim of self-defense will look at the amount of force that the defendant used, and the force used must be deemed reasonable for a claim of self-defense to remain viable. Within the traditional doctrine of self-defense, many courts have held that the use of deadly force against non-deadly force was unreasonable. This interpretation of the doctrine left women who were beaten or threatened with violence without recourse when they used a weapon to defend themselves. For example, deadly force was the key issue in *People v. Bush* (1978). The defendant was repeatedly beaten over the course of her relationship. In the midst of a severe beating, she attempted to leave the home and call the police. Her efforts not only were thwarted by her abuser, but actually reinforced her husband's constant threats to kill her. While she struggled against his violent beating, she grabbed a kitchen knife on the counter and began jabbing at her husband to fend him off, fatally stabbing him during the confrontation. She was then charged with first-degree murder. Even though the jury had been informed of the victim's reputation for violence, she was found guilty of involuntary manslaughter on the grounds that she was criminally negligent in assessing the seriousness of the danger she faced, and that resorting to a weapon to defend herself in that situation did not justify her use of deadly force. This case suggests that even a classic case of self-defense (at least in the eyes of the defendant) can go wrong when strict adherence to the doctrine is used and the jury is unable to take into account the predicament of the battered woman.

Imminent Danger

The most frequent situation in which the battered woman syndrome is used is "confrontational homicide." This is when an abuse victim kills their abuser during an actual assault, as in the *People v. Bush* case above. There is evidence that between 70 and 90 percent of homicides committed by self-proclaimed battered women involve confrontational cases (Browne, 1987; Downs, 1996; Maguigan, 1991). Another prevalent scenario is categorized as non-confrontational homicide. In this situation, a defendant may kill while the victim is sleeping. Lastly, a battered woman may arrange a contract killing, wherein a third party kills the woman's abuser (Roberts, 2003).

The issue of imminent danger is particularly of interest when a battered woman kills her abusive partner in a non-confrontational (Kinports, 1988) or murder-for-hire setting (*People v. Yaklich*, 1988). In some cases, instead of confronting her partner when he abuses her, the defendant does not take action until the abuser has finished attacking her (*Ibn-Tamas v. U. S.*, 1979; *State v. Kelly*, 1984), until the abuser threatens her with further abuse (*State v. Gallegos*, 1986; *State v. Allery*, 1984), or even until the abuser is asleep (*State v. Leidholm*, 1983). In such circumstances, juries may have a more difficult time understanding the abused woman's perceptions as they apply to the rules of self-defense.

In cases where battered women kill their partners in non-confrontational or contract killings, the element of imminent danger is often the key issue. The imminence requirement traditionally focuses on the circumstances immediately before or during the incident and does not take into account the cumulative effects of repeated violence or harm threatened in the past or future (Castel, 1990). This requirement can be particularly damaging for the defendant who committed homicide at some point after an abusive incident or during a period of threat that precedes an abusive incident. This traditional interpretation was best exemplified in the case of *State v. Nunn* (1984), wherein the Iowa State Court of Appeals held that the defendant's killing of her live-in boyfriend was not justified when the argument had ended several minutes before the stabbing and the victim was unarmed. The court found that the defendant's fear of imminent life-threatening danger was not reasonable under the circumstances (*State v. Nunn*, 1984).

Both "deadly force" and "imminent danger" impose a moral obligation upon the court to take into consideration the inherent differences between men and women (*State v. Wanrow*, 1977). The issue of whether the woman was able to defend herself during an attack comes into question when examining whether deadly force was reasonable and if the defendant felt she was in imminent danger. Similarly, to determine both "deadly force" and "imminent danger," the judge and jury must be provided with a context (life events) that can aid in assessing the defendant's state of mind. All too often, people cannot understand why the defendant did not simply leave the situation. Often, the jury will question the woman's ability to realize her alternatives, including the option of running away from the abuser, avoiding the unfortunate turn of events. The judge and jury may not be able to perceive the defendant's view of imminent danger or deadly force because they cannot imagine why she did not retreat.

Duty to Retreat

Duty to retreat, the last traditional element of self-defense, is no longer used by the majority of jurisdictions. Most now hold that the innocent party has no duty to retreat and may use deadly force if she reasonably believes the attacker will kill her or inflict great bodily harm (LaFave & Scott, 1986; Dowd, 1992; Dutton, 1992; Maguigan, 1991; Mather, 1988). In the minority view, the defendant is required to retreat, if she can safely do so, before resorting to deadly force (LaFave & Scott, 1986). Even in the minority jurisdictions, however, the defendant has no obligation to retreat from her own home (LaFave & Scott, 1986; Dutton, 1992; Maguigan, 1991). Thus, if a woman could prove that she held a reasonable perception of imminent lethal danger, she should not have a problem with the no-retreat rule in a majority view jurisdiction. For example, in *People v. Emick* (1984), the court ruled that the defendant, a battered woman, had no duty to retreat when she was attacked in her own home and was not the initial aggressor. Additional cases have also ruled that if the facts and circumstances create an honest and reasonable belief in the defendant's own mind that she cannot safely retreat from the co-habitant assailant, the use of deadly force is justified (*State v. Leidholm*, 1983; *State v. Sales*, 1985). At the same time, assault is not justified when there is a safe avenue of escape, or is practicable and the defendant failed to retreat (*State v. Corujo*, 1982). This issue was argued in *State v. Gardner* (1980), as the court upheld Gardner's conviction because Gardner shot her husband at another person's home (not her own home), hence offering her an opportunity to retreat.

Female defendants in jurisdictions with duty to retreat requirements often face difficulties (Dobash & Dobash, 1979). First, many juries continue to believe that it is the woman's duty to avoid being abused and take responsibility to leave, even though the law states that she may not have a duty to retreat from her own home. If her attacker is a co-inhabitant and not an intruder, this may affect the defendant's privilege not to retreat in a few states. For instance, some jurisdictions have generally held that the privilege not to retreat from your own home does not apply when the attacker is a co-inhabitant of the dwelling (*State v. Bobbitt*, 1982; *Carter v. State*, 1985; *State v. Shaw*, 1981, cited in Mather, 1988). Second, the battered woman might need to address her ability or inability to retreat safely from the situation. Many factors, however, could affect that ability, (economic ability, children in jeopardy, order of protection, transportation, access to social support and shelter, etc.) and the court must decide whether or not to consider them.

The Reasonableness Standard: Objective and Subjective Standards

The most crucial element of a self-defense claim is often whether the defendant *honestly and reasonably* feared unlawful bodily harm at the hands of her assailant (Gillespie, 1989; Kinports, 1988; Castel, 1990; Schneider, 1981). Most jurisdictions include both a subjective and an objective component commanding that the defendant's fear be both reasonable and honest. The objective component consists of jury instructions that call attention to whether a reasonable person would have felt the need to use lethal force under the same circumstances (Kinports, 1988). In the jurisdictions that apply subjective standards of self-defense, the jurors are given similar instructions; in order to acquit on grounds of self-defense, the jury must find that a reasonable person in the same situation, seeing what the defendant saw and knowing what she knew, would have resorted to killing in self-defense (Kinports, 1988). However, these two instructions are not mutually exclusive. The latter standard suggests that the judge and jury must incorporate the objective notion of "reasonableness." Thus, the two approaches are quite similar, merely varying in the degree to which they import the defendant's particular characteristics into the definition of the "reasonable person" (Kinports, 1988).

One case that represents the issue of objective versus subjective standards is that of *State v. Norman* (1988). In this case, the defendant was charged with murdering her husband. The defendant had been beaten on a daily basis and had often been forced to prostitute herself. Two days before the killing, the husband, Norman, was jailed for driving while intoxicated. When he returned home, he vented his anger on his wife by beating her continuously throughout the day. An officer was called to the residence, at which time the defendant told the police officer that she had been beaten all day, and that she couldn't take it any longer. However, she refused to take out a warrant, fearing Norman would kill her. Later in the evening, the defendant was hospitalized for taking an overdose of "nerve pills." On the day of the murder, beatings and threats to harm and kill the defendant intensified. That afternoon, while her husband was napping, the defendant shot him. The defendant was found guilty of voluntary manslaughter and received a six-year sentence. On appeal, the state argued that the defendant was not entitled to an instruction of self-defense because her husband was sleeping at the time of the shooting. The North Carolina Court of Appeals held that the defendant was entitled to an instruction of self-defense, as there was evidence showing that the defendant was suffering from battered spouse syndrome (*State v. Norman*, 1988). Since the courts initially did not provide a verdict option of self-defense, the Appeals court of North Carolina called for a new trial to include instructions to consider a verdict of innocent by reason of self-defense, because the evidence suggested that Mrs. Norman was a victim of abuse. The Appeals courts evidently believed that the reasonableness of her actions should be evaluated within the context of her abuse. The test of self-defense in this case consisted of four elements: whether (1) the defendant believed it was necessary to kill the victim in order to save herself from death or great bodily harm, (2) the defendant's belief was reasonable in that the circumstances as they appeared to her at the time were sufficient to create such a belief in the mind of a person of ordinary firmness, (3) the defendant was not the aggressor, and (4) the defendant did not use excessive force or use more force than necessary under the circumstances to protect herself from death or bodily harm.

The first element consisted of a subjective standard to determine what the defendant actually believed. However, an objective standard was applied to the second element that required that the defendant's belief, considering the circumstances at the time, was sufficient to create such an idea in the mind of a person of firmness. In applying the objective standard, a jury is required "to consider only the acts and circumstances surrounding the accused at, or immediately before, the time of the killing from the standpoint of a reasonable and prudent person" (*State v. Norman*, 1988). The subjective standard, when applied to the second element, on the other hand, requires the jury to decide whether the circumstances surrounding the accused were sufficient to induce an honest and reasonable belief in her mind that she must use force to defend herself. Again, both standards are quite similar to each other, and one would obviously have trouble separating the two elements. This raises the question of whether the court can indeed correctly apply an objective standard to the second element of self-defense. When placing the jury in the shoes of the defendant, the jury is prevented from answering objectively. At best, they would ask, "What would a reasonable person suffering from battered woman syndrome believe?" The extension of the objective test in this way presupposes that a person of ordinary firmness would fall prey to the syndrome. This assumption is questionable at best and is unfounded in the absence of scientific evidence at this point.

Arguing what constitutes a "reasonable person" is no easy feat. In the court system, a reasonable person is a measure of culpability. The reasonable person is one who personifies the community ideal of reasonable behavior, as judged by the jury (Kinports, 1988). The judge and jury are left to their own pre-conceived notions of what a reasonable person would do faced with the same dilemma. The objective standard then becomes an open invitation to a host of interpretations by the judges and jurors. In the subjective standard, the judge and jury are faced with placing themselves in the shoes of the defendant, but at the same time incorporating their own definition of "reasonable." The key to self-defense is convincing a jury the defendant's actions were honest and reasonable. If the defendant can prove they had an honest belief in imminent danger, yet their actions are not perceived as reasonable, then courts often recognize an alternative called "imperfect self-defense."

Imperfect Self-Defense

When a defendant can prove that they had an honest and reasonable belief in imminent death or serious bodily harm, it is possible that their actions will be viewed as reasonable in the context of self-defense. However, if the defendant cannot prove their actions were reasonable, the Model Penal

Code (a codification of criminal law developed by the American Law Institute and designed to encourage states to standardize penal law in the United States) offers a partial defense when the defendant can show they honestly believed their life was in imminent danger of death or serious bodily harm (LaFave & Scott, 1972). Imperfect self-defense is a partial defense used to mitigate the circumstances and negate malice. This defense will not exonerate the defendant, but rather mitigate murder to voluntary manslaughter (Brody et al., 2008, p. 345). In other words, courts have recognized that there are situations where defendants can have an honest but "unreasonable" belief that they would suffer death or serious bodily harm. In this regard, the courts recognize the defendant's culpability for homicide, yet understand the state of mind of the defendant serves as a mitigating factor (Brody et al., 2008).

Generally speaking, the penalty for murder far exceeds that of manslaughter. Sentences for second-degree murder can carry a potential life sentence and a determinate number of years in prison. If a defendant's actions are found to be unreasonable and imperfect self-defense is used, then it is likely that defendant's murder can be mitigated to manslaughter. In order for murder to be reduced to manslaughter, the act must be committed in the heat of passion. According to the Model Penal Code, manslaughter is "a purposeful killing that was committed under the influence of extreme mental or emotional disturbance for which there is reasonable explanation or excuse" (as cited in Brody et al., 2008, p. 396). As can be seen, imperfect self-defense might be used to effectively mitigate charges of battered women who kill, particularly in cases where women kill their abusers while they sleep or in which women provoke their abusers. Addressing evidence of past abuse can not only help assess the reasonableness or unreasonableness of the defendant's actions, but can also assist in identifying the state of mind of the defendant at the time of the crime.

How Evidence of Past Abuse Can Help to Assess Reasonableness

Whether trying to convince a jury a defendant's actions were in self-defense or imperfect defense, the mental state of the defendant is a focal issue. In order to address the mental state of the defendant, expert testimony of past abuse and battering is often admitted into the court to explain why the defendant felt as though they honestly or reasonably feared for their life or serious bodily injury. While the battered woman syndrome is not a legal defense, it is used to help judges and jurors understand the circumstances surrounding the homicide. In order to do this, bringing in evidence of prior abuse is important. When assessing the reasonableness of the defendant's actions, it is important for judges and jurors to understand the context; therefore, admissibility of evidence of prior abuse is necessary. In the past, the courts traditionally did not allow evidence of past abuse because it would "improperly focus the jury's attention on the decedent's character, rather than on the events occurring at the time of the homicide" (Federal Rules of Evidence, 702). However, in order to understand how the abused reasonably feared imminent danger and acted appropriately, the courts have come to understand that they must take into consideration the abuser's previous violent behavior.

Evidence of the syndrome and/or prior threats of violence have not been included in some courts (*Commonwealth v. Scott*, 1991; *Lewis v. State,* 1995). However, in the past 5–7 years there has been a shift in many states' legislations (Colorado, Kentucky, Louisiana, Texas, Utah, Virginia) to allow prior acts of violence or "the reputation of the deceased" into a case as a way to demonstrate justification of the abused's actions (Osthoff & Maguigan, 2004). Interestingly, while the topic of admitting evidence of previous battering has previously been at issue, courts have always allowed evidence of prior relationships with the deceased into a case to establish the defendant's subjective perception of danger and to determine whether their perceptions were reasonable given their experience with the decedent (Maguigan, 1991; Osthoff & Maguigan, 2004). This is just a small example of how courts have differed with regard to when and how evidence would or would not be offered in trials. Of late, more and more courts are allowing battered woman syndrome testimony into the courts on a regular basis, whether it is a confrontational or non-confrontational case, but the same argument supporting such testimony could be made for cases that include situations which do not necessarily fit into the typical categories of confrontational, non-confrontational, or murder-for-hire.

Changing the Standard of Reasonableness

Some theorists have argued that unless the jury is instructed to determine how a "reasonable battered woman" or "reasonable battered person" would have reacted under the circumstances, it cannot possibly evaluate whether or not the defendant's actions were reasonable (Castel, 1990; Gillespie, 1989; Kinports, 1988). Because of such discrepancies in intention and application, other theorists suggest that battered women should be exempt from the rule of self-defense (Ewing, 1990) and be entitled to other forms of self-defense (i.e., psychological self-defense, in which women kill their abusers to keep from being psychologically destroyed), which recognize the battered woman's psychological plight. Downs and Fisher (2005) suggest that more emphasis should be made on identifying the uniqueness of each situation and focus on survival skills developed by the defendant, particularly a battered woman's ability to discern whether danger is truly imminent.

While no current legislative proposal suggests separate standards of reasonableness for battered women, the scholarly debate appears to have influenced some states' application of the standard. For example, as the legal system has progressed beyond the "reasonable man" to the "reasonable person" standard of self-defense (*State v. Wanrow*, 1977), some authors have suggested a gender-neutral standard (Dowd, 1992; Mather, 1988) that considers all circumstances surrounding participants at the time of the incident, including individual characteristics and the histories of the parties involved (Dowd, 1992). To apply this standard effectively, lay and expert testimony could be used to explain an individual's violence and to dispel misconceptions about abuse. While this suggestion is admirable, the time and resources needed to consider all of these elements might make it impractical for courts. Critics (Crocker, 1985; Sheehy et al., 1992; Maguigan, 1991) suggest, however, that this standard actually may reinforce gender stereotypes by focusing on the weaknesses and idiosyncrasies of women, especially battered women. Thus, women may be judged according to who they are and what they represent, rather than the circumstances they faced.

Another alternative that has been suggested by scholars (Maguigan, 1991; Crocker, 1985) is the "reasonable woman" standard. From this perspective, it is argued that a woman's perceptions of danger, harm, and force are different from a man's perception. Thus, her actions when threatened by an abuser are different from those of a man in similar circumstances. Opponents to the use of this standard (Mather, 1988) believe stereotypes can emerge similar to those that can arise with the use of the gender-neutral standard. Thus, the use of this standard may exclude certain women from the group who don't fit the image of a "weak" or "helpless" victim (Dowd, 1992; Mather, 1988). In particular, such a standard would be especially difficult for women with histories of violence or women who are the initiators of violence, and it might also preclude men from using the defense. Use of a reasonable woman standard might also be problematic, as men have different experiences than women, and courts would then ask men to place themselves in the shoes of a reasonable woman.

The state of Wyoming enacted a statute that, while recognizing the syndrome, includes "battered woman syndrome" only as "a subset under the diagnosis of Post-Traumatic Stress Disorder established in the Diagnostic and Statistical Manual of Mental Disorders III-Revised of the American Psychiatric Association" (WYO Rev Stat, 2002), indicating that the need for medicalization of the syndrome is necessary for it to be included as testimony, though most states already make the assumption that it meets the medical basis to be included as testimony. Possibly one of the most important, yet least well-known, aspects of PTSD is that researchers and clinicians alike consider the disorder to be a common response by reasonable people who experience extreme trauma (Barlow & Durand, 1999). By addressing the reasonableness of this trauma response in court, the defense might effectively establish that the defendant's actions were, indeed, those of a reasonable person caught in an extraordinary conflict.

Finally, a more recent approach is one of understanding self-defense based on the "reasonable battered woman" standard (Dowd, 1992; Maguigan, 1991). While no current legislative proposal suggests a separate standard of reasonableness for battered women, the high courts of Kansas (*State v. Stewart*, 1988), and Wisconsin (*State v. Felton*, 1983), as well as the appellate court of Missouri (*State v. Williams*, 1990) have recognized either a "reasonable battered woman" or "reasonable prudent battered woman" standard. Legal scholars (Maguigan, 1991) suggest the reason for the court's adoption of this standard originates from some legislative proposals that attempt to set a separate standard for battered women, but which are, in fact, associated more with evidentiary issues, rather than substantive law provisions. One example is Pennsylvania's House Bill (1295), which has amended the criminal code to provide for a "Battered Person's Defense" (PA Stat. Ann. Tit. 18, 505.1(6), 1991). The provisions of the amendment relate to the admissibility of expert testimony regarding the battered woman syndrome (Maguigan, 1991). However, the intermediate appellate court of Missouri has interpreted such legislation providing for the admission of such testimony as creating a separate standard for battered women defendants (*State v. Williams*, 1990). Therefore, in lieu of using a "reasonable battered woman" standard, Missouri Statutes (Mo Rev Stat, 2001) continue to use the term "battered spouse syndrome," but stated in the Court of Appeals that application of the term "battered spouse syndrome" was not dependent upon the defendant's marital status. Other states have since incorporated the battered spouse, battered person, or battered partner syndrome into their courtrooms.

The impetus for including the term "battered partner" or "battered person syndrome" is based on an extension of the use of the battered woman syndrome to include battered men, parents, children, and those in homosexual relationships. In many states, the "battered child syndrome" is being admitted to assist jurors in understanding situations when children murder their parents or guardians (*State v. Janes*, 1993). For instance, an eight-year-old boy recently confessed to shooting his father and another man with a .22 caliber rifle in Arizona. The boy faces two counts of premeditated murder but police suspect the boy was abused. It is this type of case that the "battered child syndrome" may be admitted (CNN.com, Nov. 8, 2008). The battered person syndrome has also been used to accommodate homosexual relationships.

On one hand, the courts should be applauded for acknowledging a gender-neutral stance; on the other, extending the battered woman syndrome to all other situations can be a very dangerous move. There is too much undiscovered territory when it comes to knowing whether using the syndrome in such cases might actually work against a defendant or whether using slight variations of the syndrome (i.e., battered person, battered partner, battered woman, battered syndrome) to assess reasonability may affect judgments of culpability. At this point only the terminology used in the courts to assist judges and jurors with assessing reasonableness of a defendant's actions has been addressed. It is important to further consider the types of cases in which expert testimony of the syndrome is used, and wonder at what point such evidence would be allowed.

It should be noted that while many feminist legal scholars focus upon the doctrine of self-defense's inability to accommodate battered women who kill (Crocker, 1985; Dowd, 1992; Ewing, 1987; Kinports, 1988; Mather, 1988), one author (Maguigan, 1991) has argued that the impetus to change the law of self-defense is due to a common misconception held by legal scholars that battered women kill more often in non-confrontational settings, such as while the batterer is sleeping or incapacitated (Crocker, 1985; Ewing, 1987; Kinports, 1988). This assumption has been asserted without any empirical support or has generally been based on an unsystematic review of cases (Gillespie, 1989). In fact, as mentioned previously, research has found that between 70 to 90 percent of battered women's homicide cases actually involved confrontational situations (Browne, 1987; Downs, 1996; Maguigan, 1991). Ewing (1987) has suggested another form of self-defense, a "psychological self-defense," to remedy what he perceived to be an injustice in the application of the traditional law of self-defense.

There have been many suggestions with regard to which standard (i.e., reasonable battered woman, reasonable woman, psychological self-defense) would best help legal actors understand whether the defendants' actions were reasonable given the circumstances. Unfortunately, there is very little empirical research that has examined whether any of these standards are more effective than others. At this point, they are simply theoretical notions.

Despite the fact that the law of self-defense has come a long way from its historical roots, particularly when recognizing battered women who kill, it is imperative that researchers and scholars continue to investigate these theoretical notions, as well as extend these notions to accommodate victims of battering who are not heterosexual women. This chapter brings forth some of the difficult decisions lawyers must make when deciding to use self-defense laws when defending their clients. Lawyers can rely on expert testimony alone to convey their perceptions to a judge and jury, or they must decide whether the defendant will waive their Fifth Amendment right (to remain silent) and testify. Either way, there are constitutional issues that must be considered. Additionally, an abuser and victim are not on equal footing in the relationship. It is possible that the abused individual does not believe they can defend against their abuser unless deadly force is used. Such legal issues continue to be debated by legal scholars, even without the understanding of how the content of expert testimony of battering can influence cases.

Discussion Questions

1. Describe the three basic elements of the law of self-defense and identify who decides whether the defendant meets these requirements?
2. When is a defendant's actions justified?
3. Differentiate between confrontation and non-confrontational homicides and note how imminent danger will be evaluated differently in each case.
4. Why is mental status of the defendant so important when assessing self-defense?
5. Many scholars believe that jurors should be instructed to assess the reasonableness of a defendant's actions differently. Do you believe that if jurors were instructed to assess the reasonableness of a defendant's actions differently (i.e., via reasonable person, reasonable battered person, reasonable battered woman, reasonable battered spouse, reasonable woman, etc) this could change trial outcomes? If so, why?

CHAPTER 9

The Evolution of Expert Testimony of the Battered Woman Syndrome in the Courtroom

Flowing with the currents of the social stream of the late 1970s, the battered woman's movement and the development of the battered woman's syndrome as a body of research led to an increase in the use of self-defense as a justification for killing and an explanation for the reasonableness of a woman's use of force. During this time, the media played a large role in educating the public about battering, as many high-profile cases involving battered women were made public in the news media or movies (i.e., *The Burning Bed*, Osthoff & Maguigan, 2004). Three cases in the State of Pennsylvania (*Commonwealth v. Grove*, 1986; *Commonwealth v. Stonehouse*, 1989; *Commonwealth v. Miller*, 1993) represent a common evolutional theme that demonstrates how the battered woman syndrome became accepted in the courts.

Jesse Bell Grove was married to her abusive husband, Israel, for 22 years. She stated that while her husband was passed out, she took $400 from his wallet and shot him in the back of the head with a 12 gage shotgun, then proceeded to set his body on fire. Jessie was subsequently charged and convicted with first-degree murder and conspiracy and sentenced to life in prison, but she pleaded that her actions were justifiable based on the law of self-defense. Jessie stated that she and her daughter lived in constant fear of her husband's violent behavior. The Superior Court of Pennsylvania reviewed Jessie's appeal in the context of a self-defense claim and ruled that Jessie could not have believed she was in imminent danger of death or bodily harm, and therefore self-defense could not be at issue. However, the court did acknowledge the mental state of the defendant:

131

We find that self-defense was not properly at issue because there was no evidence presented to establish that appellant reasonably believed that she or any other person was in imminent danger of death or serious bodily injury on the present occasion when the deadly force was used. In reaching this conclusion we are mindful of the unique questions and considerations which arise in cases involving intra-familial, and especially intra-spousal, violence or abuse. In the context of a claim of self-defense by a battered spouse, our Supreme Court has explained: A woman whose husband has repeatedly subjected her to physical abuse does not, by choosing to maintain her family relationship with that husband and their children consent to assume the risk of further abuse. That woman faces a difficult choice: she must decide whether to endure continued abuse, or whether to leave her home or otherwise terminate her family relationship in order to avoid further mistreatment. Not surprisingly, some of those women who have "decided" to suffer years of abuse suddenly reach the "breaking point" and react violently. In a case such as this, in which there has been physical abuse over a long period of time, the circumstances which assist the court in determining the reasonableness of a defendant's fear of death or serious injury at the time of a killing include the defendant's familiarity with the victim's behavior in the past. ...There is no reason why a finding of self-defense should not consider the mental state of a reasonable person who has suffered repeated previous beatings at the hands of the victim [Pa. Super., 1987].

In this case it is apparent that the Pennsylvania Superior Court affirmed Grove's conviction and prison term and denied her plea of self-defense. While the court did not technically acknowledge the battered woman syndrome, it was the first time the court acknowledged the mental state of a victim of abuse.

Shortly thereafter, *Commonwealth v. Stonehouse* (1989) was the first case to mention the battered woman syndrome. Stonehouse was involved with William Welsh, whom she met at the police academy. Welsh quickly became possessive and showed up to her home and work unexpectedly, flattened Stonehouse's tires, stalked her, and made repeated death threats while holding a gun to her head in her apartment. In 1983, Welsh followed Stonehouse from a club and broke into Stonehouse's home with a firearm. Welsh beat Stonehouse, but she was able to disarm Welsh. Welsh then left the premises. Stonehouse waited on her front porch for Welsh to return, and when she saw him hiding and heard what she thought were gun-shots, she fired twice and killed Welsh. Stonehouse was charged and convicted of third-degree murder. On appeal, Carol Stonehouse argued her counsel was ineffective because they had not produced evidence that Stonehouse was suffering from the battered woman syndrome. The appeals court determined a new trial was necessary. The Supreme Court stated that "had trial counsel introduced expert testimony about the battered woman syndrome, the actions taken by appellant on the morning of March 17, 1983, would have been weighed by the jury in light of how the reasonably prudent battered woman would have perceived and reacted to Welsh's behavior" (Pa. Super., 1989).

As the courts recognized their need to accommodate battered women's claims of self-defense, one way in which they attempted to do so was to admit expert testimony. The Supreme Court had related their opinions about admitting expert testimony to explain the defendant's state of mind and evidence as to the reasonableness of the defendant's belief that deadly force was necessary in *Stonehouse*, but there had yet to be a case that determined whether expert testimony regarding the battered woman syndrome was admissible or inadmissible with regard to the defendant's state of mind.

Commonwealth v. Miller (1993) laid the evidentiary groundwork for the battered woman syndrome for the State of Pennsylvania. Andrea Miller lived with her boyfriend Mark Smith and their son. Their relationship had been tumultuous and abusive. One day, Smith and Miller were arguing, when Smith burned Miller with a cigarette, poked her in the chest, and slapped her. Later that day the arguing continued, and a knife fell out of Smith's pants. Smith threatened Miller, but when a struggle ensued, Miller grabbed the knife and fatally stabbed Smith. She was charged and convicted of third-degree murder.

The Supreme Court decided that expert testimony of the battered woman syndrome "is admissible as probative evidence of the defendant's state of mind as it relates to the theory of self-defense. The syndrome does not represent a defense to homicide in and of itself, but rather, is a type of evidence which may be introduced on the question of the reasonable belief requirement of self-defense in cases which involve a history of abuse between the victim and defendant" (Pa. Super., 1993). In the same decision, the Supreme Court also agreed that the gender neutral term "battered person syndrome" be used when pleading self-defense. Once a plea of self-defense has been entered, if battering is an issue, then it is the responsibility of the defendant claiming to be a battered person to produce an expert to testify and explain the battered person syndrome to the court.

These three cases provide a glimpse of the legal evolution toward the admission of testimony of the battered woman syndrome into the courts. In general, legal acceptance of the syndrome occurred during the 1980s through the 1990s. These dates correspond to the time that Lenore Walker's research was published and brought to the academic forefront. Faigman (1986) has noted that Lenore Walker was "the most active [domestic violence expert] in relating battered woman research to the legal context, and it [was] her work that courts most often relied on in their decisions" (p. 622). Walker's work, coupled with an increase in the amount and variety of media and research on the topic, helped to aid the syndrome as the most widely recognized explanation for domestic violence (Rothenberg, 2003).

By admitting expert testimony on the battered woman syndrome, the law of self-defense need not change. With a clinical solution to the problem (a verified "syndrome"), the law itself could remain unchallenged (Faigman, 1987; Schuller, 1994). Consequently, it is not surprising that courts were so quick to give legal acceptance to the theory of the battered woman syndrome. Although there are differences in various courts' reactions to the testimony, since expert testimony on the battered woman syndrome was first introduced in *Ibn-Tamas v. U.S.* (1979, 1983), there is clear evidence of a trend in favor of admitting battered woman syndrome evidence in trials of battered women who have killed their abusive husbands (Kinports, 1988; Schuller & Vidmar, 1992).

Who Are the Experts and What Is the Focus of the Testimony?

Expert testimony of the battered woman syndrome in a self-defense case is typically presented by one or more clinical psychologists or psychiatrists who are knowledgeable about the topic of abuse, with the content of their testimony relying heavily on the work of Lenore Walker (1979, 1984) and her theory of the battering cycle. This testimony is used to describe the psychological traits that typify battered women and their perceptions of the potential dangerousness of the abuser's violence (Blackman, 1989). As applied in the context of criminal cases, the syndrome testimony offers the defense attorney a way to explain the conduct of a woman in a battering relationship who fights back and kills her abuser. Given the potential interplay between jurors' beliefs and the lack of fit between the woman's actions and the existing laws of self-defense, establishing the reasonableness of the woman's behavior is a formidable task.

In most homicide cases where it is relevant, expert testimony is typically allowed to discuss the mental state of the defendant to help understand whether the defendant's perceptions and actions were reasonable at the time of the crime. In order to enable this assessment, experts and attorneys address violence, coercion, and prior abuse to provide a richer context of the situation for jurors to evaluate whether the defendant's perceptions and actions were reasonable at the time of the killing. While most experts who testify are clinicians, testimony can also come from other sources, such as social workers, advocates, psychologists and psychiatrists (Osthoff & Maguigan, 2004). By examining the history of the abuse, legal actors can better understand whether the defendant's perceptions were reasonable given the circumstances. There are three main goals in admitting syndrome testimony as evidence (Follingstad, 2003). The first goal is to evoke sympathy for the battered woman. The second goal is to assist judges and jurors in understanding the psychological effects associated with how battering distorted the defendant's perceptions of the situation, affected her abilities, and hindered her ability to leave the abuser. The third goal is to attempt to convince judges and jurors that her reactions were reasonable given the circumstances.

Traditionally, expert testimony focused on the medical model and was more likely to discuss whether or not, based on an interview with the defendant, she "fit the syndrome" or exhibited signs of mental instability. However, the use of the medical model did not necessarily help battered women who killed. If a battered woman defendant was to convince a jury her actions were reasonable and not the product of a mental disorder, then a shift from the medical model to social framework was necessary. One scholar (Slobogin, 1998) noted a fundamental shift in expert testimony leading away from the traditional medical model and departing from mental disabilities to describe what scientists know to be true based on empirical research data. Contemporary experts are more likely to offer evidence that addresses research on domestic violence and link that evidence to supporting data on social contexts associated with the defendant.

Initially, when expert testimony of battered woman syndrome was allowed as evidence, many scholars and clinicians believed it could create a new defense for battered women. Unfortunately, when they testified, they typically portrayed and promoted battered women as pathological. During testimony, they would focus on the women's incapacity, inability for proper cognitive functioning, and inability to reason. Experts also used diagnostic language that helped to create models into which all affected women may not fit (Biggers, 2005). They basically promoted a "stereotype" of the battered woman as pathological (Crocker, 1985; Downs & Fisher, 2005; Dutton, 1993; Osthoff & Maguigan, 2004; Schneider, 1986; Stubbs, 1992), helping to perpetuate a perception of battered women as irrational and dysfunctional, as well as unreasonable. The question of the reasonableness of a battered woman's actions was particularly difficult to overcome, as a double standard had been created in which it was then necessary to explain how a woman experiencing pathological symptomology could react in a reasonable manner.

Feminists (MacKinnon, 1982) made it clear that such double standards within the legal system often lead to the disadvantaging of the women they are actually designed to protect. Now, experts who had just explained the pathological aspects of the defendant had to explain how the same defendant's actions were reasonable and justified given the circumstances in accord with self-defense law. Osthoff and Maguigan (2004) stated, "Reverting to the stereotype of battered women as damaged human beings can be particularly problematic for women who kill their abusers, because reasonableness is central to their self-defense claims" (p. 236). Osthoff and Maguigan (2004) further reported five "mistaken categories" (p. 236), errors or misperceptions of abused women's legal defenses that have persisted over time, yet are not rooted in reality. These misperceptions can be held by experts, legal actors or laypersons. First, many believe that there exists a "battered woman's defense" or "battered woman syndrome defense," though, the syndrome is used only to support a defense claim of self-defense, not as a defense itself. Second, many believe this defense has its roots in either vigilantism or insanity. Third, many understand expert testimony to be the most important aspect of a battered woman's defense. According to the authors, "Expert testimony is not introduced in every battered woman's case. When it is offered, it is generally one of many pieces of evidence introduced to support a woman's defense claim," and, "In the overwhelming majority of cases where expert testimony is used, this testimony addresses a range of social and psychological issues related to the reasonableness of a defendant's use of force to protect herself. It does not focus on the woman's incapacity or lack of reason" (Osthoff & Maguigan, 2004, p. 237). Fourth, many individuals believe that the expert testimony provided is only about the syndrome. Finally, they often believe it is provided to focus primarily on the woman's victimization, denying her ability and responsibility (Osthoff & Maguigan, 2004).

Despite these perceptions, testimony is allowed on a case by case basis. When testimony is allowed, it is more likely to pertain to the effects of battering in order to provide a context for judges and jurors to evaluate whether the defendant's actions were justified, given her perceptions of the situation. Courts also allow testimony on battering to provide an explanation for why a woman may have remained in an abusive relationship or why she may have acted under duress. Testimony is not intended to deny the responsibility of her actions, but rather to demonstrate the woman's state of mind at the time of the crime. It is also admissible to address common myths and misperceptions about battered women, to speak to diminished capacity or lack of intent, bolster the credibility of the defendant, or demonstrate mitigating factors (U.S. Department of Justice, 1996). Many people also believe that defendants' use of testimony of the battered woman syndrome places the focus of the crime onto the victim, thus exonerating the defendant.

Research suggests that battered women actually do not get off easily. Research by the U.S. Department of Justice (1996) found that 63 percent of state court cases (out of 152) on appeal involving battered women affirmed the original courts' conviction or sentence, despite the fact that testimony of battering was admissible in 71 percent of the affirmed cases. It is difficult to tell whether testimony of battering led to more lenient verdicts for battered women. The data in this sample is limited by the fact that defendants acquitted by self-defense were not included; the sample shows appealed court cases in which the defendant was convicted, and an appeal occurred. However, it is likely that the decisions which were affirmed on appeal, for the most part, did not lead to more lenient verdicts for battered women.

More recently, scholars and practitioners have argued for the need to shift the focus away from using the battered woman syndrome. There are two reasons for this. First, with the syndrome comes the possibility of subjecting women to labels that stereotype abused women. These labels can never capture the complexity and diversity of women's individual situations; instead, they portray them as debilitated, weak, and vulnerable (Crocker, 1985; Dutton, 1993; Osthoff & Maguigan, 2004; Schneider, 1986; Stubbs, 1992). In the last ten years or so, scholars have, for the most part, successfully convinced some legal actors and advocates to move away from the battered woman syndrome and to shift the heart of the evidence to the effects of battering (Bradfield, 2002; Ferraro, 2003; Follingstad, 2003; Osthoff & Maguigan, 2004) instead of the woman's pathology. However, there are many states that continue to refer to the battered woman syndrome in state statutes and legal precedent. Second, Stubbs and Tolmie (1999) point out an additional critique of the use of the battered woman syndrome in that while it had been "a useful construct as a focus for women's self-defense work ... it is now outmoded" because it does not adequately reflect the state of knowledge and practice (p. 713).

Shifting the Focus of the Testimony to Social Framework

Terminology associated with learned helplessness has led to increased attention to a woman's passivity (Schuller & Rzepa, 2002), and ultimately, to the creation of the stereotype of the battered women (Schneider, 1986). Many scholars believe social framework, or expert testimony explaining battering and its effects, would be more effective than using terminology associated with the syndrome, such as being passive or submissive (Osthoff & Maguigan, 2004). Such testimony places the emphasis on the effects of battering, the survival strategies used by the battered woman, and the unique ability to predict her partner's actions, rather than focusing on the battered woman's pathology (Osthoff & Maguigan, 2004). Social framework testimony does not take into consideration the specific individual, but rather addresses cutting-edge research in order to provide a context for a particular situation. In fact, the combination of case-specific relevant information and social framework evidence of battering and its effects can be helpful for the defendant who claims her actions were in self-defense.

The recent call for reform and a major shift from the use of the term "battered woman syndrome" to the effects of battering and the social context in which it occurs has dominated the majority of theoretical discussions over the last ten years. While there is a great deal of research and scholarly interest on the first issue—shifting focus from the use of the battered woman syndrome to incorporating a social framework perspective—there has been a substantial lack of scholarly and legal interest in the extent to which the battered woman syndrome actually reflects the state of knowledge and practice in the scientific world today. The shift away from its use was precipitated by a study authorized by the U.S. Congress under the Violence Against Women Act of 1994 to identify the validity of the battered woman syndrome and its effects in criminal trials (U.S. Department of Justice & U. S. Department of Health and Human Services, 1996). The report revealed strong validity and relevance for including information on battering and the resultant effects on the victims of intimate partner violence. However, the report also suggested that the term "battered woman syndrome" was too constricted and had negative connotations. The report further elaborated that the syndrome fell short of reflecting the empirical research on the topic of battering.

The purpose of social framework testimony pertaining to battered women was to provide jurors with an alternative perspective (Biggers, 2005; Bradfield, 2002; Follingstad, 2003; Monahan & Walker, 1993; Schuller, 1992; Stubbs & Tolmie, 1999). Social framework as evidence in the form of expert testimony is meant to provide jurors with a more thorough understanding of the defendant's experience and circumstances (Bradfield, 2002). Proposing a shift from traditional to social framework testimony, Stubbs and Tolmie (1999) suggested that expert testimony should refrain from focusing on "whether or not a woman might have BWS" and instead focus upon "broad social framework evidence to provide the context within which to understand the issues in a given case" (p. 34). In order to provide this perspective, Walker and Monahan (1987) have pointed out the commonly accepted legal use of social science in establishing either legislative (general questions of law and policy) or adjudicative (concerning only the case at hand) facts. These authors have also noted that the more recent social science research should be used in cases involving battered women because many of these cases do not conveniently fit in either the legislative or adjudicative category. Therefore, Walker and Monahan (1987) proposed the concept of social framework as a frame of reference for deciding factual issues that are crucial to resolving specific cases.

The key issue for the defense is to demonstrate how and why battered women believe there to be few, if any, alternatives to homicide. Research has revealed that the average juror cannot understand many aspects of the nature of the battering relationship or other aspects of what is reasonable behavior for a battered woman. Most people are incapable of intuitively understanding what it is like to live within a violent home; therefore, they may evaluate normalcy or reasonableness of response based upon their own perceptions of *reasonable*, which are created out of their own often limited experience. Thus, experts are needed to dispel any misconceptions that jurors may have about the dynamics and consequences of abuse, and to explain to the jury and the judge exactly how the defendant's behavior does conform to the requirements of self-defense by describing what is reasonable for someone in that situation.

Of critical importance is the content of expert testimony; jurisdictions differ in the extent to which expert testimony is admissible. For example, the content of what an expert can say in court varies depending on how it can specifically address the defendant's behavior. In some situations, courts have allowed experts only to explain general research findings regarding the battered woman syndrome and provide a clinical opinion regarding whether or not the woman on trial "fits" the syndrome, to the exclusion of any information pertaining to the woman's perceptions at the time of the killing (e.g., *LaValee v. Regina*, 1990; *Commonwealth v. Jones*, 1993), while in other instances, experts have been allowed to give evidence regarding only general research findings without offering evidence of whether or not the woman on trial fits the syndrome (e.g., *State v. Thomas*, 1981). In addition to cases of homicide, expert testimony pertaining to the battered woman syndrome, battered spouse syndrome, or battered person syndrome is also often permitted in cases of duress, coercion, and many other related situations.

The Battered Syndrome Used to Explain Duress and Coercion

In recent situations, the issue relating to the reasonableness standard has been one of providing (or not providing) evidence that the syndrome is relevant in demonstrating a context for coercion or duress. While these examples are not exhaustive, some of the more common types of cases in which the battered syndrome has been used include child murder, sexual abuse or neglect, conspiracy to commit murder, tax evasion and/or fraud, cult murders, purchase of illegal firearms, delay or omission in reporting rape or murder,

contract killings, and civil cases such as child custody, post-nuptial agree-
ments, or tenant issues.

The law of duress excuses a defendant's actions if they can show that
they would not have committed the crime if they were not threatened by
another person with bodily harm to themselves or another person. In other
words, the law cannot hold someone responsible for a crime they were forced
to do against their will (Brody et al., 2008). However, the law does not allow
duress as a defense against charges of intentional murder. While some states
allow a duress defense for a felony that precedes a felony murder (a murder
that is committed during the commission of a felony), half of the jurisdictions do not allow this defense at all if the defendant is charged with murder, including felony murders (LaFave & Scott, 1972).

With regard to the topic of duress and coercion, society is currently at
the forefront of the most pivotal time in the history of the battered woman
syndrome. In February of 2006, the Supreme Court agreed to hear the case
of *U.S. v. Dixon* (2005), which addresses the issue of duress and coercion.
Keshia Cherie Ashford Dixon, a resident of Dallas, Texas, contends that she
was pressured by her boyfriend to purchase guns illegally. She agreed that
in 2003 she bought seven guns at gun shows because she feared her boyfriend
would kill her and her daughters if she didn't. Her boyfriend was a felon and
unable to purchase guns himself. Dixon was allowed to purchase guns by
providing false information (i.e., incorrect address, hiding a criminal history), when, in fact, she was under indictment for a check-cashing scheme
at the time. Dixon claimed that she suffered from the battered woman syndrome. The district court judge instructed the jury that Dixon had to prove
her duress defense by a preponderance of the evidence. She was convicted
of lying to purchase firearms and receiving guns while under indictment and
imprisoned.

On appeal, Dixon claimed that the U.S. should be required to prove
beyond a reasonable doubt that the defendant did not act under duress and
that her rights were violated when the judge did not allow jurors to hear evidence regarding the effects of domestic violence. When the Supreme Court
heard the case, the only issue they considered was whether the U.S. or the
defendant had the burden of proving duress. The Supreme Court affirmed
Dixon's conviction and stated that Congress had intended the petitioner to
bear the burden of proving duress by preponderance of the evidence (*Dixon
v. U.S.*, 2006). The Supreme Court only considered whether a defendant must
prove he or she was under duress, or whether it is the responsibility of the
prosecution to prove beyond a reasonable doubt that a defendant was not
under duress. J. Craig Jett, Dixon's attorney, told the *Dallas Morning News*
that the Supreme Court would not address the question of whether expert

testimony should be allowed in cases involving women who experience battered woman syndrome. He further stated, "It's really a legal issue, unfortunately, and that's too bad, because I had the opportunity to really make a statement about the law and how the law is going to treat what it is to be battered" (Newsflash, Feb. 15, 2006). Unfortunately, this case does not appear to address the crucial issue of whether expert testimony should be allowed in cases involving persons who are battered or experience the battered woman syndrome.

Some civil cases include issues such as child custody. Testimony is used to find evidence of the defendant's mental instability, and based on allegations of spousal abuse, mandate evaluations of the defendant's parenting skills, and testimony is often included regarding the effects of battering on children (*Kaliher v. Kaliher*, 1990). *Heck v. Heck* (1986) used the syndrome testimony to explain why a post-nuptial agreement was signed under duress. A self-proclaimed battered woman reported she signed it after a battering incident.

Child Murder, Neglect, and Sexual Abuse

In *Labastida v. State* (1999), a self-proclaimed battered woman defendant appealed her conviction of second-degree murder and child neglect of her 7-week-old infant son, who died of injuries inflicted by her boyfriend. The defendant claimed she did not know the father was abusing the child. In fact, the boyfriend admitted that he didn't tell the defendant of his abuse toward the child, yet she was convicted; and during appeal, her conviction was upheld because the courts could not believe that the defendant, who was breast-feeding, could not know that her child was being abused.

Other interesting cases fall under the duress or coercion statutes where self-proclaimed battered women use the syndrome as a defense because they were under their abusers' domination. In cases of murder and claims of duress, any actions made by the defendants are claimed to be motivated by the need to protect themselves from injury or death. There are many cases that fall under the category of child abuse, murder and/or neglect. For example, in *Commonwealth v Beeler* (1993) the defendant was accused and convicted of assisting her boyfriend in sexually assaulting her 14-year-old daughter. The defendant's defense was duress and coercion due to years of abuse she experienced by her boyfriend. The defendant's actions in assisting him were claimed to be motivated solely to protect herself and children from further harm.

There are many cases where defendants claim duress and/or coercion and argue that the battered syndrome is necessary to provide a context for their behavior, whether it is for acting as an accomplice in the assault of children (*Echols v. State*, 1991), for failure to intervene and stop the abuse of a minor (*People v. Hernandez*, 2000), or for killing. In *State v. Wyatt* (1996), Wyatt was charged and convicted of child abuse and neglect with bodily injury, malicious assault, and murder of a child by failure to provide medical care to her boyfriend's 2½-year-old son. The defendant was not allowed to provide evidence of the battered woman syndrome to explain her failure to protect the child or seek medical care. On appeal, the state reversed her conviction and remanded the case for a new trial that would include battered woman syndrome testimony.

In *State v. Long* (1995), a husband and wife were tried together in the killing of their 8-week-old son. The wife was convicted of aiding and abetting the perpetrator. On appeal, the defense argued that the defendant did not use the self-defense plea or the battered syndrome to show that she was under considerable duress. The appeals court disagreed and her conviction of first-degree murder was affirmed. Similarly, in *State v. Maupin* (1991), the defendant appealed her conviction of first-degree murder in her boyfriend's killing of her 2-year-old son. On appeal, her case was reversed and remanded for a new trial because the mother wasn't even present when the boyfriend killed the son. However, in her new trial, it was clear that she had witnessed earlier abuse, so her original conviction for first-degree murder was reversed to a lesser sentence of second-degree murder or manslaughter.

It should be noted that when a battered woman is a mother charged with child murder, neglect, or sexual abuse their actions may be scrutinized differently than women who do not have children. In most situations when a mother kills or abuses her own child, society is more often surprised and angry. The media will also capitalize on stories that depict women who kill or hurt their children much more often than men. Aren't women supposed to be nurturers and protectors of their children? Unfortunately, there is little research on the topic of how battered women in these types of cases are perceived by jurors. These are complex issues that must be addressed by scholars in the future.

Conspiracy and Accomplice to Murder

In *People v. Callahan* (2004), the defendant was convicted of felony murder for her participation in killing another person. Callahan believed her defense made a series of errors of omission including (1) failing to present evidence on duress, (2) not reporting the defendant had a drug habit, (3) the codefendant did the killing and prevented her and the victim from leaving, and (4) that she believed she would be killed if she didn't comply with his orders to dispose of the body. In addition, there was previous evidence of abuse and threats made to the defendant by the codefendant. On appeal, based on the fact that she claimed to be a battered woman and no evidence of the effects of battering had been introduced in the original trial, she was granted a new trial.

Similar cases have included complicity to commit murder or simply committing murder itself. One interesting case was that of McBride, who was charged with complicity to commit murder. She and her husband lured homeless men onto their farm to work and later killed them for their money (*State v. McBride*, 1982). McBride claimed she had to acquiesce to her husband, and claimed she was abused and under duress. The court believed otherwise, and she was convicted of several murders.

In another case, Dunn and her boyfriend fatally injured a police officer and were charged and convicted of first-degree felony murder, aggravated robbery, and battery on a police officer, and were each given four concurrent life sentences. In her first trial, the court denied funds for an expert on the battered woman syndrome. On appeal, Dunn received a new trial to include the syndrome as an explanation that she was under duress from her boyfriend at the time of the murder (*State v. Dunn*, 1992; *Dunn v. Roberts*, 1999).

There have been cases where defendants have been charged with aiding and abetting husbands or boyfriends with the killing or disposing of bodies of family members (*People v. Bazzetta*, 1990) and torturing and murdering sexually abusive family members (*Marley v. State*, 1996). For example, Lundgren was married to a man who was a religious fanatic involved in cultish behaviors. These behaviors led to the executions of their own children as a sacrifice. Lundgren was charged with complicity in her abusive husband's cultish church (*State v. Lundgren*, 1994). Lundgren claimed that her actions were the result of a domineering and abusive husband.

In *People v. Yaklich* (1988) a self-proclaimed battered woman was acquitted in a contract murder case. Yaklich hired a third party to kill her husband. The killer shot Yaklich's husband as he exited his truck in his driveway while Yaklich was asleep in the house. The trial court admitted testimony of the battered woman syndrome. The defense presented testimony that the defendant was a battered woman and the people's expert provided opinions suggesting Yaklich did not fit the profile of a battered woman. Yaklich was acquitted of murder in the first degree, but found guilty of conspiracy to commit murder in the first degree and sentenced to 40 years in prison. On appeal (*People v. Yaklich*, 1991) the people sought to review the process of the trial court, suggesting the trial court erred when it let admitted self-defense instruction. The appeals court believed that the trial court erred by admitting self-defense instruction, claiming self-defense instruction is not available in a contract-for-hire situation.

In another case, Frazier was convicted of failing to prevent a crime from being committed as she sat and watched her mentally retarded child being raped, assaulted, and eventually killed by her boyfriend (*State v. Frazier*, 2002). A Massachusetts court reversed the decision of rape and indecent assault on a mentally retarded person, believing that the mother's failure to prevent the boyfriend's sexual assault of her retarded daughter did not make her an accessory before the fact to those assaults (*Commonwealth v Raposo*, 1992).

In *State v. Ciskie* (1988) a male defendant was convicted of raping his girlfriend multiple times over the course of their relationship. Ciskie appealed to the high court, claiming that the trial erred by admitting expert testimony on battered woman syndrome in an effort to explain why the girlfriend didn't report the abuse sooner. The Supreme Court of Washington agreed the testimony was relevant and admissible and affirmed the conviction.

Recent U.S. Supreme Court Rulings

There have been several recent Supreme Court rulings that may affect cases of domestic violence. On March 22, 2006, the Supreme Court examined the constitutionality of whether police could search a home if there were two people living in a dwelling and only one consented to a search. In the past, police needed to obtain consent from any habitant of the home. However, the court ruled that this would be a violation of a co-habitant's Fourth Amendment rights against unreasonable search and seizures if police searched a home when one resident invited police in, but another refused police entry. While many consider this a victory for our Fourth Amendment rights against unreasonable search and seizures, others fear that this ruling may have an adverse affect on police responses to domestic violence calls. While this doesn't prevent police from protecting victims of domestic violence, it could possibly make life more difficult for a victim of abuse.

The Supreme Court recently examined another case that would have significantly bolstered legal protection for divorced battered women and their children. After coming home and not finding her children there, Jessica Gonzales suspected her husband had taken them. She phoned the police five times and physically went to the police station over an eight-hour period to get the police to find her daughters and arrest her husband. The police declined to act and suggested she wait until her husband brought her children home. Mr. Gonzalez arrived at the police station and opened fire with a semiautomatic handgun he had purchased earlier that evening. Police shot and killed Gonzalez. They then found the bodies of his three daughters, ages seven, nine, and ten, in the cab of his truck, murdered by their father.

The main issue for the Supreme Court was whether Mrs. Gonzalez's protective court order created a constitutionally-backed entitlement for prompt enforcement by the police. In 2004, the 10th U.S. Circuit Court of Appeals in Denver ruled that the protective order did entitle her to such enforcement. However, the Supreme Court reversed that decision, claiming a domestic restraining order did not create a "property interest" in prompt police enforcement of the order. Justice Scalia stated, "A benefit is not a protected entitlement if government officials may grant or deny it in their discretion." The majority claimed that even though the law directed police to "use reasonable means to enforce a restraining order," the state law did not make it mandatory according to Colorado's existing statute. The claim was based on whether the town of Castle Rock failed to adequately enforce her protective order (*Castle Rock v. Gonzales*, 2005). Thus, the Supreme Court ruled that domestic restraining orders do not provide a constitutional right to government protection against harm from private individuals.

Further, on June 19, 2006, the United States Supreme Court handed down its decision in the joint cases of *Hammon v. State of Indiana* (2005) and *Davis v. Washington* (2006). While domestic violence was the basis for the cases, the legal aspects involved more of a determination as to whether 911 calls or on-scene testimonials would be admitted into testimony in lieu of the victim testifying against her abuser. The court ruled in both cases that 911 calls were considered non-testimonial statements and were not subject to the confrontation clause (the defendant's right to confront his accuser). In *Hammon*, the Supreme Court reversed the state's ruling, saying that on-scene statements made to police were considered testimonial and were subject to restrictions of the confrontation clause. The court ruled on-scene statements were considered testimonial because 1) the emergency had ended when the statements were taken, and 2) the inquiries made by the police were not to assess an emergency but rather to gather evidence for future legal proceedings. The decisions in these cases created an objective test to assist judges and jurors in determining whether statements made to law enforcement during a 911 call or on-scene questioning constitute testimony in lieu of a victim testifying in court against her abuser.

These recent Supreme Court rulings may ultimately have some impact on domestic violence in the future. Two of the three outcomes of these cases possibly place the victim of domestic violence at increased risk. The fact that courts now require both individuals at the home to consent to a search can have detrimental effects for a victim of domestic violence. Similarly, even when women have restraining orders against their violent partners, the government does not necessarily have to act promptly.

These cases may appear tangentially related to expert testimony of battering, but there are many cases where an abuser violates an order of protection and the victim calls for prompt enforcement by police. If police response is not prompt, then it is very possible that either the victim or the abuser will be injured or killed in a dispute. If the victim of abuse kills their abuser, their actions will then be called into question in a court of law. A case of self-defense is likely, and expert testimony of abuse will also most likely be used. When the larger picture of battering and its effects are contemplated, one must extrapolate the possible effects of these rulings. When Supreme Court judges make decisions, they often argue the legal issues involved and are less likely to consider the larger picture in how domestic violence played a significant role in the case.

Over the years, the laws have extended the use of expert testimony on battering and its effects or the battered (woman, person, or spouse) syndrome and how it can be used to explain the context of many situations. Legal precedent in the early 1980s (*Ibn-Tamas v. U.S.*, 1981) led to the inclusion of the syndrome into the courtroom. Alternatives to testimony about the battered woman syndrome help us to better understand the context of battering and how abuse affects individuals. Unfortunately, research has only just begun to investigate the efficacy of these alternative forms of testimony. Even if the context of the expert testimony changes to include battering and its effects, many statutes continue to label such testimony "battered woman syndrome," "battered spouse syndrome," or "battered person syndrome." It is possible that legal actors, as well as the general public, will continue to adhere to ideas or misperceptions associated with the syndrome. It is vital to understand how these alternative perspectives interact with public perceptions of battered victims so that researchers can understand how victims are perceived, particularly in cases of self-defense. From the plethora of research conducted on battered women, researchers continue to try to separate myth from reality. It is evident from research that stereotypes of battered women exist; however, researchers are still trying to tease out exactly what characteristics are true and which are myths. Until reality can be discerned from myth, the legal standards for admissibility of expert testimony regarding the syndrome need to be carefully considered. In particular, the following chapter will demonstrate the importance of relevance and reliability and its relation to the syndrome. This reliance on relevance and reliability should reflect the importance of re-examining the syndrome within the contemporary context of the law as this discussion continues.

DISCUSSION QUESTIONS

1. Who provides expert testimony of battering in the courts and describe the content of such testimony.

2. What are the three main goals of admitting expert testimony in trials of self-defense?

3. How did expert testimony of the battered woman syndrome create a stereotype of women as pathological, and how can this stereotype be at odds with claims of reasonableness of her actions?

4. What is social framework, and how does it differ from previous forms of expert testimony of battering?

5. Identify and discuss how expert testimony has been used in various cases of duress, coercion, and other related situations. Can you think of additional cases where expert testimony of battering might be relevant?

CHAPTER 10

The Admissibility of Evidence: Understanding Legal Standards

Before expert testimony on the battered woman syndrome may be admitted into a trial, a number of legal requirements must be met. Legal methods are used to determine what evidence is allowed in court, and judges must evaluate the extent to which social science evidence meets these legal requirements (Monahan & Walker, 1993).

In the past, courts have held that the battered woman syndrome was scientifically undeveloped and inconclusive, thereby rendering it inadmissible as a part of expert testimony (*State v. Thomas*, 1981; *Burhle v. State*, 1981). However, despite controversy surrounding its use, the emerging position has generally supported the use of the testimony as scientifically reliable and relevant to the defendant's claim of self-defense (Aron, 1993; Lafferty, 1990; *State v. Kelly*, 1984; *State v. Hundley*, 1985). Over the years, states have actually incorporated the battered woman syndrome into their statutes as "a matter of commonly accepted scientific knowledge ... which is not within the general understanding or experience" of laypersons (Ohio Rev Stat, 1990).

Since the admission of expert testimony in such cases defines the present state of affairs, the issue has since shifted to how the jury should consider expert testimony (Aron, 1993; Lafferty, 1990). However, many scholars and legal practitioners argue that due to the vagueness and ambiguity associated with standards of admissibility, the standards should be re-examined and restructured to produce a more accurate means of assessment.

Admissibility of Expert Evidence

In order to explore admissibility of evidence in the form of expert testimony, an examination of its history in the courts should first be considered. States differ with regard to which standard they use to assess admissibility. Some states use the historic "Frye" standard, or elements of the Frye standard, while others use "Federal Rules of Evidence" or its contemporary, the federal standard of the "Daubert trilogy."

Before an expert can testify in a case, the judge must decide whether to admit the testimony based on specific criteria set forth by the courts using one of the standards above as the defining criteria. The judge decides on whether to admit the expert based on their credentials and the content of their testimony. For example, if the expert will testify about test results or research, these must be evaluated by the judge.

The Frye standard (*Frye v. U.S.,* 1923) requires that scientific validity of evidence must be generally accepted by experts in a particular field. The defendant in the Frye case wanted to admit expert evidence regarding the use of a lie detector, though evidence of its efficacy was not yet scientifically developed and "generally accepted" by the scientific community. The court rejected the evidence and provided a new standard of admissibility of expert testimony that would be used for the next 50 years. The Frye standard also requires that the evidence be relevant and that the methods used to obtain it are compatible with the discipline from which it was obtained. For example, if a psychologist were potentially to provide expert testimony on the battered woman syndrome, in order to be admitted, the courts must determine that the content of the testimony is generally accepted within the field   of psychology, the testimony is relevant to the case, and that the research methods that are discussed by the expert are approved within the discipline of psychology. In addition, before 1975, in order to admit "opinion" testimony, the information provided had to be specialized information that was "beyond the ken" (i.e., beyond the understanding) of the jury. The Frye test was used as a basis regarding whether to allow expert testimony until 1976, when Congress enacted a new standard incorporated in the Federal Rules of Evidence.

In 1975, Congress provided a new standard of admissibility for expert testimony. According to Rule 702 of the Federal Rules of Evidence (FRE) or the state equivalent, the admission of expert testimony has to satisfy three other standards of admissibility (Monahan & Walker, 1993). While there is a lot of variability within courts' interpretations of each of these standards, the basic list of the requirements include: 1) the expert must be sufficiently skilled or qualified, either by education or experience in the particular field of inquiry, 2) the testimony must be scientifically reliable, and 3) the testimony must provide the jurors with unique information that would be beyond the ken of the common juror (*Dyas v. U.S.,* 1977; Monahan & Walker, 1993). A court will require that the testimony meet either the three criteria set forth in *Dyas v. United States* (1977), the criteria of Rule 702 of the Federal Rules of Evidence, or the state equivalent (Coffee, 1986; Monahan & Walker, 1993). Therefore, FRE adopted elements of *Dyas* (i.e., an expert can testify only if the information presented was beyond the ken of the average person, the testimony provides legal actors with information beyond the understanding of laypersons, and helps them to reach a legal decision), but also required expert testimony to include the qualifications of the expert and scientific reliability.

The differences between the Frye and FRE tests are that FRE no longer required the standard of "general acceptance," though it now required relevance (material to the case) and reliability. In addition, all three criteria had to be met in order to be admitted. For instance, even relevant information could be excluded if it was believed the information provided might bias the jury in some way. In other words, judges also had the task of determining the probative value of the testimony or whether expert testimony might sway a jury too much as to prejudice their decision. In addition, the change from admitting evidence that is "beyond the ken" of the jury to admitting opinions based on "scientific, technical or other specialized knowledge" to "assist" jurors may appear to be a subtle difference, but the language used in FRE suggests a broader concept of what constitutes expert evidence. It was believed that the FRE would relax the standard associated with Frye and provide a greater acceptance of expert testimony. FRE stated that experts could testify if their testimony was based on "scientific, technical or other specialized knowledge" and needed only to "assist the trier of fact to understand the evidence or to determine a fact in issue" (Federal Rules of Evidence, 702). Some courts used the FRE criteria and some states used the Frye standards, while other states made up their own criteria in line with both Frye and FRE. For years, it was generally unclear as to what constituted admissibility of expert testimony based on these two tests, but the Daubert trilogy provided some clarity on the issue.

Daubert v. Merrill Dow Pharmaceuticals (1993), *General Electric v. Joiner* (1997), and *Kumho Tire Co. v. Carmichael* (1999) constituted the Daubert trilogy. These cases together provided a new standard used by the federal courts to decide whether expert testimony should be admitted in a case. In *Daubert,* parents and their two infants sued Merrill Dow Pharmaceutical Company, claiming that the drug Benedictin, used to curb nausea during pregnancy, caused serious birth defects. In the trial, an expert testified that research on the drug showed Benedictin was not a risk factor for birth defects. The jury found the drug company was not responsible. On appeal, the court used the Frye standard and affirmed the trial courts' decision.

The federal and state courts had used the Frye standard until 1976, when the FRE standard was provided. Following the adoption of the FRE standard, there was a controversy between the federal courts and the state courts over whether "general acceptance" was still applicable. *Daubert* solved this controversy when the case went to the U.S. Supreme Court. Using the FRE as a basis of their decision, the appeal court's decision was overturned, with the Supreme Court stating that "a rigid general acceptance" requirement would be at odds with the "liberal thrust" of the Federal Rules and their "general approach of relaxing the traditional barriers to 'opinion' testimony" (p. 2794). The Supreme Court also added that "general acceptance is not a necessary precondition to the admissibility of scientific evidence under FRE" (p. 2799). The Supreme Court then gave explicit rules about how FRE should be used in the court systems and how judges should evaluate whether or not to include expert testimony. The rules and guidelines included: 1) whether admission of expert testimony is relevant to the case, 2) whether the probative value of the testimony would outweigh its prejudicial impact, 3) whether the testimony would assist the judge or jury in its determination, and 4) whether the witness qualifies as an expert (for a great depiction of this decision model, see Roesch, Hart, & Ogloff, 1999).

In essence, in *Daubert*, the Supreme Court supported the Federal Rules of Evidence and did not dispose of the general acceptance rule, but rather suggested that general acceptance be considered when assessing whether something is reliable, and that general acceptance should not be a necessary component. Following the *Daubert* case, the Supreme Court evaluated the *Joiner* case, where Robert Joiner, an electrician from Georgia who smoked and had a family history of lung cancer, sued defendants General Electric and Monsanto, arguing his lung cancer was the product of exposure to electric transformers and toxic chemicals (i.e., PCB's dioxin). A judge in the lower court refused to admit experts who would testify that the chemicals were responsible for Joiner's cancer. The case was moved to a federal court and a summary judgment (disposing of a case without a trial) was issued. Yet, when Joiner appealed to a higher federal court they ruled that the judge had erred by not letting the experts testify. When the case met the Supreme Court, the court unanimously ruled that the initial judge had not erred by excluding expert testimony because two of the four original experts could not specifically say that Joiner's lung cancer was the direct result of PCB's. The judges also excluded two other experts who were willing to testify that

Joiner's cancer was the result of PCB's because the studies they were basing their results on were not directly related to the case. The Supreme Court stated in *General Electric Co. v. Joiner* (1997) that if a judge carefully analyzed the scientific evidence before it was offered as evidence, the Supreme Court would trust the judgment of judges unless it was clear that the judge abused the discretion of allowing or not allowing expert testimony. In *Kumho Tire Co. v. Carmichael* (1999), an engineer's testimony whether a faulty tire was the cause of a car accident was questioned because it was considered technical and not scientific. The Supreme Court ruled that all expert testimony (i.e., scientific, clinical, or technical knowledge) was subject to the *Daubert* standards of relevance and reliability (Bartol & Bartol, 2004).

In this trilogy, the courts explained that judges are in charge of deciding admissibility of scientific evidence by examining its "helpfulness," which is dependent on "whether the reasoning or methodology underlying the testimony is scientifically valid and ... whether the reasoning properly can be applied to facts in issue." The courts further defined validity by examining the "falsifiablity" or "testability" of the theory and methodology underlying it, the error rate associated with the theory or procedure, the extent to which it has been subject to peer review and publication, and the extent to which it has been generally accepted by the relevant field.

Most states continue to use the Federal Rules of Evidence, but by 2000, 30 states had used the *Daubert* standard or an equivalent (Parry & Drogan, 2000) when deciding to admit expert testimony, and some states continue to use the Frye standard of general acceptance (Bartol & Bartol, 2004).

Relevance and Reliability

So, what were the implications and effects of *Daubert*? The Daubert trilogy helped to define criteria for admissibility of expert testimony. Judges must evaluate relevance, the reliability (or the scientific validity), the probative value, and helpfulness of the testimony.

The admissibility of any evidence provided in the form of expert testimony must be material, and it must be relevant (McCormick, 1972, cited in Coffee, 1987). The relevant evidence must bear on the issues or facts to be decided in the case (i.e., render some issue at trial more or less probable) (Monahan & Walker, 1993; Roesch et al., 1999; Schuller & Vidmar, 1992). The component of relevance is usually referred to as "probative value" or "logical relevance" (Monahan & Walker, 1993). In other words, "more probable or less probable than it would be without evidence" suggests that even if social science evidence addresses the facts of the case, it cannot be admitted unless there is substantial data that supports the basis of the fact. Thus, the evidence must be offered to prove a proposition that is at issue and must also provide support for the existence of that proposition (Monahan & Walker, 1993).

Before addressing a discussion of reliability, distinctions in terminology need to be made. For instance, when courts speak of reliability in the context of a scientific field of interest, they are referring to what social scientists would label as "validity." The essential issue is whether or not there is a general acceptance of the theoretical basis and methodology used to support the theory (Schuller & Vidmar, 1992). Courts also use reliability in the sense that it has diagnostic ability, or the ability to accurately classify individuals as meeting specific criteria associated with mental disorders or traumatic reactions with minimal potential for error (Monahan & Walker, 1993; Schuller & Vidmar, 1992). For example, if a psychologist gave a defendant the MMPI (Minnesota Multiphasic Personality Inventory), a common personality assessment used to assess personality disorders, the judge would have to assess the instrument's reliability. This would include examining its theoretical basis, publication and peer review, when the test was made, its reliability (consistency) across time and samples, its ability to classify persons reliably (i.e., the extent to which physicians agree upon a diagnosis), the error rate of the test, and whether other specialists in the field use it.

Scholars (Bartol & Bartol, 2004; Slobogin, 1998) caution that judges are not likely to challenge issues of reliability or validity of issues that have established legal precedent. Unfortunately, most lawyers may not know if something is unreliable or whether the research methods are condoned by the discipline in question. Daubert motions cost time and money, requiring legal actors to also act as scientists. This is asking a lot of people who are already required to know and interpret the ever-evolving, highly-complex legal system.

There are major disagreements as to the extent of knowledge judges and lawyers have and their ability to be the "gatekeepers" of the validity or reliability of research methodology. Judges and attorneys don't usually have backgrounds in research methodology. Kovera, Russano and McAuliff (2002) conducted a study of judges, jurors, and attorneys and found that they were similar in their ability to identify a flawed experiment. Kovera and her colleagues (2002) found that legal actors and jurors don't understand the need for control groups or the importance of sample sizes and error rates. One study asked judges and attorneys to evaluate research studies with various methodological flaws that compromised the validity (study that measures what it intended to measure) of the study (i.e., study missing a control [comparison] group), confound in study (identifying alternative explanations for research findings), and a non-blind confederate (a research assistant that knows the hypotheses of the study, which can bias interpretation of data). Judges were asked whether they would admit the potentially flawed studies as evidence and lawyers were asked if they would file a motion to exclude the evidence. Their results found that judges admitted flawed research into evidence as much as valid research. Attorneys mostly reported they would file a motion against admitting all studies (regardless of validity), but whether or not they would file a motion did not depend on how valid the study was. Kovera et al., (2002) cautioned that her results show that "junk science" may be getting into our courtrooms.

One legal scholar believes that reliability rarely plays a role in determining admissibility of testimony (Slobogin, 1998). Even though Daubert requires analysis of scientific validity (psychologists refer to this as reliability), courts don't place much value on scientific validity, particularly when it comes to psychiatric testimony (Slobogin, 1998). According to Richardson et al. (1998, cited in Slobogin, 1998), "Courts are not generally engaging in scientific reviews of the proffered syndrome; most typically, the focus is on general acceptance and the qualifications of the expert, and even then the judicial review tends to be cursory" (p. 12).

An additional example of the lack of reliability in the courts today is the courts' handling of PTSD (Slobogin, 1998). PTSD has been used in the courts as testimony for Vietnam veterans, battered women, abused children, and rape victims. If it were assumed that PTSD is the same diagnosis at issue and reliability was the basic test for acceptance into a case, then admissibility of PTSD should be equal in each case (Slobogin, 1998). However, judges have sometimes not allowed PTSD testimony for alleged rape victims because the courts perceive this evidence only to prove a criminal act occurred or to improve a victims' credibility. Evidence of PTSD is often not admitted in cases of diminished capacity (Slobogin, 1998). Scholars argue that if PTSD is a reliable diagnosis, it ought to be admitted consistently across cases (Slobogin, 1998).

Similarly, legal scholars consider the issue of relevance and how it is inconsistently applied in courts. For instance, there is an abundance of research regarding eyewitness ability. Studies on this topic are valid and reliable across samples over time. However, testimony regarding this topic is not always allowed in court. In this case, relevance becomes an issue. If experts testify in an eyewitness case, they usually provide social framework testimony, basically addressing the research findings associated with eyewitness ability. In many cases, courts haven't allowed this testimony, claiming that it does not deal specifically with the defendant (is not relevant to the individual defendant), and the general scientific nature of the testimony might confuse jurors (Slobogin, 1998).

When issues associated with admissibility are examined, how does the battered woman fare in all of this? Overall, battered women have done very well in getting testimony about the battered woman syndrome admitted. Researchers in one study (Blowers & Bjerregaard, 1994) reviewed 72 state appellate court decisions between 1979 and 1994 and found that courts questioned the scientific methodology used in defining the battered woman syndrome or its general acceptance in the scientific community only in 15 out of 72 cases. However, the shift in allowing battered woman syndrome testimony into the courts was evident, as Blowers and Bjerregaard reported, "After 1985, only one court ruled that the state of the art was not sufficiently developed" (1994, p. 551). This suggests that once expert testimony was allowed into the courts after 1985, very few courts questioned the general acceptance of the theory within the field of psychology. While the credentials of an "expert" are rarely challenged, once relevance of testimony is established, the reasons why testimony is admitted varies (Blowers & Bjerregaard, 1994). Blowers and Bjerregaard noted that the content of expert testimony was usually used to explain characteristics of battered women, identify patterns of abuse, address misconceptions and myths associated with abuse, reinforce or clarify the diagnosis of the defendant, and aid in establishing the defendant's state of mind at the time of the crime.

Testimony regarding the battered woman syndrome has become the norm, though if legal actors were to re-examine the syndrome, they would find that, by contemporary standards, it may fall short of meeting the Daubert criteria. The syndrome is based on outdated methodology and theory that most likely would not be considered reliable or valid by contemporary standards. With this in mind, expert testimony is progressing toward offering social framework evidence associated with the effects of battering instead of using the term battered woman syndrome. However, the courts and legislation have allowed and continue to allow expert evidence of the syndrome, and many legal actors have yet to question whether the admissibility of the syndrome as evidence meets the criteria set forth by Daubert.

Questioning the Reliability of the Battered Woman Syndrome

The Case of Ibn-Tamas v. United States

In February 1976, Dr. Yusef Ibn-Tamas, a neurologist, was shot to death in his home. Beverly Ibn-Tamas, his wife of three and a half years, was charged with second-degree murder. Beverly met Yusef while she was working as a nurse and he was a resident in neurology in a hospital. When they met, Yusef was married. After divorcing his wife, Yusef and Beverly were married. They moved into a home where Yusef maintained a private practice in neurology. The marriage was tumultuous, vacillating between violent episodes and harmonious love. Beverly became pregnant and had a daughter. During and after her pregnancy, Beverly continued to experience abuse including bruises, broken bones, verbal abuse, and threats that Yusef would kill her if she left him. According to the defendant, on the morning of the murder, a fight broke out during breakfast. Beverly was pregnant with their second child at the time, and Yusef had promised he would not hurt her. As the fight progressed, Yusef began hitting her in the head with a magazine, and then used his fists. He then dragged her up a flight of stairs into their bedroom and pulled out a suitcase and instructed her to pack her bags and get out. Beverly resisted and Yusef began to hit her again. The doctor then grabbed a .38 caliber revolver, held it to her face and told her she'd be "out of here one way or another." The doctor then left the room and returned to his office downstairs. Beverly's young daughter came into the bedroom and stayed with her. Beverly tried to reason with Yusef again, yelling down to him from the top of the stairs to no avail. The doctor then came back to the main part of the house. There are conflicting stories between the doctor's secretary, who came in during the fight, and Beverly's account of the event at this point. According to Beverly, the doctor returned to the bedroom and continued the attack, at which point Beverly was pushed into a bureau. Beverly knew the top drawer of the bureau held a gun and feared Yusef would attempt to grab the gun, so she picked it up. At that point, Beverly begged him to leave her alone and aimed the gun toward the bottom of the door, firing it with the intention of scaring him away. Yusef left the room, and Beverly grabbed her daughter and headed down the stairs to leave the house. As Beverly stood at the landing of the stairs, the doctor grabbed her from behind, and Beverly shot two more times. Unbeknownst to Beverly, one of the shots hit Yusef, yet he did not show signs of bleeding and continued to stand. As the doctor headed toward his office, she began to exit the premises with her daughter. "Daddy!" their daughter screamed, chasing after her wounded father. Beverly followed her daughter into the exam room, where she saw her husband crouched down with what looked like a gun in his hand. She then shot her husband in the head, killing him.

The battered woman syndrome was first addressed by the courts in this case, *Ibn-Tamas v. U.S.*, in 1979. In 1977, Ibn-Tamas was charged with second-degree murder and convicted for killing her husband. In the first appeal (*Ibn-Tamas v. U.S.*, 1979), the defense attempted to overturn the judge's ruling that expert testimony pertaining to battering was not allowed because the expert would not be expressing her opinion on the question of whether the defendant actually believed she was in imminent danger when she shot her husband. The court was also unable to determine whether the expert (Lenore Walker) was qualified and whether the state of scientific knowledge on the topic of battering was sufficient to allow expert testimony. The court ruled that the testimony was not admissible. The second appeal also attempted to overturn the ruling, which had been based on the fact that the methodology Walker used was too novel and underdeveloped and was not generally accepted in the psychological community (that the testimony did not meet the Frye standard).

Four years later (*Ibn-Tamas v. U.S.*, 1983), with the help of the submission of a brief condoning the methods used by Walker written by the American Psychological Association, an appeals court made a ruling to admit testimony of the syndrome. This inspired other courts to recognize battered woman syndrome as an aid for criminal defense and for establishing claims of self-defense. The courts then struggled to define what constitutes admissibility relating to the syndrome. In time, instead of pondering what constituted admissibility, they looked only to legal precedent to guide their decisions and conclusions. Once legal precedent was set, it provided a safe haven for judges and legal actors. A blanket approach was easier than the formidable task of assessing each case on its own merit and risking being overturned on appeal. In addition, re-assessing the admissibility of testimony on the battered woman syndrome would be a task that could have major repercussions. If the testimony was re-assessed and found not to meet the standards put forth by Daubert, this would have unfathomable consequences for all legal actors, victims, and perpetrators of domestic violence. Instead of erring on the side of not admitting expert testimony, courts have erred on the side of admitting testimony and expanding its use to include other defenses.

The decision to admit or prohibit expert testimony regarding the syndrome remains within the discretion of the trial judge. To prove self-defense, the woman must first prove that she reasonably believed she was in imminent danger of injury, harm or death before she can present expert testimony regarding the syndrome (Buzawa & Buzawa, 2003; Brewer, 1988; Schuller & Vidmar, 1992). In addition, she must use the expert testimony of the syndrome to show the reasonableness of her beliefs. More recently, due to political pressures, many jurisdictions not only allow the testimony, but guarantee the testimony through legislation. For example, to ensure a more consistent application of judicial treatment of battered woman syndrome testimony, the State of Missouri was the first to embrace a more consistent application to the judicial treatment of the battered woman syndrome testimony. Missouri legislature passed a bill that stated, "Evidence the actor was suffering from the battered spouse syndrome shall be admissible upon the issue of whether the actor lawfully acted in self-defense or defense of another" (Mo Rev Stat 563.033, 1988). Other states have since guaranteed the use of the battered syndrome in their legislation not just for self-defense, but also for cases of duress and/or coercion of the battered syndrome defense through their legislation.

The purpose of the law was to embrace a more consistent application to the judicial treatment of the battered woman syndrome testimony by taking the decision of whether to admit expert testimony on the syndrome out of the trial judge's discretion (Brewer, 1988). While most states require the admission of expert testimony regarding the syndrome to be determined by the trial judge, the Missouri statute eliminates this dilemma. The Missouri law allows a battered woman to demonstrate the reasonableness of her actions in the situation and to perhaps "fit" her case into the self-defense model. Theoretically, a statute such as this helps the defendant to sustain her self-defense claim and warrant jury instruction regarding self-defense (*State v. Fincher,* 1983, cited in Brewer, 1988). Furthermore, the evidence aids the jury in its determination of the reasonableness of the defendant's conduct and the determination of her honest belief in the necessity of her actions (*State v. Kelly,* 1984). According to such statutes, evidence for the battered spouse syndrome should be admissible when a defendant "injects the issue" of self-defense into a homicide case (*State v. Goforth,* 1986, cited in Brewer, 1988). To inject the issue, the defendant must make a prima facie (a sufficiently strong case to establish a favorable finding for one side unless contradicted by other evidence) showing the elements of self-defense (*State v. Goforth,* 1986). Once the issue is properly injected by the defendant, the state has the burden of proof to demonstrate beyond a reasonable doubt that the defendant did not act in self-defense. Of course, the matter of injecting the issue of self-defense becomes more problematic when the homicide that has occurred has been non-confrontational (Brewer, 1988; Mo Rev Stat 563.033, 1996).

While some states have guaranteed that evidence of the syndrome can be admitted into a trial, in the majority of states it is still up to the trial judge to determine whether battered syndrome evidence will be admitted.

The Issue of Probative Value and Helpfulness

The issue of probative value and relevancy of the battered woman syndrome in the court systems has a relatively short history, yet, despite the syndrome's short history in the legal system, its validity seems to have fared well. There has been implicit support found in the work of many researchers and legal commentators working in the area of domestic violence law (Kinports, 1988). In addition, the American Psychological Association (APA) became involved by writing Amicus Briefs regarding its endorsement of the validity of the syndrome within the scientific community (*State v. Kelly,* Amicus Briefs, 1986, cited in Schuller & Vidmar, 1992). In *State v. Kelly*

(1984), it was argued that judicial opinion and legal commentary supported the admission of expert testimony on the battered woman syndrome. By 1983, a substantial number of courts had accepted the testimony, and much of the legal commentary applauded its methodology and use in the courtroom (Kinports, 1988; Schuller, 1994).

However, based on the many problems inherent in the syndrome theory, Faigman (1986) recognized the limitations associated with the syndrome and claimed that it had "little evidentiary value in self-defense cases" (p. 647) for battered women on trial for killing their abusers and strongly believed the syndrome should not be admitted as expert testimony.

Further criticism came in a report conducted by the Federal Government in 1994 to investigate and describe the content of expert testimony and its effects of criminal trials where women kill their abusers. It demanded an examination of "medical and psychological testimony on the validity of battered woman's syndrome as a psychological condition" (VAWA, 1994, as cited in Rothenberg, 2003). The results of the study (Dutton, 1996) revealed that "Among the most notable findings was the strong consensus among researchers, and also among judges, prosecutors, and defense attorneys interviewed for the assessment, that the term 'battered woman syndrome' does not adequately reflect the breadth and nature of the scientific knowledge now available concerning battering and its effects. There were also concerns that the word 'syndrome' carried implications of a malady or psychological impairment and, moreover, suggested that there was a single pattern of response to battering." Further, the authors believed the terminology associated with the syndrome (learned helplessness, cyclical theory of violence) was "no longer useful or appropriate" (p. vii). Most importantly, the report stated what most critics of the theory had previously believed: that "the phrase 'battered woman's syndrome' implies that a single effect or set of effects characterize the responses of all battered women, a position unsupported by the research findings or clinical experience" (p. vii). This led to the most critical analysis in the report, one which suggested that the term "battered woman syndrome" promoted a stereotype of battered women as helpless, passive, or psychologically impaired (p. viii). These findings led VAWA to recommend that "battering and its effects" be admissible as expert testimony, but not "the syndrome" or its associated terminology. Rothenberg (2003) believes this report negatively impacted the success of the battered woman syndrome in subsequent criminal trials.

Despite the general shift to testimony of battering and its effects, what remains problematic is that the content of such testimony depends on the expert who is testifying. Some experts have altered the content of their testimony to reflect the social framework aspect, but others may continue using syndrome terminology. The courts also tend to believe that the probative value of the testimony helps jurors evaluate to the context of the event. Even if information is probative, evidence should not be admissible unless it assists the jury. Information should be probative (helpful), but it is a difficult task for judges to determine whether or not testimony might actually bias jurors.

Beyond the Ken of the Average Juror: The Helpfulness of the Testimony

As a requirement of the Dyas test, the subject matter of expert testimony must be beyond the understanding of the average layperson (McCormick, 1984). The first case to address this "beyond the ken" requirement in detail was *Ibn-Tamas v. U.S.* (1979). In this case, the court held that the subject matter of the battered woman syndrome was beyond the ken of the average person. Since *Ibn-Tamas*, there appears to be a trend that the majority of courts have held that the battered woman phenomenon is beyond the ken of the juror (Mather, 1988; Schuller, 1994), as courts have repeatedly admitted expert testimony on the basis of finding that the battered woman syndrome is beyond the understanding of the average person (*State v. Allery*, 1984; *Smith v. State*, 1981; *State v. Ibn-Tamas*, 1979). The fact that many courts allow expert battered woman syndrome testimony for an increasing number of situations suggests that they believe that the context of battering should be explained to jurors. Specifically, these courts have admitted testimony to dispel common misconceptions that a normal or reasonable person would not remain in an abusive relationship (*Smith v. State*, 1981), for the purpose of bolstering the defendant's position and lending credibility to her version of the facts (*State v. Ibn-Tamas*, 1979), and to show the reasonableness of the defendant's fear that she was in imminent threat of death or serious bodily injury (*State v. Allery*, 1984). In the past, some courts have disallowed expert testimony regarding the syndrome based on the belief that the unique fears experienced by a battered woman were not beyond the understanding of the average juror (*State v. Thomas*, 1981), and that any evidence of battered woman syndrome admitted might prejudice or confuse the jury (Kinports, 1988).

Critics who suggest expert testimony can prejudice jurors have based their assumptions on the fact that the testimony may persuade the jury to vote to acquit the defendant simply because she was a battered woman, and that they will be prejudiced in the defendant's favor because the evidence at trial will portray the homicide victim as a mean and well-deserving victim (Kinports, 1988). While evidence of previous abuse is now entered as evidence in most states, research with regard to whether this may impact the jury has yet to be conducted, and those who make such arguments have little or no empirical evidence to support their assumptions. In fact, the number of cases in which battered women are convicted suggests that concerns about prejudice are generally overstated (Kinports, 1988). Because the woman who resorts to violence is often in conflict with the jury's concept of appropriate female behavior, they may actually use more stringent decision-making standards than they would if it were a man who committed murder. Yet, research on this topic is mixed, as some researchers have found that conviction rates and sentences for female defendants often exceed those for male defendants who committed similar crimes (Bowker, 1993; Browne, 1987), while in contrast, others (Mann, 1994) have found that women receive lighter sentences than men, particularly in violent crimes. With regard to scientific evidence, it appears that expert testimony may indeed be beyond the average ken of many laypersons. However, the question of whether or not the introduction of the battered woman syndrome testimony unduly influences jurors has yet to be definitively answered.

When testimony is introduced, does it impact jurors' decisions or interpretations of the woman's claims of her perception of fear, the reasonableness of her actions, and final verdicts? Anecdotal accounts have been documented by those who have served as expert witnesses, and some psychologists have asserted that their expert testimony has impacted trial outcomes. For example, after testifying in over 150 trials of battered women who kill, Walker (1989) found that in over 25 percent of those 150 trials in which she had testified, the women were fully acquitted. However, because of the range of variables in such trials, it is impossible to assess the exact role that such evidence plays in the trial process (Schuller, 1994). Similarly, Ewing's (1987) review of 44 trials involving battered women who attempted to introduce expert testimony found that of the 26 cases in which testimony was allowed, one-third of the women were acquitted, while all of the remaining 18 cases where testimony of the syndrome was not included were convicted.

Earlier experimental studies conducted to examine the effects of battered woman's testimony have met with mixed results. For instance, researchers (Follingstad et al., 1989; Finkel, Meister & Lightfoot, 1991; Kasian et al., 1993; Schuller & Hastings, 1996) found no difference between presence or absence of expert testimony on trial verdicts. However, while the presence of expert testimony did not alter verdicts, Finkel et al. (1991) found that the testimony *did* influence the way in which jurors perceived the case, wherein jurors tended to shift their verdicts to "diminished capacity and insanity." While more recent studies have found that the use of the battered woman syndrome evidence has led to more lenient sentences, there were also problems, such as women being perceived as psychologically damaged or unstable (Schuller & Hastings, 1996; Schuller & Rzepa, 2002; Terrance & Matheson, 2003). The discrepancy among research findings can be attributed to many factors, including the number and types of variables examined and the level of sophistication present in research techniques that allow for the examination of interactions among variables.

Researchers are also investigating alternate forms of testimony (i.e., social agency, social framework, combatant, PTSD), their possible interactions with stereotyped typicality of the defendant, and confrontational or non-confrontational situations (Russell & Melillo, 2006; Schuller & Hastings, 1996; Schuller & Rzepa, 2002; Schuller, Wells, Rzepa, & Klippenstine, 2004; Terrance, Matheson & Spanos, 2000; Terrance & Matheson, 2003). Overall, current research suggests that expert testimony (all types) leads to more lenient sentences for battered women; however, there is overwhelming evidence that such testimony also leads mock jurors to believe the defendant is psychologically unstable.

While these studies provide some insight into the impact of battered woman syndrome evidence on jurors' decisions, there are other important factors. Studies have consistently found that female mock jurors are more likely to be more lenient in their verdict decisions of battered women compared to men (Russell & Melillo, 2006; Russell, Ragatz, & Kraus, 2009; Schuller, 1992; Schuller & Hastings, 1996; Schuller, Terry & McKimmie, 2001; Schuller et al., 2004; Terrance et al., 2000; Plumm & Terrance, 2009).

One research study (Blackman, 1989) found that a defendant's social class played a significant role in the admission of expert testimony, which ultimately related to rates of acquittal. Outcome data suggested that when defendant social class was examined in isolation, it did not relate to the outcome of the case. However, expert testimony was found to be accepted more often in cases when the defendant was not considered to be in the "welfare class." Similarly, women who were not poor and who were offered expert testimony were most likely to be acquitted (or not indicted), while women who were poor and were offered expert evidence were significantly more likely to be convicted or indicted (Blackman, 1989). In addition, women who were poor and did not receive expert testimony were acquitted in 42 percent of the cases, while those who were not poor and did not have expert testimony fared the worst, with a 20 percent acquittal rate (Blackman, 1989). The results of this study bring forth the importance of understanding the many factors that interact to affect legal decisions. It also becomes apparent that the presence of expert testimony of battering increases the chances for an acquittal. Moreover, judges' decisions to admit testimony of battering were affected by social class. It is possible that poor women were perceived as less credible and were therefore less likely to have expert testimony admitted in their case. This negatively affected the outcome of their cases. In contrast, judges may have perceived women in higher social classes as more credible, increasing their chances for expert testimony and higher acquittal rates.

Reliability and Diagnostic Accuracy

The issue of admitting expert testimony on the battered woman syndrome becomes important when experts go beyond describing general characteristics of battered women and the nature of battering relationships to offer an opinion of whether or not the defendant actually suffers from the syndrome. Thus, the question for the courts is the diagnostic accuracy of the experts and their conception of the battered woman syndrome (Schuller & Vidmar, 1992). However, research regarding the diagnostic accuracy of the syndrome is lacking. Further, diagnostic accuracy has never really been an issue of importance for the courts (Dutton, 1992; Schuller & Vidmar, 1992), despite the fact that according to Daubert, diagnostic accuracy should be of great importance.

Courts tend to understand and admit testimony that is related to medical terminology. The medical model gives power to psychiatric experts, but doesn't necessarily help battered women. Scholars argue that diagnosing battered women with a psychological illness is like blaming the battered woman rather than focusing on the abuser's actions (Rothenberg, 2003), and more importantly, the bigger picture of societal inequality that leads to battering. For instance, MacKinnon (1989) believes that inequality among the sexes causes women to be the target of sexual objectivity. MacKinnon (1989) states, "If the sexes were equal, women would not be economically subjected, their desperation and marginality cultivated, their enforced dependency exploited sexually or economically. Women would have speech, privacy, authority, respect, and more resources than they have now" (p. 215).

Many social scientists believe that there are too many unanswered questions remaining concerning the internal reliability (consistency) of the symptoms and the degree to which the syndrome characteristics overlap with other mental disorders (Schuller & Vidmar, 1992). For example, some researchers have suggested that many of the symptoms presented by battered women have often been confused with schizophrenia or borderline personality disorder, ultimately leading to misdiagnosis (Rosewater, 1987, cited in Schuller & Vidmar, 1992). It is likely, however, that at least some battered women do have symptoms of schizophrenia or borderline personality disorder.

Levit (1991) showed that some of the findings on psychological testing for diagnostic accuracy should also be considered with caution. For example, while Levit identified a distinctive similarity between the manifestations of the battered woman syndrome and PTSD, there were marked differences in the manifestations of PTSD symptoms between battered women and non-battered women. This research indicated a difference between women who had committed a homicide or assault against a spouse in simple self-defense and claimed they were not battered compared to battered women who claimed self-defense. Results found that women who claimed self-defense as a reflection of the battered woman syndrome often displayed characteristics of PTSD, and that trait dependency, alcohol, and drugs frequently played a major role in their crimes. Battered women were more likely to experience acute symptoms of PTSD for several weeks to several years.

In contrast, women who committed simple self-defense without a history of battering did not show the same psychological patterns. Women without a history of battering experienced PTSD symptoms only for a short period of time after the homicide or assault occurred, and symptoms diminished quickly over time to a point where they fully disappeared. In addition, alcohol and drugs did not play a major role in the homicide when women did not have a history of battering. When simple self-defense was the primary factor, women who committed homicide typically did not experience panic or acute depression and felt less remorse for the homicide or assault (Levit, 1991).

Non-battered women who committed homicide as self-defense had higher educational and socioeconomic levels and had less dependency on their spouses compared to battered women who committed homicide. Furthermore, women who had been battered and killed in self-defense but were not representative of the "syndrome" made greater efforts toward independence, were employed, and made more attempts to leave the abuser (Levit, 1991). These results suggest that it is essential for psychologists to make clear differentiations when evaluating different defendants.

Judges evaluate expert evidence to determine its admissibility. While there are criteria set to assist judges in determining whether expert testimony should be allowed, the decision is clearly wide open to interpretation. Much of the criteria set forth in Frye, FRE, and the Daubert trilogy require judges to become amateur scientists themselves. When the battered woman syndrome was allowed into court, the syndrome theory was believed to be reliable and generally accepted by the scientific community. However, the methodological shortcomings associated with the research from which the theory stems is highly questionable. When the criteria set forth by the Daubert trilogy is considered, it is clear that reference to the syndrome should be questioned and certainly re-examined with regard to its acceptance, helpfulness, and particularly, its reliability. One key criterion is the diagnostic ability (reliability) to describe a battered woman. Empirical research suggests this ability is elusive at best. Battered women and other individuals who experience battering may react differently depending on their personality and the circumstances of the event. There is no simple and exclusive definition for battered women (Rothenberg, 2003), yet, in order to admit testimony of battering, the woman (or individual) must convince legal actors that she suffers from battered syndrome. If she is unable to fit the profile of a battered woman, then testimony of battering and its effects (or the battered syndrome) may be inadmissible. This can have significant implications for the defendant when she attempts to explain her circumstances to a court of law. If the testimony is allowed, the actions of the battered woman defendant are evaluated against the backdrop of stereotypes of battered women in general, as stereotypes and prior beliefs play a significant role in the fate of victims of battering, particularly in the courtroom.

DISCUSSION QUESTIONS

1. Who decides whether an expert will testify and the content of such testimony in a legal case?

2. Compare and contrast Frye, FRE, and Daubert standards. Which standards are used most often?

3. What are the implications and effects of Daubert and the Daubert trilogy with regard to questioning the reliability of the battered woman syndrome?

4. Explain the results of Dutton's 1996 study and VAWA's recommendations about the use of the battered woman syndrome in the courts.

5. There is a fine line between determining what is helpful (probative value) to jurors but will not bias them. Can you think of a logical way to provide evidence to jurors about battering that will not bias them? Please explain.

CHAPTER 11

Theories of Jury Decision Making: The Role of Prior Beliefs and Social Cognition

I have been verbally and psychologically abused, I've been threatened with bodily harm, I've been threatened to be shot right between the eyes, I've been kicked, I've had to watch my ex sexually molest my daughter and not dare interfere for fear of retaliation.

I was married for 13 years to someone who did everything in their power to hurt me mentally, physically, financially, and sexually. In the past few years, they changed. As I started my business, they tried to stop me, and the better I did, the more controlling they became. They started not paying bills, withholding sex, and calling me names. One night, I woke up to them yelling at me at 3 A.M., a knife clenched in their hand. On more than one occasion, I woke up because I was being hit.

These are familiar stories. If you were to conduct an Internet search for stories of domestic violence, you would find a plethora of stories such as these. As you read these stories, what did you imagine? Who did you picture as the victim in each situation? Did a woman quickly come to mind for one or both of the stories? The first story was actually found on a website designated for battered men (http://www.batteredmen.com), while the second was found on a website for female victims of domestic violence (http://www.mental-health-today.com). This chapter explains how prior beliefs, stereotypes, and cognitive processes affect legal decision making.

The Role of Prior Beliefs, Stereotypes and the Use of Categorical Information

Münsterberg (1908, cited in Dane, 1992) was the first to speculate that an individual's prior beliefs and assumptions associated with categorical information inferred from different groups of people might affect the way jurors evaluate evidence during trial. Social psychologists (Fiske & Taylor, 1991) have regarded this as a categorization process or a way to describe how individuals classify and identify individual instances as members of larger groupings. Although Münsterberg's published work, *On the Witness Stand*, brought to the forefront the issues of prior beliefs and their effect on eyewitness testimony, his ideas about the extent to which existing knowledge is used as a filter for new information served as the first attempt to understand the roles of prior beliefs in jury decision making. Recently, such incidents of previous knowledge and its effects on juror decision making have been documented extensively. For example, social psychologists have demonstrated that individuals tend to search for information that confirms their perceptions (i.e., confirmation bias). Research has shown that confirmation bias exists with respect to socioeconomic labels, race, and gender.

An individual comes to court with a picture already in his or her mind related to social and cultural stereotypes (Lippman, 1992). Some scholars (Stangor & Schaller, 1996) consider stereotypes as culturally shared beliefs about social groups. Stereotypes are often negative and obtained unconsciously at an early age, continue throughout one's lifetime, and are resistant to change (Devine, 1989). Cultural stereotypes acquired at an early age seem to come to mind easier and are more likely to be acted upon.

Research has also consistently shown that preconceived perceptions are associated with characteristics of victims and defendants, and ultimately affect juror verdicts (Blackman, 1989; Dane & Wrightsman, 1982; Smith, 1991, 1993; Willis, 1992). Many researchers have found that when jurors discover that a defendant, victim, or other legal actor is male, female, black, white, rich, or poor, this often results in jurors using stereotypes or prior beliefs to filter preliminary information about the likelihood that the crime occurred in the manner described by the prosecution or defense (Dane, 1992).

For instance, African Americans are often perceived as more likely to commit such crimes as assaults, muggings, and grand theft auto compared to Caucasians, while Caucasians are associated with such crimes as embezzlement, child molestation, fraud and rape (Sunnafrank & Fontes, 1983). Research has shown that defendant race, type of crime, and strength of evidence all play a role when evaluating defendants accused of race stereotypic crimes. Experimenters who manipulated the race of the defendant in hypothetical cases revealed that defendants accused of race stereotypic crimes (e.g., embezzlement = Caucasian stereotypic; assault = African American stereotypic crimes) were more likely to be perceived as a typical offender and found guilty than defendants accused of race non-stereotypic crimes (Gordon, 1993; Sunnafrank & Fontes, 1983). In both of these studies, more severe judgments were handed down to defendants who were perceived as having committed race-stereotypic crimes than to defendants accused of race non-stereotypic crimes. Similarly, one study on race and crime congruency manipulated a defendant's race (Caucasian or African American) and crime stereotype (auto-theft or embezzlement). Results found that Caucasians were more often judged guilty when it was a crime congruent act (charged with embezzlement), and African Americans were also more frequently found guilty when it was a crime congruent act (grand theft auto). There were also no racial differences in guilt when the crime was incongruent (African Americans committing embezzlement or Caucasians committing grand theft auto), but African Americans received harsher punishments than Caucasians for grand theft auto, while Caucasians did not receive harsher punishments than African Americans for embezzlement. These results suggest that when the crime was not congruent with race (African Americans and embezzlement) ratings of punishment actually increased for African Americans, but not for Caucasians (Jones & Kaplan, 2003).

Before setting foot in a courtroom, jurors are influenced by previous knowledge about groups of individuals, as well as the legal system. For instance, many people believe that a criminal record, a history of violence, and dishonesty are all characteristics of a guilty defendant. These characteristics are all part of a "guilty" stereotype. As Rauma (1984) stated, "good cases have good victims and bad offenders" (p. 384). Not all defendants have a previous criminal record, history of violence, or pattern of dishonesty, yet if the defendant does have any one of these "guilty" stereotypes, she or he is often perceived as guilty just the same. In fact, the more stereotypes a defendant has, the more likely jurors will vote for conviction. Dane (1992) opined, "To the extent that a defendant's characteristics match the traits contained in a given stereotype, one would expect jurors to be more likely to vote for a conviction simply because the defendant matches the prototype of a guilty defendant" (p. 34).

The concern about prior beliefs and the development of stereotyping in the legal system is justified in many ways. For example, it is often believed that the procedures of voir dire (jury selection process) and peremptory challenges (the ability of the defense or prosecution to exclude jurors during the selection process) should help to weed out those who hold prior beliefs that would be discriminatory to the defendant and legal process. However, many individuals withhold blatantly discriminatory views during jury vetting, and it is unusual for a prospective juror to volunteer information that suggests that he or she harbors racist or discriminatory views, unless they were attempting to avoid jury duty. More recently, issues of modern racism have become more subtle (Devine, 1989), and people are less apt to admit to discriminatory prejudices, or many times sincerely believe they are not discriminatory, when in fact, they embrace some discriminatory attitudes. Either way, applying what is known about prior beliefs and the juror decision making process may increase our understanding of that process beyond the obvious point that categorical information about defendants affects jurors' decisions (Dane, 1992).

Research has yet to examine whether "gender" stereotypic crimes actually exist. Based on research of race stereotypic crimes, it would appear that women would be prosecuted more leniently if they committed a non-gender stereotypic crime (perhaps domestic assault); however, this would counter feminist theory that suggests that women would be prosecuted more harshly for such crimes because they are stepping outside their prescribed gender roles. However, as a recent study suggests, female offenders of domestic violence were judged less harshly than male offenders of domestic violence (Henning & Feder, 2005). The authors believed that the more lenient treatment of female defendants in their sample probably reflected the perception that men are more likely to be the perpetrator and females are more likely to be the victims.

Gender Roles

Once a woman commits a homicide, she has crossed the traditional boundaries associated with her gender role of a "good" woman. Researchers (Jenkins & Davidson, 1990) provided college students with scenarios that depicted a battered woman as either a "good" woman, who fulfilled traditional gender roles, or a "bad" woman, who was depicted as a drug abuser who nagged her husband, watched TV, and bought items the family couldn't afford. In each scenario, the woman killed her husband in a confrontational act. They found that the "bad" wife was perceived as more culpable for her actions. This study also reported that attorneys often use traditional gender roles to depict their clients. Prosecutors will often try to demonstrate how the defendant was a "bad" wife, while the defense will show how she was a "good" wife. Overall, research shows that women who deviate from gender roles are perceived more negatively.

A meta-analysis of perceptions of gender and evaluation skills of leaders and managers found that overall there was a small favoritism toward men as having more effective leadership skills (Eagly, Makhijani, & Klonsky, 1992). However, women leaders or managers were evaluated less favorably when they acted in a more masculine manner or were in primarily male dominated positions. Others (Schuller et al., 2001) have used this research as a basis to explore whether legal decision making would vary as a function of expert gender. Researchers believed that mock jurors use heuristics (mental shortcuts used to make judgments that are "good enough") to guide their decision making, suggesting they are more receptive to information and cases that are congruent within the jurors' area of expertise. The authors proposed that experts would be more persuasive in cases that were congruent with their gender and examined this theory by manipulating a civil case where the primary issue was awarding damages for price fixing (Schuller et al., 2001). Schuller et al. examined a male-dominated industry (a construction company) and a female-dominated industry (a women's clothing company). She manipulated the gender of the expert in each case. A female expert in the woman's clothing company would be considered gender congruent and a male expert in the construction case would be considered gender congruent. Her results found that the strength of the plaintiff's case was more convincing when there was gender congruency. In other words, when the expert was a female presenting evidence for the plaintiff in the women's clothing company, she was more convincing than if the evidence was provided by a male. Similarly, there were more favorable judgments of the plaintiff in the male congruent case (construction) when the expert providing information for the plaintiff was a male. This idea can be extended to the use of expert testimony and battered women defendants.

A series of additional studies (Schuller & Cripps, 1998; Schuller et al., 2001) examined the function of gender stereotyping and heuristics in an attempt to explain some of the gender differences found in judgments of civil and criminal trials. In particular, Schuller's research found evidence that credibility of the expert differed depending on the context of their testimony and the case. For instance, Schuller and Cripps (1998) found that the gender of the expert played a significant role in verdict decisions associated with battered women. Mock jurors in this experiment were asked to assess the guilt of a woman that had committed homicide and pleaded self-defense. Schuller and Cripps varied the gender of the expert. Their results found that when expert testimony of the battered woman syndrome was provided by a female, mock jurors were more lenient in their verdicts and were more likely to believe the defendant acted in self-defense compared to when a male was the expert.

An additional important aspect associated with gender roles is the gender difference found in verdict decision making. With the exception on one recent study (i.e., Huss, Tomkins, Garbin, Schopp, & Kilian, 2006), studies have consistently found that males tend to award harsher punishments compared to women when evaluating battered women (Russell & Melillo, 2006; Russell et al., 2009; Schuller, 1992; Schuller & Hastings, 1996; Schuller & Cripps, 1998; Terrance et al., 2000; Plumm & Terrance, 2009). These gender differences were found despite using subjective (taking the perspective of a "reasonable battered woman") or objective evaluations (taking the perspective of a "reasonable person") of battered women.

Relying on Prototypes for Juror Decision Making

People rely heavily on their general knowledge of social psychological reality and law when making legal decisions (Smith, 1991, 1993; Wiener, 1991). While a juror's duty is to attend to and make sense of evidence presented at trial, to heed judges' instructions of the law, and to ultimately integrate these facts and law into an objective and legally valid verdict (Smith, 1993), research has found that jurors' decisions are the product of both the trial facts and prior knowledge of the physical and social world (Pennington & Hastie, 1986; Smith, 1993; Wiener, 1991).

As empirical research has revealed and legal scholars have argued, the impact of legal actors and jurors' extra-evidential biases can result in a less-than-impartial decision making process and legal system. The way information is interpreted is affected by constraints imposed by history, socialization, class, race, gender, or a complex interaction of these factors. Even when effects of history, socialization, and culture are not expressed explicitly, assumptions about them are operating because the significance of individual actions is often understood within the context of the group (Martinson, Mac-Crimmon, Grant, & Boyle, 1991).

Individuals tend to process and interpret individual action through generalizations about the group to which the individual belongs, asserting something is likely to be true about a given class or group. However, while this cognitive process aids in simplifying many aspects of life, it is quite often prone to error (Fiske & Taylor, 1991). Such generalizations are often framed within a schema, or a cognitive model (Fiske & Taylor, 1991). A schema is a generic knowledge structure which encodes "prototypical" (representing the most typical or average category member) properties of a concept (Fiske & Taylor, 1991). Thus, before one can apply schematic prior knowledge to any social judgment, one must first classify that person or situation as fitting into a familiar category. While social psychologists (Fiske & Taylor, 1991) have made distinctions between stereotypes, schemas, prototypes, exemplars, scripts, decision heuristics, and similar concepts, for the purpose of simplicity, this text will focus specifically on categorical knowledge and prototypes and the simulation heuristic within these cognitive structures as they apply to juror judgments of the battered woman.

Both categories and prototypes aid in decision making processes when impression formation occurs. Attributes that are identified as diagnostic of a category membership may influence attitudes and impressions heavily (Fiske & Taylor, 1991). Researchers (Lambert & Wyer, 1990; Lord, Desforges, Fein, Pugh, & Lepper, 1994) have suggested that in relation to social categorization, attitude formation follows a similar process. For example, when a person is introduced to a member of a previously categorized group about which they have strong opinions, the cognitive representation may act as a filtering system to assess the typicality of the category member. As typicality (or prototypicality) is assessed, attitudes will either be reinforced or altered according to the situation.

One study examined the effects of prototypes or schemas (referred to as typicality effects) toward social policies and found that proponents of capital punishment made more references to the type of person who would be executed, made direct and deeper associations to the type of people who would be executed, and assigned harsher sentences to murderers who fit the typical profile than did opponents of capital punishment (Lord, Desforges, Ramsey, Trezza, & Lepper, 1991). In addition, the researchers (Lord et al., 1991) found that individuals who are more experienced with a category treat all category members approximately in line with their general attitudes, whereas individuals who are inexperienced in using a particular category as an organizing concept and know comparatively little about that category treat only typical members in line with their general attitudes.

These results suggest that the effects of categorical information and the prototypes they evoke may have effects on matters such as judgments of culpability in battered women defendants, especially if jurors have formed prior attitudes or concepts of battering which contain prototypes of the "typical" battered woman. Furthermore, the results of Lord's (1991) study offer an intriguing explanation for the differential perceptions of battered women consistently found between men and women. Research has consistently found that men embrace more misconceptions about the nature of battering relationships and the victims of such relationships (Aubrey & Ewing, 1987; Dodge & Greene, 1981; Ewing & Aubrey, 1989; Greene et al., 1989; Schuller, Smith, & Olson, 1994). While it is unknown exactly how men define the "typical" battered woman, from this perspective, it is possible that because men may have less experience utilizing the category of "battered women" and know comparatively little about battered women, men may treat only typical battered women in line with their general attitudes. These effects can also be explained by research in the attitudes literature showing a biasing effect of attitudes on the interpretation of attitude-relevant information, such that ambiguous information is interpreted as being consistent with existing attitudes (Eagly & Chaiken, 1993).

The Cognitive Structure of Juror Judgments: Prototype Theory

Prototype theory describes the process by which people categorize knowledge. One accepted notion of categorization is that particular categories do not entail specific, necessary, and sufficient attributes (Fiske & Taylor, 1991). Rather, category members or social concepts often are derived from "fuzzy boundaries," from which it is not always clear which instances belong in a particular category (Fiske & Taylor, 1991). The process of categorization occurs when one perceives some instances as being more typical or atypical than others. The prototype may be represented by the more typical or best instances of the category. For example, if asked to name a bird, for most of us the prototype (i.e., best instance of that category, "typical example") might include small birds such as robins and sparrows. Less likely to come to mind (depending on one's experience with these birds) are examples of birds such as parrots and ostriches, which also fall within this category. In the same sense, a prototype of a battered woman might represent a battered woman as exemplified by a summary consisting of features abstracted from individual experiences (e.g., isolated from friends and family, passive, victim of abuse, made previous efforts to call police, etc.) (Feigenson,1995). The extent to which a defendant "fits" a crime category is dependent upon a cognitively based variable that refers to the degree of goodness of membership of an exemplar within a category (Casey, 1992). The more target features that are characteristic of the prototype, the more likely it will be perceived as a member of that category. Categories have a graded (or probabilistic) structure in that the more typical features the target possess, the more representative of the category it is perceived to be (Smith, 1991). With regard to decision making, prototype theory then proposes a judgmental heuristic, which suggests the decision maker, because of limited processing abilities, often resorts to making inferences and decisions which are "good enough," rather than reflecting on "optimal" resources which lead to the best possible inferences and decisions (Feigenson, 1995; Fiske & Taylor, 1991).

Thus, when confronted with a decision making task, the cognitive simplification process of classifying a person or event occurs. The person making the judgment compares features of the person or event to the characteristic features of the prototype and will classify the person or event as a member of the category if she appears to resemble the "typical" aspects of the prototype constructed (Feigenson, 1995; Fiske & Taylor, 1991).

Recent examinations of simulated criminal cases have demonstrated that mock jurors reason by using these types of prototypes. In other words, judgments of culpability are made on the basis of how evidence corresponds to pre-existent prototypical conceptions of the offense or offender, rather than being based on legal confines as established by elements of the law (Feigenson, 1995; Smith, 1991, 1993; Wiener, 1991). While mock jurors' prototypes are sometimes in accordance with the law, the degree to which jurors reach the same decision is relative to the manner in which prototypes are applied (Feigenson, 1995; Smith, 1991, 1993).

For example, in a series of experiments, one researcher (Smith, 1991, 1993) found that jurors have "naive representations" of legal concepts from which crime categories are formed, and this prior knowledge of crime categories often conflicts with proper legal decision making. The conflict occurs when verdict decisions are influenced by people's prototypes (or typical exemplars) of crime categories, when they should be based on a set of specific legal conditions. In addition, the features believed to be characteristic of a crime are often irrelevant under the law (Smith, 1993). For instance, in order to obtain general characteristics of crime categories, Smith (1991) first asked participants to list features they believed characterized crimes like assault, kidnapping, and robbery. Participants readily supplied attributes of the victim, perpetrator, and the actions, intentions and motives of the criminal in each crime category. For example, when describing a general category such as robbery, participants would often list features such as the taking of money or other valuables from a home or by an armed perpetrator. By contrast, the law defines robbery as the taking of property from a victim by force or threat of force (Smith, 1993). So, while the participants were correct in assuming that robbery involved the "taking" of possessions, under the law, the item taken need not be a valuable, the location doesn't necessarily imply the home, and the perpetrator need not be armed (Smith, 1993). In addition, while most participants believed robbery occurred when the owners were away, the law requires the victim to be present when the object was taken. The implications of this research suggest that, indeed, participants did construct representations of crime categories, but much of the content of those representations was legally incorrect or irrelevant, and could pose a potential problem when interpreting judges' instructions.

In another study, Smith (1991) measured readily assessable cognitive prototypes about crimes and found that people use these prototypes to decide whether they fit the crime category membership. Most importantly, Smith (1991) found that jurors were most likely to convict when facts of the case closely matched their schemata of the crime category. In other words, scenarios more closely relating to the layperson's prototypical crime revealed higher conviction rates than did less prototypical scenarios. Furthermore, Smith (1993) revealed that participants who heard the judge's instructions on the actual elements of the crime before being presented with the case reached the same verdicts as those who did not. This suggests that mock jurors rely on preexisting prototypes instead of judges' instructions when determining culpability. However, Smith (1993) did find that while mock jurors rely on prototypes, judgments can be improved in "atypical" cases when jurors are instructed that certain features of the prototypes often held by the public are not legal elements of the crime (Smith, 1993). This suggests that while instructions about potential biases can assist jurors to make more informed decisions, regardless of factual circumstances, stereotypical thinking colors perceptions of, and ultimately shapes, objective reality in legal decisions.

While there is no research that demonstrates that jurors hold prototypes of self-defense, it is likely that they do hold pre-existing prototypes of the elements of self-defense in general, in the same way that they have prototypical conceptions of other crimes. When jurors think in terms of self-defense when a woman claims to have been battered, it is likely that they would think in terms of prototypical scenarios for events like the nature of abusive relationships and images of reasonable behavior under the circumstances. Prototype theory would lead us to expect that jurors will determine culpability by comparing the evidence to their prototype of a battering relationship and comparing the characteristics of the woman on trial to their prototype of a battered woman, rather than by analyzing each element of the prima facie case (i.e., the verdict categories such as second-degree, manslaughter, or self-defense) (Feigenson, 1995).

Narrative Structures as Prototypes

Jurors in a self-defense case involving battering are often asked to evaluate the incident in the context of a series of events leading up to the killing. Prototypes in the form of scenarios or stories are another way jurors might conceptualize an incident or events leading up to an incident (Pennington & Hastie, 1986). The relevant cognitive schemas for reasonableness of the defendant's actions may include narratives or stories about how such incidents might "typically occur," as well as category exemplars (e.g., characteristics of the defendant in relation to race, SES, employment, etc.).

The way in which people create and arrange story elements (the development of a narrative structure) depends on their knowledge obtained by experience or through other sources (e.g., media, others' opinions, etc.) (Lurigio, Carroll & Stalans, 1994). Individuals construct many unique stories that can adequately fit the same facts (Pennington & Hastie, 1986). Differences in stories come to arise due to ambiguity within the case, or case actors' motives or intentions. Furthermore, differences result from variations in the kinds of stories people prefer.

Indeed, there exists a considerable amount of research that indicates that jurors typically organize complex evidence into a narrative or story form. Jurors recreate the series of events in a way that best tells a story about what occurred based on evidence provided in the courtroom. In addition, jurors' judgments and their confidence in their own judgments depend on the ease with which they can generate acceptable stories from the data they are given (Pennington & Hastie, 1986). This may be attributed to our general tendency to organize experiences in terms of stories (Feigenson, 1995).

According to Pennington and Hastie's (1986) story model, jurors examine the pertinence of evidence by constructing stories during the trial. Once the potential verdict categories (i.e., guilty of second-degree murder, manslaughter, not guilty by self-defense) are announced, jurors reach their decision by matching the accepted story to the verdict category and deciding if the story "fits" the potential verdict. The story model involves prototypical reasoning at the story development stage, wherein the best story is chosen after a conceptual comparison has been made between prior knowledge of how such stories should play out and the actual evidence provided (Pennington & Hastie, 1992). The final stage also includes prototypical reasoning in which there is a conceptual "goodness of fit" between the accepted story and verdict category.

The story model proposes that when jurors are presented with evidence, they create stories in their minds to make sense of the information that is provided. In the example used in their research, Pennington and Hastie (1993) provided mock jurors with a case scenario of a man named Johnson who stabbed and killed a man named Caldwell during a bar fight. Johnson was charged with first-degree murder, but claimed the incident was self-defense. The key to deciding first-degree murder was whether Johnson had intended to kill Caldwell. Johnson did not dispute that the event occurred or that earlier in the evening the two men had exchanged words that led to an argument in a bar. During the argument, Caldwell threatened Johnson with a razor blade. Johnson left the bar and came back later in that evening. When Johnson returned, he and Caldwell had a fist fight outside the bar. During the fistfight, Johnson pulled a knife and stabbed Caldwell once, causing Caldwell's fatal injury. Pennington and Hastie (1993) examined the thought processes associated with those who found the killing was in self-defense compared to those who viewed it as first-degree murder. Mock jurors who believed the incident was self-defense believed Johnson feared for his life and pulled the knife to prevent Caldwell from killing him. In contrast, those who gave a verdict of first-degree murder inferred that Johnson had been angry and humiliated by the earlier argument, went home to get his knife, and came back to the bar with the intention of killing Caldwell.

Jurors listen to the evidence and construct stories as they obtain information (Pennington & Hastie, 1993). If information is missing or contrary to the story that they have created, then they fill in the missing pieces by constructing what they believe would be the most convincing story. At the end, when jury instructions are provided, jurors will choose a verdict that best fits the story that they have created in their own minds. This model has been used to understand various types of trials, such as murder, rape and harassment (Pennington & Hastie, 1993; Huntley & Costanzo, 2003).

The way a juror evaluates the case at hand is dependent upon the degree to which jurors' stories differ from their expectations, leave gaps or contradict their scripts or prototypes. The extent to which a person's story model differs from the elements instructed by the law is an important issue (Feigenson, 1995). The more a story differs from expected scripts, the less credible the story, as described by the prosecution or defense, may appear (Bennett & Feldman, 1981, cited in Feigenson, 1995).

The role of creating stories in self-defense cases is not limited to matching events to prototypes; it also includes distinguishing the differences between the jurors' prototype and evidence. Some jurors' scripts correspond to stock scripts of battering that occurs in "some families." When elements of a stereotype are missing or require reinterpretation in light of case information, deviations from routine decision making are likely to occur. One big deviation would be the killing of the accused batterer. When thinking about a case, individuals are more likely to try to find information that supports their point of view (confirmation bias), rather than objectively assessing the case. Therefore, people are less likely to pay attention to information that conflicts with their prototypes or scripts in order to maintain their existing schemata (Farrell & Holmes, 1991). These information-processing strategies may diminish or amplify the significance of the defendant's actions, and thus we label the individual as generally legitimate and deserving of a more favorable decision, or truly deviant and deserving of a less favorable decision (Anderson, Lepper & Ross, 1980).

Research in story comprehension has found that people will attempt to explain a deviation from a prototypical story (or script) by searching for another deviation and then trying to find a causal connection (Feigenson, 1995). Feigenson (1995) has stated that when such deviations are apparent, attorneys must then try to construct a plausible or "normal" background scenario. Each attorney attempts to emphasize that his or her client behaved normally and that the other party was the one who deviated from the script in some way (Feigenson, 1995).

Lastly, stories are an ideal way of justifying deviant behavior within cultural norms. Stories allow us to understand motives and intentions within contexts and enable us to understand the defendant's justifications for their deviant behavior (Feigenson, 1995). Therefore, defense attorneys would be expected to try to persuade jurors that their client's seemingly deviant behavior was actually a reasonable response within social norms, thereby rendering the defendant blameless. In self-defense cases where battering is a primary issue, both sides of counsel attempt to evoke prototypes of a reasonable person, and attempt to characterize the evidence in ways that enhance the fit for their client. This is a formidable task for attorneys defending a battered woman, because most people believe the battered woman's actions are unreasonable because she remained in a relationship that "reasonable" people would have rejected (Schaffer, 1990). Therefore, the crux of the defense becomes one of intuitively detecting what is considered "normal or exceptional" in jurors' perceptions, then "normalizing" the defendant's behavior and evoking prototypes (or stories) consistent with a reasonable person's response to the circumstances at issue.

Categorization, stories, and prototypes allow court actors to readily differentiate exceptional (or deviant) from routine cases (Farrell & Holmes, 1991). Exceptionality depends upon the degree to which a case is different and cannot be readily interpreted using the category. Cases that deviate only slightly from the stereotyped category are readily supplemented with stereotypical imagery and often pose little problem for decision makers (Farrell & Holmes, 1991).

Atypical cases can be evaluated in two ways (Farrell & Holmes, 1991). First, unusual cases can be seen as more serious when the defendant's social attributes violate what would normally be expected. Second, atypical cases can be found to be less serious when alternatives to the offender's actual behavior can be imagined (i.e., if the battered woman left the situation before the violence escalated or if the offender and victim did not have a gun on the premises), but the imagined alternative resists stereotype application or the victim's status attributes are directly associated with the category or prototype. Because exceptional cases require a more extensive search for explanations, surface information that legitimizes the alternative imagined heightens doubt regarding culpability.

When jurors are subjected to atypical or exceptional cases, they often look to the imagined alternatives of the actual behavior of the defendant as a basis from which to compare their conceptual representation of the defendant. Because the typical case represents a juror's conceptualization of the crime or defendant, this representation becomes the "normal" standard to which defendants are compared. In other words, if jurors have an unusual case, they would first need to ask themselves: "What would the normal (or typical) battered woman do in this situation?" They would then need to compare the battered woman defendant with the normal standard they have created. Jurors then compare the normality of the event or outcome with prior knowledge or expectations, as well as the available imagined alternatives to the actual events, and subsequently decide defendant culpability. The process by which people imagine alternative events or outcomes is a form of heuristic processing called the "simulation heuristic," which is embraced within the theoretical framework of Norm theory (how people decide what is normal and, by exclusion, what is surprising and, therefore, emotion-producing) (Kahneman & Miller, 1986).

Stereotypes are rampant in the legal system and serve an important purpose; cases that are stereotypical routinely come through the legal system and are quickly resolved. Despite the popular saying "innocent until proven guilty," court actors often assume guilt and efficiently determine a verdict (Farrell & Holmes, 1991). It is the exceptional cases that pose a problem for the legal system. For example, when the defendant's or victim's social status is inconsistent with the stereotype, cognitive dilemmas occur. When faced with exceptional cases, information-processing strategies are used to redefine the case so that it fits within existing schemata. Legal actors may diminish the significance of the defendant's actions, thereby allowing for a more favorable decision, or they may amplify the significance, allowing for a less favorable decision. If the exceptional case is unable to be redefined in the above manner, other alternatives statuses (such as ethnicity or class) may be examined and used in the determination of guilt or innocence. If an offense is atypical, questions about whether the crime actually occurred may arise. For instance, in cases where a man claims he committed murder of his abusive female partner and uses the battered partner syndrome, jurors may question whether this is truly possible. The nature and motives of the offender will also be more closely examined when a case is atypical.

Heuristics: The Formation of Norm Theory and Counterfactual Alternatives

It is clear that heuristics play a key role in the juror decision making process. Tversky and Kahneman (1974) reasoned that because people are limited processors, they often rely on heuristics or "rules of thumb," which serve to simplify complex problem-solving and streamline judgmental operations. Heuristics constitute a fairly standard mental shorthand device which makes use of meaningful information and excludes less salient, but at times, equally relevant and diagnostic information (Wiener & Pritchard, 1994). While such heuristic judgments are sometimes prone to error (Kahneman & Tversky, 1982), they are also efficient in that they are often "good enough" to make adequate inferences and decisions in everyday life. Kahneman and Tversky (1982) suggest that people's standards of efficiency often rely on two classes of mental operation: the retrieval of information and previous experience, and the construction of scenarios.

The Simulation Heuristic: An Examination of Counterfactual Thinking

The construction and use of alternatives to an event are based on the cognitive heuristic of mental simulation (Kahneman & Tversky, 1982), otherwise known as counterfactual thinking. In other words, people mentally simulate alternative outcomes and alternative paths to actual outcomes. People evaluate dramatic scenario outcomes by producing mental simulations of events that are analogous to the running of a computer simulation program (Kahneman & Tversky, 1982). The simulation does not necessarily produce a single story with definite outcomes; rather, the outcome is dependent upon the ease with which the program or person can produce different outcomes, given the initial conditions and natural parameters surrounding the individual. People construct hypothetical scenarios in an attempt to predict, determine causality, and to evaluate what "might have been," particularly in situations of near-misses (i.e., had the defendant left the batterer, the action could have been avoided) (Kahneman & Tversky, 1982). The cognitive and affective reactions to this and other dramatic scenarios are dependent upon the extent to which alternative scenarios easily come to mind (Kahneman & Miller, 1986).

It has been suggested (Kahneman & Tversky, 1982) that propensity, probability, and the accompanying effects (emotional reactions) are often based on the mental simulation of events. For example, Kahneman and Tversky provided a classic example of the simulation heuristic, presenting subjects with two airplane travelers who missed their flights because their limousine was caught in traffic. Subjects predicted the traveler who just missed his plane by five minutes would be more upset than the traveler who missed his plane by thirty minutes. The authors argued that the participants found it easier to imagine how the traveler who was five minutes late had more of a chance to catch his flight than the traveler who was thirty minutes late, thus assuming the traveler who nearly missed his flight would be more upset.

The simulation heuristic and its ability to generate "if only" conditions can be used to understand the psychology of near-misses and the frustration, regret, grief, or indignation they may produce. This counterfactual construction appears to have a broad range of effects on judgment. It may be used to assess causality by trying to identify the unique or unusual specific factor that produced the dramatic outcome (Wells & Gavansky, 1989). It also influences the affective response to a particular event's outcome (Kahneman & Miller, 1986; Kahneman & Tversky, 1982) by providing visions of "what might have been." For example, abnormal or exceptional events lead people to generate alternatives that are normal, and thus dissimilar to the actual outcome (Kahneman & Miller, 1986). This contrast between the exceptional circumstances and the normal situation intensifies the emotional reaction to the unusual situation. For instance, a battered woman on trial for killing her partner had a history of being passive and never fighting back against her aggressor, yet on the day of the killing yelled and attempted to hit the abuser. Jurors might be inclined to imagine alternatives to her behavior such as "if only she didn't yell or fight back, then the incident might have been averted."

Norm theory (Kahneman & Miller, 1986) conceptually and empirically relies on the simulation heuristic. The central idea of norm theory suggests that norms are computed after the event, rather than in advance. Judgments of normality are made after consulting pre-computed expectations of "what should be" and post-computed representations of "what might have been" (Miller, Turnbull & McFarland, 1990). In other words, when something unexpected occurs, these events are easy to undo in our minds. When someone imagines what otherwise might have occurred, they tend to mentally undo things in the direction of what they perceive to be normal (Kahneman & Tversky, 1982; Miller & McFarland, 1986).

Norm theory identifies the factors that determine the ease by which alternatives to reality can be imagined or constructed. For example, researchers (Kahneman & Miller, 1986) presented subjects with a scenario of two soldiers, both of whom were killed in a plane crash. One victim was killed on the last day of the war on his way home, while the other was killed six months before the war ended. Although the outcome is obviously the same for both victims, these events produced remarkably different reactions. The authors (Kahneman & Miller, 1986) offered an explanation of this difference. They contended that the affective impact of an event is influenced by its normality, which they define as the ease with which an alternative event can be imagined. The more strongly events evoke alternative outcomes, the more abnormal the events are and the stronger the elicited emotional reaction tends to be.

Normality of an outcome differs from its probability. Judgments of probability are pre-computed expectations, whereas judgments of normality are post-computed. Therefore, judgments of normality do not reflect what was expected, but rather what the event itself evoked (Miller & McFarland, 1986). Consequently, in the previous scenario relating to the plane crash, it is not the pre-computed probability that differentiates the two versions, because the probability of being killed in the plane crash is the same. What separates the two versions is the post-computed availability of a more positive alternative (Miller & McFarland, 1986). The post-computed availability of positive alternatives represents a mental mutation, or the cognitive undoing of events. To the extent that events are more easily mutated, research has shown that these events lead to increased perceptions of abnormality as measured by judgments of affect and victim compensation (Kahneman & Miller, 1986; Macrae & Milne, 1992; Miller & McFarland, 1986), causality, (Wells & Gavansky, 1989), and the negligence of alleged defendants (Wiener et al., 1994). It is possible that more mental mutations are made when a battered woman who kills does not fit the stereotype. For instance, a battered woman who kills who has no children, is gainfully employed, or has a social network may invoke more mental mutations of her opportunity to leave her abuser without killing. Similarly, mental mutations may be more likely when battered women kill in non-confrontational situations (e.g., "Why didn't she just leave?").

According to counterfactual theorists, there are a number of factors that appear to determine the normality of events and people's ability to generate or mentally mutate counterfactual alternatives to these events. Selective events that are mentally mutated are often governed by rules of exceptionality, temporal order, commission, and constraint.

It has been established that it is easier to imagine or generate counterfactual alternatives for exceptional or unusual events (Gavanski & Wells, 1989; Kahneman & Miller, 1986). It is also generally easier to imagine alternative outcomes to acts of commission compared to acts of omission (Gleicher, Kost, Baker, Strathman, Richman & Sherman, 1990) and under situations of constraint versus unconstrained behaviors (Wells & Gavansky, 1989). While temporal order (the order of events as they occur) has also been found to influence mutability, the impact of exceptionality, commission and omission, and constrained vs. unconstrained behaviors will be explained here because of their applicability to cases of battered woman self-defense.

In demonstrating the link between exceptional events and emotional amplitude, Kahneman and Tversky (1982) presented study participants with a scenario depicting two individuals who had been killed while driving home from work. One group of participants read that the driver had been killed while taking his normal route home. A second group of participants read that he had died driving on a route he only took when he wanted a change of scenery. Despite having suffered identical fates, subjects reported the "change of scenery," or exceptional story as more upsetting than did participants who read the "normal route" scenario. The authors explained that the difference in emotional amplitude was related to the greater accessibility of the alternative fate in the second scenario (not being killed) than in the first. Thus, the discrepancy between "what might have been if only he had..." and what actually happened was responsible for eliciting predictions of greater emotional upset.

A series of additional studies (Miller & McFarland, 1986) were conducted to test the hypothesis that the abnormality or exceptionality of the victim's fate affects the sympathy that the victim receives from others. Their results further supported evidence of the exceptionality of events, as participants granted greater compensation to the victim of a robbery who was injured in a store he rarely frequented, as opposed to the store he frequented often. Therefore, events which are viewed as routine are less likely to stimulate counterfactual thinking, while exceptional and negative events increase the likelihood (Kahneman & Miller, 1986). A battered woman who never fought back against her abuser, yet who uncharacteristically retaliated the night she killed him, might bring about more mental mutations and greater sympathy for the abuser.

Kahneman and Tversky (1982) presented evidence showing that alternatives to negative outcomes are easier to imagine if they are due to the victim's action rather than inaction. In their investigation, participants were presented with two scenarios: investor A, who lost money because he had switched his stock to a company whose fortunes were later lost, and investor B, who thought about moving his stock out of the company that eventually lost value, but who ultimately decided against this action. Respondents believed that stockholder A, who had switched his investment, would feel more regret than investor B.

In addition, researchers (Gleicher et al., 1990) also presented participants with scenarios about individuals who experienced monetary gains and losses as a result of taking action and changing investments or deciding not to take action. The authors (Gleicher et al., 1990) found participants rated individuals who lost money on the basis of action were judged as feeling worse than those who lost money on the basis of inaction. Future research studies will need to examine whether remorse or sympathy for a battering victim would vary as a function of her actions or inactions. For example, if a battered woman left her abuser and was subsequently killed by her batterer, would her actions evoke different attitudes toward her killer?

There is also increased likelihood for counterfactual thinking if it is perceived that a greater, rather than lesser, number of options existed prior to the negative outcome. Wells and Gavansky (1989, study one) presented participants with two different versions of how a young woman had died from an allergic reaction to ingesting wine. The young woman's dinner partner, unaware of her wine allergy, had ordered her a meal that contained wine. In the first part of this study, the dinner partner selected the fatal dish among two dinners containing wine. In the second part of the study, the dinner partner had the option of choosing a dinner with or without wine. Despite identical outcomes (the young girl died as a result of her allergy to wine), participants reading the second version as compared to the first believed more strongly that the ordering decision caused the young woman's death. This disparity was explained by the greater availability of the alternative action, i.e., not ordering the fatal dish in the second scenario.

This can be related to the battered woman in many ways. For instance, if jurors are constrained to a scenario in which a battered woman is prevented from leaving her partner, then they will be less likely to invoke mental mutations to leaving the batterer. Furthermore, the more jurors perceive that options were available to the battered woman who kills her abuser, the more likely mental mutations will be made that mentally undo the killing and lead to greater blame. Introduction of expert testimony which educates jurors on the difficulties women face in leaving their batterers can help jurors understand how the defendant did not consider alternatives to killing. It is therefore possible that expert testimony plays a significant role in reducing mental mutations or alternatives to the event, leading to greater sympathy and ultimately more lenient verdict decisions. While it seems likely that expert testimony of battering and counterfactual thinking plays a role in evaluating culpability, this theory has yet to be empirically tested in relation to battered women.

The Role of Affect and Causality
in Counterfactual Thought

Affect is determined by the specific counterfactual elicited. A comparison is made between the counterfactual that is generated and the actual outcome of the event. Affect is amplified or attenuated depending upon the extent to which the counterfactuals and realities differ (Gleicher et al., 1990). When the counterfactual constructed is opposite to that of the actual event and the counterfactual can be easily simulated, affect will be amplified. For example, since many people believe that a battered woman can leave her abuser at any time, a juror's counterfactual thinking that the incident need not have occurred may be enhanced.

A considerable body of evidence supports the contention that counterfactual thinking amplifies people's emotional reactions to events. In particular, counterfactual thinking increases the sympathy and antipathy directed toward the event's participants. This, in turn, affects a range of subsequent incident-related judgments. Studies (Macrae & Milne, 1992) have examined the influence of empathetic focus and event exceptionality on affective and behavioral response to injury. Participants read about a woman who suffered food poisoning after dining at a restaurant she regularly frequented or one she rarely frequented. Empathetic focus was manipulated by having participants identify with either the woman diner or with the restaurant. The investigators (Macrae & Milne, 1992) found that identification with the victim magnified affective reactions, while identification with the restaurant attenuated them. Among the specific findings were that participants who read the story from the perspective of the young diner as opposed to the restaurant felt more sympathy for the victim, awarding her higher compensation and giving a stiffer fine to the restaurant. The authors (Macrae & Milne, 1992) concluded that sympathetic responses mediated the effects of counterfactual thinking on subsequent judgments. An important implication of this study is that influencing a jury to adopt the perspective of the litigant could have profound consequences on the outcome of the trial. According to research by Macrae and Milne (1992), trial lawyers defending battered women who kill would be more effective when they have jurors put themselves in the shoes of the battered woman, whereas prosecutors could be more effective by having jurors empathize with the victim.

The concept of *foreseeability* has been found to be related to counterfactual thinking and attribution of responsibility or blame. "The ascription of responsibility by virtue of foreseeability requires that the perceiver believe that Y would not have occurred if the target had not done X, and that the target should have known that X could have led to Y" (Miller et al., 1990, p.

311). Therefore, it is reasonable to assume that there is indeed a possible relationship between imagining counterfactual alternatives and assignment of blame. The easier it is for observers to imagine alternative outcomes to a tragic event, the easier it is to construe that the target could and should have done more about preventing the tragedy and the more the target will be blamed for the outcome (Williams et al., 1993).

There is an increasing body of evidence that supports the relationship between imagining counterfactual alternatives and ascription of blame. Wells and Gavansky (1989) found that participants attributed greater responsibility for a negative event to a target individual when the available counterfactual "undid" the outcome than when it did not. For example, one study found that participants were more likely to find a rape victim blameworthy after imagining how she might have avoided the rape (Branscombe & Coleman, 1991, cited in Boninger, Gleicher & Strathman, 1994). Moreover, others (Macrae, Milne, & Griffiths, 1993) have found that when counterfactual alternatives were readily available, subjects considered the incident to be more serious, felt greater sympathy toward the victim, and punished perpetrators more severely.

Once causality is ascribed to the simulated (or mutated) event, this might actually detract from the truth of what actually occurred. If the imagined alternative to a given target's actual behavior mentally averts or undoes the real outcome, then the target is regarded as the causal agent (Wells & Gavansky, 1989). In contrast, the target would be judged as less causal to the degree that imagined behavior alternatives (or mutations) fail to undo the outcome. Judgments of causation are guided by a comparison between reality and knowledge of, or belief about, what might have been (Wells & Gavansky, 1989).

In two experiments, Wells and Gavansky (1989) manipulated the salient (default) counterfactual alternatives to events resulting in negative outcomes. For example, participants read a story where a cab driver refused to transport a disabled couple, who then took their own car and were involved in a fatal accident on a bridge. Participants read that the cab driver either drove off the same bridge as the couple did, barely surviving the incident, or that he crossed the bridge without incident. In the former instance, the disabled couple's survival was difficult to imagine, even if the cab driver had transported them. However, in the latter instance, the disabled couple's survival proved easy to imagine if only the cab driver had given them a ride. Wells and Gavansky (1989) found that participants judged the driver as more causal of, and responsible for, the couple's deaths in the latter scenario than in the former.

The previous examples illuminate how exceptionality (abnormality) and availability of counterfactual alternatives influence judgments of blame and causality. We have also addressed the implications of how abnormality of a victim's fate affects the sympathy that he or she receives. Thus, judgments of guilt or innocence may follow from, as well as influence, affective reactions to the suffering of others. In fact, researchers (Wiener & Pritchard, 1994) have addressed the implications of counterfactual thought and its influence on decisions of tort law. They also found that after participants were asked to mentally mutate a civil negligence injury case, participants who created more mutations against the defendant rated the defendant's behavior as less normal and more responsible for the injury. These findings suggest mental mutations of battered women could have implications for the battered woman defendant. There is little to no research on mental mutations and battered women or battered women who kill. It is likely that in cases where battered women are "exceptional" (or atypical) to the stereotype associated with battered women, or exhibit an action (i.e., retaliation) not consistent with past behavior, such issues may lead to increased mental mutations and greater blame. Similarly, when a battered woman's actions are constrained, less mental mutations are made, possibly evoking sympathy. The following chapter will investigate whether the battered woman syndrome has been helpful in replacing misconceptions, responsible for creating a new stereotype to which all battered women are compared, or a degree of both.

DISCUSSION QUESTIONS

1. Name some of the ways in which prior knowledge plays a role in jury decision making.

2. What are some prototypes of victims of battering?

3. Using your understanding of prototype theory, what are some of the ways in which individuals evaluate typical and atypical cases?

4. Compare and contrast prototype theory with norm theory. How might attorneys use these theories to present their case to the courts?

5. Counterfactual thinking has been found to be related to blame and guilt. Explain how counterfactual alternatives can influence judgments of blame and causality in cases of self-defense.

CHAPTER 12

The Battered Woman Syndrome and Social Cognition: Creating a Stereotype or Effectively Replacing Misconceptions?

Shortly following the introduction of battered woman syndrome into courtroom testimony, scholars began to note the testimony's potential limitations (Crocker, 1985; Schneider, 1986). This issue has become the focus of a controversy regarding both the informational value and potential impact of syndrome evidence on the trial process and outcome (Blackman, 1989; Crocker, 1985; Easteal, 1992; Jenkins & Davidson, 1990; Schneider, 1986). Concerns center on the testimony's inability to address the apparent contradiction between a woman's use of force and the characteristics associated with the syndrome. The difficulties originate largely from the testimony's focus on incapacity and learned helplessness, which is often at odds with perceptions of reasonableness (Dowd, 1992; Schuller, 1994). Qualities associated with the syndrome, such as passivity and inaction, lead one to wonder why the woman would perpetrate homicide. The only rational explanation would be that her actions were the result of someone who was insane or who lost psychological control. Coupled with the aforementioned problems, others (Dutton, 1992; Jenkins & Davidson, 1990; Schneider, 1986) have argued that the clinicalization of the term "syndrome" itself connotes images of an "irrational or emotionally damaged" woman, thus making the reasonableness of her actions more questionable.

Results of jury simulation studies offer good reason to be concerned. As previously mentioned, studies have found that when expert testimony of

188

the syndrome was presented, jurors more often believed that the women had "lost control" (Schuller, 1992; Russell et al., 2009), or was functioning in a diminished capacity (Finkel et al., 1991) and generally psychologically unstable (Schuller & Hastings, 1996; Schuller & Rzepa, 2002; Terrance & Matheson, 2003). Many scholars agree that when the battered woman syndrome is used as a descriptive term to explain the experiences of *some* battered women, then problems are minimized (Dutton, 1992; Dowd, 1992; Stubbs, 1992). However, the problems occur when the syndrome is used to describe all battered women (Stubbs, 1992). Those who advocate the use of syndrome as evidence generally acknowledge that not all women conform to the symptomology of the syndrome or the pattern of abuse (Blackman, 1989; Dutton, 1992; Walker, 1984). The main concern is that the courts "treat the battered woman's syndrome as a standard to which all battered women must conform rather than as evidence that illuminates the defendant's behavior and perceptions" (Crocker, 1985, p. 144).

One theorist (Rothenberg, 2003) argues that the syndrome was effective at calling attention to battered women and creating a legal response that would demonstrate that their actions were reasonable and justified given the circumstances. The syndrome, as first introduced, attempted to explain that these were innocent women in need of assistance. Over time, the media, the courts, and society have opened their eyes and realized the need to recognize and accommodate battered women. Unfortunately, now that the syndrome is more widely recognized within the legal system and society, most of the characteristics associated with the syndrome are firmly rooted in the public consciousness and are resistant to change, despite the attitudinal reforms that have taken place.

It has been noted that individuals use social cognitive processes to categorize information and ultimately make decisions. Any woman going against this stereotype, such as by exhibiting aggression toward her abuser, was "in danger of having her sympathy revoked" (Rothenberg, 2003, p. 783). Women who did not fit into what society had coined a battered woman might lose resources generally allocated to battered women. For example, one feminist theorist (Loseke, 1992) reported that women have been denied access to shelters or temporary housing because of their characteristics, such as access to financial resources. The determination of "who counts" as a battered woman is made by shelter workers, as well as society (friends, family, media, etc.) (Loseke, 1992). In essence, while the syndrome was effective for bringing attention and sympathy to the plight of the battered woman in the beginning of the woman's movement, it fell short in representing the diversity and complexities associated with domestic violence, and the biggest consequence of this stereotype is for women (or other victims) who kill their abusers (Rothenberg, 2003).

Prior Beliefs and Legal Decision Making

The significance of psychological theories as they relate to battered women and legal decision making is apparent. With regard to battered women claiming self-defense, prevalence of stereotypes held by the general public and the legal system have been addressed at length (Aubrey & Ewing, 1987; Dodge & Greene, 1991; Ewing & Aubrey, 1989; Greene et al., 1989; Reddy et al., 1997; Worden & Carlson, 2005). Research has also revealed that prior beliefs play a major role in all aspects of the legal decision-making process. For example, one study (Schuller et al., 1994) found that individuals more informed about the dynamics of abuse were more believing of the battered woman's account of what happened. Furthermore, there seem to be negative stereotypes related to African American battered women beyond those associated with battered women in general (Allard, 2005).

Stereotypes about African American women who kill their abusers are more negative than for than women of other ethnicities (Allard, 2005; Harrison & Esqueda, 1999; West, 2002). Researchers (Harrison & Esqueda, 1999; West, 2002) have found that people tend to believe that African Americans are more violent, accustomed to violence, and aggressive than other ethnic groups. They argue that racist stereotypes of black battered women create a disadvantage when a black battered woman kills her abuser in self-defense. Some (Allard, 2005) believe that there is a larger socio-cultural force at work where racism and sexism promote stereotyping. African American women do not tend to fit the stereotype of the passive, weak, fearful, white middle-class victim of domestic violence, and as such, are often allotted harsher penalties (Allard, 2005). At the same time, there has also been contradictory research (*Melior Group, v. Kramer & Associates*, 2001) suggesting that judges were more lenient in self-defense cases for African American women than white women. It is necessary to keep in mind that geographical location, methodology, and sampling strategies can play a role in research findings. Despite the contradiction in results, it is clear that when categorical information about a defendant or victim is relied upon to determine the defendant's guilt, this process can become extremely biased, infringing on the constitutional guarantee of due process (Dane, 1992).

Stereotypes and the Typical Battered Woman

Scholars (Crocker, 1985; Schaffer, 1990) have noted that the court's previous reactions to cases in which testimony on battered woman syndrome was ruled inadmissible is evidence that people may not be as receptive to testimony in less "prototypical" cases. In *State v. Anaya* (1983), the admission of expert testimony on the battered woman syndrome was deemed inadmissible because the defendant had on a previous occasion stabbed her boyfriend, was employed, and did not manifest the characteristics that battered women most frequently exhibit, such as reacting passively and being dependent. In addition, a battered woman could be challenged for both trying and not trying to protect herself by means less drastic than homicide. While not calling the police or seeking help from family or friends could be a prerequisite for "fitting" into the battered woman stereotype, the prosecution may also use the lack of evidence of such attempts to substantiate its claim that the abuse was trivial or non-existent (Crocker, 1985; Jenkins & Davidson, 1990). Determining the existence and severity of abuse is especially crucial in such cases. For example, research has found that rates of acquittal have occurred more often in conditions of severe abuse as opposed to moderate abuse (Kasian et al., 1993).

Domestic violence knows no boundaries. It can be found in all socioeconomic levels and across all ages. However, its presence is perhaps least surprising when the couple involved is relatively young and of low socioeconomic status. One study (Greene et al., 1989) examined how jurors' opinions might change when these demographic characteristics changed. Jurors were presented with a brief scenario describing an incident of domestic battering. The socioeconomic status (high v. low) and the age (20 or 50 years) were manipulated in the scenarios. Although age of the couple had no effect, jurors' responses were more in tune with experts of abuse in the scenario depicting the low SES couple, as opposed to high SES couples. Experts were less likely than jurors to believe a battered woman could easily leave her batterer or was masochistic, and believed battering could happen to anyone (Greene et al., 1989). Given that one of the myths surrounding wife abuse is that it occurs only among low SES couples, this finding suggests that lay knowledge regarding wife abuse may be contextually bound to the degree of similarity to the "prototypical" battering relationship.

Regina Schuller is a pioneer who studied the effects of expert testimony for battered women. Her research was the first to examine the controversial nature of a defendant's passivity. When a defendant deviates from these perceived typical characteristics, her motives are intensely scrutinized. One study (Schuller & Hastings, 1996) presented scenarios to mock jurors in which the defendant's prior response history (active v. passive) was manipulated. Half of the participants in the experiment received a depiction of a defendant as having a history of fighting back against her abuser (active), while the other half received a portrayal of a defendant with a history of being passive toward her abuser (passive). In addition, the content of the expert testimony was manipulated in the following manner: (1) testimony presented about battered woman syndrome that gave reference to PTSD and learned helplessness, (2) testimony presented about social agency, which made no references of PTSD or learned helplessness, but stressed that behavior must be understood in the context of the batterer's domineering and coercive behavior, and (3) a "no expert" control group. The results found that both forms of expert testimony yielded more favorable evaluations of the defendant's claim of self-defense compared to the no expert control group. Surprisingly, the woman's prior response history (active v. passive) had little effect on the legal decision-making process, suggesting that a woman's previous history of fighting back against her abuser did not affect verdict decisions. Thus, this research suggested that defendant typicality ("typical" passive characteristics) did not play a significant role in jurors' responses. However, this finding can be attributed to the fact that there is typically more than one variable (active vs. passive) that affects legal decision making; it is more likely that defendants have multiple attributes that help to define a person's prototype of who constitutes a battered woman.

Additional research (Schuller & Rzepa, 2002) examined response history (active v. passive), expert testimony (expert testimony v. no expert testimony), and nullification instructions (nullification instructions v. no instructions). Jurors have the power to nullify the law; this means that jurors can base their verdicts on their own reasoning and morals and disregard jury instructions. The results found that mock jurors gave more lenient verdicts when nullification instructions and expert testimony were provided. The authors (Schuller & Rzepa, 2002) also found that when the defendant had an active (history of violence) history, there were fewer verdicts of self-defense compared to when the defendant was depicted as passive. Furthermore, when there were no nullification instructions and the defendant was depicted with an active history, she was more likely to receive a verdict of guilty, while respondents given nullification instructions and who assessed a depiction of the defendant as passive assigned significantly more verdicts of self-defense. In addition, when the defendant was portrayed as passive, mock jurors were more likely to believe that the defendant's belief of fear of imminent danger was more plausible and less likely to believe she had options when expert testimony was provided. Lastly, participants receiving expert testimony were more likely to find that the defendant was psychologically unstable.

Researchers (Terrance et al., 2000) also varied the threat of imminence where the defendant killed her husband while he was sleeping or during a direct confrontation, and they varied whether mock jurors received instructions to evaluate the defendant in a subjective manner (putting themselves in her shoes) or an objective manner. Their results found that when the defendant committed homicide while the victim was sleeping, there were significantly more guilty verdicts unless they were held to a subjective (as opposed to an objective) test of reasonableness of the defendant's self-defense plea.

In a series of studies (Terrance et al., 2003, Plumm & Terrance, 2009) researchers examined defendant "typicality or atypicality" and expert testimony. In the first study, mock jurors evaluated a video-taped simulation of a case of self-defense where a woman shot her husband (Terrance et al., 2003). To determine the effect of typicality, the researchers varied the stereotypical aspects of the defendant (based on her social support system: friends and family v. no family and friends) and examined alternate forms of testimony (battered woman syndrome, PTSD, or no-expert). They found that neither stereotype of support network or expert testimony affected verdict decisions, nor did they aid in viewing the defendant's actions as justifiable from the perspective of a reasonable person. However, perceptions of credibility and mental stability were affected by expert testimony and a defendant's support system. When participants were provided with expert testimony of the battered woman syndrome and the defendant had little to no social support network, the defendant's story was perceived as more credible. When battered woman syndrome and PTSD evidence were provided, overall, participants perceived the defendant as being driven insane, out of her mind at the time of the crime, mentally unstable, and less fit for child rearing. This study found that compared to a no-expert condition, PTSD evidence strengthened mock jurors' belief of the defendant's credibility as a battered woman and that she was dominated by her husband. Thus, in general, battered woman syndrome and PTSD expert testimony was better than no expert testimony; however, the negative effects suggested that with such evidence, mock jurors viewed the defendant as mentally unstable. Mock jurors receiving expert testimony on PTSD were more likely to think that the defendant was mentally unstable and should therefore be more successful pleading insanity rather than self-defense.

A more recent study examined the extent to which empathy and expert testimony could affect attitudes toward battered women who kill (Plumm & Terrance, 2009). Mock jurors examined a case in which a battered woman killed her abuser. The researchers varied the expert testimony (social agency—no reference to learned helplessness or the cycle of violence or battered woman syndrome or no expert condition) and empathy instructions (asking jurors to imagine themselves as the defendant). Their results showed that while women believed that the defendant's actions were reasonable across conditions, men were more likely to find the defendant's actions reasonable when the expert provided social agency testimony compared to the battered woman syndrome or control conditions. Similarly, men were more likely to find the defendant's actions justified in the social agency condition compared to the battered woman expert or control conditions. Female respondents were more likely to rate the defendant as mentally unstable compared to male respondents, and empathy induction played a significant role in mental instability, wherein participants who were asked to empathize with the defendant were less likely to find the defendant mentally unstable compared to no empathy conditions. Finally, results also found that participants who received the battered woman syndrome expert testimony and empathy induction were least likely to believe the defendant suffered from mental instability.

Additional studies (Russell, 1999; Russell & Melillo, 2006) examined the extent to which laypersons actually embrace stereotypes and how these stereotypes affected legal decision making. Not only did the researchers find that individuals embraced many stereotypes about battered women, but these stereotypes affected perceptions of defendant culpability. There was persuasive evidence that judgments of guilt or culpability were directly influenced by whether the defendant fit or does not fit the stereotype of a battered woman. As with any research, there were many limitations to this study, but most importantly, the earlier research did not examine the effects of expert testimony in relation to the typicality of the defendant. While earlier research had established a strong relationship between typicality and judgments of guilt (Russell, 1999; Russell & Melillo, 2006), it had not investigated the interactive effects of whether expert testimony of the syndrome could help or harm an atypical defendant. Therefore, a subsequent series of research studies were conducted to examine the effects of expert testimony of the syndrome and judgments of culpability when the defendant deviates from a battered woman. In other words, the next logical step was to investigate how mock jurors evaluated heterosexual males or same-sex couples in abusive relationships that lead to killing.

Examining Stereotypes Associated with Defendant Sexual Orientation and Gender

In this series of research studies, researchers (Russell, Ragatz, & Kraus, 2009, 2010) expected that sexual orientation and gender of the defendant would promote stereotypical images of victims of battering. For example, while it is known that battering occurs in homosexual relationships, no one has examined whether expert testimony on battering might affect (or work against) a homosexual who uses battering evidence as part of their defense in a homicide case where they kill their abuser. In addition, it is also acknowledged that male heterosexuals are victims of domestic violence, yet no research had been conducted assessing whether heterosexual men would benefit from having evidence of battering in their trials when they commit homicide against their abuser. Homosexuals might be considered atypical with regard to the syndrome, and heterosexual men perhaps would epitomize the most atypical situation. While it was clear that "atypical" defendants are more likely to receive judgments of guilt compared to "typical" defendants, it was much less clear how homosexual and heterosexual male defendants would fare. The researchers explored whether evidence of battering using the battered partner syndrome would actually backfire in atypical cases, such as homosexual cases or heterosexual male cases.

Russell et al. (2009) conducted a study to evaluate the hypothesis that female defendants in heterosexual relationships would be most likely to meet the requirements of self-defense compared to male defendants in heterosexual relationships or female and male defendants in homosexual relationships. Participants were provided with a case scenario that began by describing the violent abuse that had been ongoing and perpetrated by the defendant's partner in the relationship. Subsequently, the scenario described how the abused individual was planning on leaving the relationship. When the abused individual came home from work, they found their abusive partner coming at them with an object that looked much like a knife. The abused individual pulled a gun from their bag and shot their partner. At the close of the scenario, the deceased abusive individual is found to be holding a letter opener in one hand and a cell phone bill in the other hand.

The relationships of the defendants and victims were varied (i.e., heterosexual female who kills heterosexual male, heterosexual male who kills heterosexual female, homosexual male killing homosexual male, homosexual female killing homosexual female), as well as the use of expert testimony of the battered person syndrome (or no expert conditions).

Analyses of guilt ratings partially supported the hypotheses. Overall, heterosexual females did receive the lowest ratings of guilt compared to all other defendants. However, interaction effects between participant gender, expert testimony, and sexual orientation found that female participants were more influenced by expert testimony and variables such as defendant gender and sexual orientation than male participants were. Female respondents were more likely to give heterosexual female defendants and homosexual males lower ratings of guilt when expert testimony was provided. Interestingly, when female participants received expert testimony they rated culpability similarly high for heterosexual males and homosexual women. In fact, when expert testimony was provided, ratings of guilt actually increased for heterosexual males. These results suggest that heterosexual women (and to some extent homosexual males) are more likely to fit the stereotype of a victim of battering. It is important to note that at least with female participants, expert testimony assisted homosexual males, but not homosexual females or heterosexual males. This is perhaps due to the fact that individuals may perceive homosexual males as sharing more feminine sex role attributes and therefore more likely to be similar to a woman. In contrast, a homosexual female might be perceived as sharing more characteristics with a heterosexual male. These results are in line with the typicality argument, wherein heterosexual females are more likely to fit the general perception of a "typical" victim of battering, while homosexual couples, and particularly heterosexual males who do not necessarily fit the "typical" depiction of a battered person, may not fare as well using the syndrome. In this case, expert testimony did not assist the atypical heterosexual male, but did assist others (some more than others). These findings support research demonstrating that participants tend to have more favorable views and are more inclined to view the battered woman's acts as self-defense when expert testimony is included at the trial (Schuller & Hasting, 1996; Schuller et al., 2004; Schuller et al., 1994), though this does not appear to apply to heterosexual males.

In a similar study, researchers (Russell, Ragatz, & Kraus, 2010) investigated perceptions of various attributes normally associated with interpersonal violence victimization. It was expected that heterosexual female victims of battering who committed homicide and claimed their actions were in self-defense would be more likely to be believed that they experienced attributes more commonly associated with the battered woman syndrome. The researchers examined the extent to which mock jurors believed the defendant should have left the relationship, was a victim of severe abuse, repeated abuse, their actions not under their control, and experienced learned helplessness. They found that heterosexual female defendants were more likely to be believed they lacked control, they had no control of their actions, and experienced learned helplessness. However, there were no effects found for belief that the defendant should have left the relationship or the extent to which the defendant experienced severe or repeated abuse. While previous research has consistently found that when expert testimony of the battered woman syndrome is used in cases of self-defense, mock jurors are more likely to believe the defendant is less credible, less believable, and mentally unstable (Schuller, 1994; Terrance & Matheson, 2000), this study found no interaction effects with expert testimony that would suggest the use of the battered person syndrome could actually lead to increased perceptions of pathology. In other words, simply being a heterosexual female was enough to evoke the stereotype of a woman out of control and helpless.

A predominant theme throughout these studies shows that when a defendant is a heterosexual female, she is more likely to meet all the legal requirements of self-defense compared to heterosexual males and same-sex couples. In effect, heterosexual men are less likely to be believed that they experience abuse compared to female defendants. Furthermore, respondents are more likely to believe the actions of heterosexual men and homosexual females are under their control compared to heterosexual females and homosexual males.

With the culmination of this new research, arguments suggesting that jurors' misconceptions about battered women are merely being replaced by a stereotype of the "typical" battered woman (Crocker, 1985; Jenkins & Davidson, 1990; Schneider, 1986) may have some credence. When critics of the syndrome (Crocker, 1985; Schneider, 1986) first made this claim, they did so without empirical evidence to support their assumption. Only recently has research come to the forefront to suggest that a stereotype does exist and that this stereotype of the "typical" battered woman affects legal decision making, yet research on the topic remains in its infancy. There is still much to be learned about what constitutes an "atypical" defendant, and at what point the use of expert testimony of battering actually helps or hurts the defendant's case.

Defendants are often caught between two conflicting stereotypes that include "the judicial construct of the battered woman based on the syndrome testimony and the prosecutorial model that uses myths about battered women to prove their unreasonableness" (Crocker, 1985, p. 144). Ironically, the work of feminist social scientists who first wrote about battered women inadvertently created a standard to which battered women defendants are often held.

Conflicting images are evoked merely by the contradiction between the syndrome characteristics and the woman's actions. This problem is coupled with general beliefs about socio-sexual stereotypes. For instance, while the prosecution may attempt to discredit the defendant for not living up to the standard of a "good woman or mother," the defense often counters these issues with equally distorted portrayals of the defendant as ultra-feminine, passive, or helpless (Jenkins & Davidson, 1990). None of these stereotypes allows a battered woman to portray the reasonableness of her actions accurately to the jury (Crocker, 1985). The ability to take a life is often outside the confines of both the "good woman" and "battered woman" stereotypes. Therefore, examining the gendered appropriateness of the defendant's behavior often results in turning the focus to "who she is" or "what she did" and whether or not the defendant "fits" the stereotype of a battered woman, rather than whether or not she is guilty of a crime.

The biases and myths which are brought into the courtroom are often used as a filter through which legal decisions are made (Schuller & Vidmar,

1992). Such misconceptions have operated to prevent battered women from presenting acts of homicide or assault against batterers as reasonable self-defense (Dodge & Greene, 1991; Ewing & Aubrey, 1987; Greene et al., 1989). The culmination of these biases leaves women defendants who attempt to justify their behaviors on the basis of the battered woman syndrome at a disadvantage when their characteristics or experiences deviate from any one of these standards (Blackman, 1990). This leads to the question as to whether jurors are similarly influenced by the defendant's behavior. More importantly, what happens when a defendant on trial is "atypical or exceptional" with regard to the characteristics of the syndrome and femaleness in general?

While the legal application of battered woman syndrome evidence in trials of battered women who kill has been seen as a significant advancement for battered women in self-defense cases, the impact of such evidence is the basis of much controversy. Social psychological dynamics are included in assessing both typical and atypical cases. Both are evaluated and compared to prevailing stereotypes, often including myths and misconceptions. Typical cases may be evaluated and disposed of routinely, while exceptional cases often present cognitive dilemmas for jurors (Farrell & Holmes, 1991). Therefore, the extent to which testimony of battering may be effective in exceptional cases is unknown. In fact, some preliminary research suggests expert testimony of battering may actually work against heterosexual males who use the battering to bolster their pleas of self-defense. The question becomes one of whether individuals and society can rise above the tendency to stereotype individuals.

DISCUSSION QUESTIONS

1. Why would it be a problem if courts "treat the battered woman syndrome as a standard to which all battered women must conform"?

2. Based on the research reviewed in this chapter, does type of expert testimony play a role in how battered woman defendants are evaluated?

3. What does the research suggest regarding the use of expert testimony of the battered woman syndrome and female defendants?

4. What does the research suggest regarding the use of expert testimony of the battered person syndrome and defendant sexual orientation and gender? Based on this knowledge, what might be some of the implications for a defendant who is not a heterosexual female?

5. What are the two conflicting stereotypes of the battered woman syndrome and the myths about the syndrome that the prosecution may use to cast doubt on the reasonableness of her behavior?

CHAPTER 13

Syndrome or Excuse:
A Critical Analysis of
the Use of the Syndrome

Women have struggled for the rights they currently have. The lives of women have changed tremendously over time, and undoubtedly, the battered woman syndrome has helped bring tremendous attention to the problem of domestic violence. Are those who use the syndrome in the courts requesting special treatment from the law? Evidence of battering and its effects is used increasingly in trials involving situations such as conspiracy or accomplice to murder, child abuse and neglect, and acts of duress, which can be helpful for judges and jurors to understand the situation, but this same evidence can also be a vehicle for excusing irresponsible behaviors. Many scholars would argue that the syndrome was effective in helping women in the fight toward human liberation, yet one must ask whether the function of the syndrome has become outdated.

Questioning the Existence of the Syndrome

When Walker (1979) coined the term "battered woman syndrome," she claimed that, based on her research, battered women exhibited a group of co-occurring symptoms. Since research has found that women may or may not display the symptomology Walker had outlined, and in fact, their psychological and behavioral characteristics are so widely diverse, justification for a syndrome is lacking. In response to calls for a more precise, rigorous definition, Walker (1995) claimed, "The definition is still evolving ... so it may be too soon to codify one" (p. 33). Consequently, one can imagine the diffi-culty in obtaining reliability when studying the syndrome. If individuals, researchers, theorists, and experts define the syndrome differently, or even describe battering differently, then there is no way to establish reliability. If there is no clear set of symptoms and no clear way to identify whether an individual has the "syndrome," can it really exist? Interestingly, while researchers and clinicians are having difficulty defining exactly who is a bat-tered woman (or person) or what exactly constitutes being a victim of bat-tering, in most cases, a person simply has to introduce the issue to the courts and expert testimony is summarily admitted.

Even if the syndrome's overlap with PTSD (Dutton & Goodman, 1994) might allow it to be subsumed under the diagnostic category of PTSD, not all battered women report having PTSD symptomology attributable to abuse (Cimino & Dutton, 1991; Resnick et al., 1993). Thus, suggesting that battered women all fall under the umbrella of PTSD can also be misleading and inap-propriate. Yet, despite this lack of consensus, some courts have actually cho-sen to include legislation that defines the battered woman syndrome as "a subset under the diagnosis of PTSD" (Wyoming State Statute, 1993).

The difficulty of the syndrome's lack of a consistent set of symptoms has been a major problem for researchers and scholars, but not necessarily for the courts. This lack of consistency can lead to dangerous and biasing testimony. Some have argued that instead of a diagnostic tool, testimony on the syndrome merely describes the effects of battering on a woman (Schuller & Vidmar, 1992); but even as a descriptive tool, it lacks scientific rigor and reliability, yet it continues to be introduced as expert testimony in courtrooms across the world.

The Search for Equality
and the Need for a Syndrome

It has been suggested that the battered woman syndrome was a "cul-tural compromise" that helped to bring attention to battered women and pro-vide recognition, funding, therapy, and shelters, and changed the laws of self-defense to explain why battered women's behaviors were rational and reasonable (Rothenberg, 2003). However, many feminists believe the issue of abuse will not be rectified until there are wider structural and cultural changes made in our patriarchal society (Rothenberg, 2003; MacKinnon, 1989).

Some feminist scholars believe women are victimized multiple times: first, by a patriarchal society filled with power and inequity, then by their abusers, and finally, by the legal system (Rothenberg, 2003). A greater recognition of equality is necessary before societal change can occur and equality can begin. While this explanation is useful in theory, it may be too simplistic and circular in nature. Suggesting that the solution to the problem of domestic violence is to alleviate inequality could be viewed as narrow and simplistic. Having one specific solution may actually lead us to ignore the very diversity and complexity associated with the causes of domestic violence that most feminists deem important.

Feminists may argue that because of the patriarchal power differences inherent within society, women need to be accorded special protections or benefits based on their unique status as women. The issue of equality is supported by all feminists, yet the applications may differ. For instance, feminists who believe in equal treatment theory (e.g., MacKinnon, 1982) stress the similarities among the sexes and suggest that the law must be applied equally (Levit & Verchick, 2006). Equal treatment theorists believe that issues such as maternity leave are considered special treatment which some men may not receive. Similarly, many states are now allowing same-sex couples with live-in spouses to obtain insurance benefits for their partners, while heterosexual cohabitating couples are not able to do so. Some feminists would argue that because these populations require special attention under the law, they are considered disadvantaged, and therefore can never be equal (MacKinnon, 2001). Yet, some cultural feminists (e.g., Gilligan, 1982) suggest that the law should consider differences between the sexes (e.g., biological or cultural). In order to equalize women's status, special treatment may be necessary. Such gendered arguments, and those regarding race and affirmative action, have been debated by scholars and feminists for years, and there doesn't seem to be a solution on the horizon.

As long as women are perceived as victims needing special rights, equality will be elusive; however, our judicial system was historically geared for conflicts between men and has been slow in changing to reflect gender equality. Scholars (e.g., Downs & Fisher, 2005) assert that there is a slippery slope with the use of the battered woman syndrome that can lead to "victim ideology." Scholars (Downs & Fisher, 2005) have pointed out that many advocates of battered women refuse to believe battered women are responsible for their behavior; yet, equality is compromised when individuals fall into this victim mentality.

Some feminists might argue that in order to be equal, individuals should all be treated the same, regardless of gender. However, others (MacKinnon, 1989) would claim that being treated the same implies that everyone is then treated by a male standard. For instance, MacKinnon suggested that when genders are treated the same, men are less likely to feel the repercussions because of the gender hierarchy. However, preliminary research results have found that mock jurors who hear evidence of the battered person syndrome in a case of self-defense of a battered heterosexual male are more likely to offer harsher sentences. Scholars (MacKinnon, 1982; Rapaport, 1991) have remarked that double standards applied within the law for the sake of equaling the playing fields have often worked against women and minorities. If equality is to be obtained, then personal responsibility for actions and behaviors must be accepted. Some (Downs & Fisher, 2005) suggest that in order to achieve equal citizenship, society must learn to balance empathy for victims of abuse with personal responsibility and equal treatment under the law.

Legal feminists (MacKinnon, 1979, 2001) have been particularly effective in revealing social inequality between men and women and in facilitating changes in the legal realm to better reflect gender equality. Feminists should be applauded for their efforts to promote change toward equality; yet, the quest for equality brings with it the need for change. Postmodern feminist legal theorists tend to move beyond comparing the differences between the sexes and focus on the notion that the concept of gender is multi-dimensional and that there is no one answer that can explain differences, nor should we try. Post-feminists believe men and women are both different and have different experiences and perspectives, and therefore society should move beyond the categorization of the genders (Levit & Verchick, 2006). The recent shift from the battered woman syndrome, moving away from stereotyping what a battered woman should act or look like, into focusing on the effects of battering represents a compromise of equal treatment theory and postmodern feminism.

Society and the judicial system need to acknowledge issues of inequality in order to make necessary changes. Sometimes acknowledging the inequalities leads to identifying the issues that lead to dramatic change. For instance, the courts have evolved to acknowledge the social problem of battering, and after many years, the battered woman syndrome was adopted by the courts, though the syndrome was associated with women only. The concept of battering was considered unique to women and it is generally understood that women tend to share a unique sexual fear of men, therefore the judicial system should be provided with a context that assists them when trying to understand legal issues such as self-defense. Still, battering is recognized as a national problem in the United States, and victims often fall into a societal structure that imparts its own ideologies and stereotypes onto the victim. Therefore, raising the public consciousness of abused women inadvertently created a stereotype by which these individuals are judged. These stereotypes are now a topic of rigorous scholarly debate, as they can create additional victimization and perpetuation of the belief that only women are victims.

A reasonable battered person should respond similarly, despite gender or sexual orientation, yet the concept of battering beyond a female victim and male abuser is difficult to comprehend. Some courts (*Ellison v. Brady*, 1991) and scholars (Maguigan, 1991; Crocker, 1985) believe that a "reasonable woman" standard should be used to evaluate cases of battering in cases of self-defense because a woman's perceptions of danger and sexual assault are different from a man's. The opponents to the use of such a standard (Mather, 1988) believe its use may exclude certain women from the group who don't fit the image of a "weak" or "helpless" victim (Dowd, 1992; Mather, 1988).

As this book has discussed, anyone can become a victim of battering, despite gender or sexual orientation. Researchers have yet to learn whether victims who are not heterosexual women also fall prey to multiple forms of victimization. The battered persons syndrome has been used in hundreds of cases by battered women, yet the same syndrome has yet to be used in the United States by a heterosexual man who claims self-defense against their female partner.

Will We Ever Overcome Prejudice, Stereotypes, and the Need to Categorize?

In the search for equality, most of us would agree that society has made great strides in reducing prejudice, racism, and sexism. Reducing these stereotypes and prejudices took hundreds (if not thousands) of years, and it may be a long time before these iniquities are eliminated (if this is even humanly possible). Human cognitive functioning will continue to use prototypes, heuristics, and stereotypes as a function of survival, and the use of these cognitive tools seems to be largely unconscious (Devine, 1989). Moreover, because individuals are usually not aware that they hold these stereotypes, they often don't realize that their behavior is influenced by them. In general, most individuals do not consider themselves prejudiced or realize that many of the decisions they make in life are based on prototypes or heuristics.

As much as many people would like to believe that society has been liberated from sexism and/or prejudice, it is important to realize that blatant and subtle racism, elitism, and sexism continue to exist within society. Whether thoughts and behaviors are implicit or explicit, these traditional perspectives continue to plague our thoughts, sometimes consciously and sometimes unconsciously. Society has a long way to go to change traditional gender stereotypes, as well as stereotypes that have been created for battered women. It seems clear that stereotypes exist for victims of battering, and it is likely that stereotypes exist for homosexuals and heterosexual men, but it is unknown whether stereotypes exist for sub-categories of abused homosexuals or heterosexual men. Furthermore, researchers and legal actors are only just beginning to examine theses issues and have yet to identify what the implications of using battered partner syndrome evidence in trials of self-defense would be in these cases or whether syndrome evidence used to address issues of duress and coercion would help or hinder these atypical battered defendants.

Society's embrace of the battered woman syndrome originates from the human need to categorize information and predict behavior. Placing information into categories is necessary to allow us to make judgments about others. Being able to predict behavior allows individuals a certain sense of control over their lives. When one is unable to predict human behavior, this can lead to a sense of helplessness and the perception that we lack control. Being able to label individuals with a syndrome allows us greater perceived control over our own lives.

Syndromes help us to better predict potential behaviors of victims and perpetrators. If one assumes that victims and perpetrators of abuse demonstrate recognizable patterns of behaviors and thoughts, then it becomes easier to believe that we can identify a potential abuser and steer clear of becoming a victim of abuse ourselves. Unfortunately, this form of thinking can lead us to believe that if a victim does not display the behaviors we expect from a victim, then they cannot be a victim. Many people believe this. Victims of rape also share the same problem. But how are victims supposed to act? Everyone has preconceived ideas of how victims should react. If a victim's reaction differs from what is expected, they are less likely to be believed.

Our need for syndromes is part of our human nature to want to predict and control our own destinies, but they are often used to explain behavior in the legal system. The question becomes one of whether the use of a syndrome excuses defendants from personal responsibility or whether it simply provides a context of abuse in which behavior can be evaluated.

The Battered Woman Syndrome: Abuse or Excuse?

Of primary interest is not whether a battered woman claiming self-defense or duress is guilty, but whether her actions were justified. For an action to be justified, the defendant must prove to the court that they were responsible for their actions and mentally competent during the crime (Follingstad, 2003). Justification is different from an excuse. An excuse entails committing a crime without taking responsibility for one's actions because one was mentally incapacitated during the event (Mahoney, 1991; Morse, 1998). In this regard, the key question is whether the defendant's actions were justified (permissible) given the circumstances, or whether being a victim of abuse rendered the defendant incapable of knowing what she was doing during the crime (Morse, 1998). In other words, the gist of the argument lies in whether expert testimony of the battered woman (partner/spouse) syndrome provides evidence suggesting that the defendant was mentally incapable at the time of the crime, and therefore not responsible for her actions, or whether her reactions were a reasonable response to the abuse. Most feminists and scholars would agree that battered syndrome testimony should focus on the latter. However, critics argue that in the majority of situations in which testimony has been admitted, testimony has tended to focus on the defendant's mental state at the time of the crime. It seems reasonable that in cases where the mental state at the time of the crime is the primary issue at hand, diminished capacity would be a more appropriate defense. Even if social framework evidence is admitted and no mention of mental instability is made, jurors may continue to perceive battered women defendants as mentally unstable when syndrome evidence (or alternatives) are offered to provide a context for the case.

Critics argue that non-confrontational cases of self-defense lead to major problems, particularly when it comes to the element of imminent danger in self-defense. Because the majority of self-defense cases are direct confrontation, issues of justification are rarely disputed (Osthoff & Maguigan, 1998). Critics who believe the syndrome is used as an excuse tend to focus on the minority of cases that are non-confrontational. They have argued that the legal system rarely considers the time interval between the physical attack and the woman's fatal attack. This is an important point for the legal system to address. Roberts (2003) brings attention to the importance of defining exactly what qualifies as imminent danger. Should the element of imminence expand to consider extenuating circumstances such as frequency and severity of abuse? Recent cases that have included syndrome evidence (i.e., non-confrontational cases, contract killings, and duress) suggest that courts are considering such extenuating circumstances (i.e., frequency and severity of abuse) and admitting syndrome evidence. Critics argue that when syndrome evidence is used, particularly in cases of non-confrontational homicide, this may provide battered women with a "license to kill" (Dershowitz, 1994; Downs, 1996). Critics claim that the use of expert evidence of the syndrome for battered women who kill in non-confrontational cases is merely an excuse for their behavior.

Dershowitz (1994) clearly states his distain of the use of the battered woman syndrome. He claims that while the syndrome has been used to explain to jurors how a battered woman who killed could not perceive options other than staying with her abuser, he is more dissatisfied with the use of the syndrome in cases where battered women might have more options. In other words, he believes it should not necessarily be used in cases where women do not fit the stereotype of a battered woman. For instance, Dershowitz states, "Though we may be sympathetic with a childless, financially independent woman who is abused by her boyfriend, or husband, a history of abuse does not justify killing the abuser, regardless of how unsympathetic he may be" (p. 16).

Dershowitz's interest in the battered woman syndrome as an "abuse excuse" was piqued in 1987, when Stella Valenza used the battered woman syndrome as evidence in her case of self-defense and was acquitted for the attempted murder of her husband. Stella admitted to hiring three men to kill her husband. After three unsuccessful attempts, she and the three men were charged and tried with attempted murder. This case demonstrated the use of evidence of previous abuse as a justification for murder-for-hire. Dershowitz believes that the overuse of "syndromes" as an "excuse" in the courtroom is a product of society, one that abdicates individual responsibility and perpetuates a form of vigilantism. Defense lawyers testing the waters have since used novel syndromes such as "rape trauma syndrome" or "black rage defense" to shift the blame from the individual to someone or something else, and some of these testimonies have been quite effective as evidence for the defense.

Osthoff and Maguigan (1998) caution readers that there is no evidence that supports the critics' view. They discuss their concerns regarding the critics' perspective that the syndrome is simply an "abuse excuse" and claim that the critics' assumptions are based on flawed logic. Because critics base their assumptions on a small minority of cases (non-confrontational) and mental incapacity of the defendants, they neglect to mention that the testimony is an appropriate defense for justification in the majority of situations. Those who embrace the notion of an "abuse excuse" claim the use of the syndrome in all cases erodes the aspect of individual responsibility and generally dilutes the law of self-defense.

Even with the shift to the use of social framework as expert testimony, critics (Downs, 1996) claim simply using the word "victim" within testimony presents two problems. First, when defending their client in a self-defense case, lawyers (presenting social framework testimony) have a propensity to blame the victim (the batterer). This evokes images that suggest that the batterer deserved what he got. The word "victim" also connotes that the defendant was a victim of an abusive batterer. In fact, other scholars have noted that social framework testimony should include the notion of "multiple victimization" (Rothenberg, 2003), depicting the battered woman defendant as a victim of not only her batterer, but the judicial system, and society. This interplay with victimization has been at the heart of most self-defense trials. Using this perspective, the defense paints the picture of the battered woman as justified in her actions because she believed she was in imminent danger of bodily injury and there were no reasonable alternatives to killing her abuser (Downs, 1996; Osthoff & Maguigan, 1998).

Imminent danger suggests that the defendant perceives an attack is coming (Roberts, 2003). Advocates of the battered woman syndrome believe the defendant lives in a constant state of fear of imminent attack from her abuser. This theory would seem to justify a killing that occurs at any point before, during, or after a battering incident (Roberts, 2003). If one considers the issue of imminence in non-confrontational cases, coupled with the fact that there is no single profile of a battered woman, then where does this leave the battered woman who kills? Many would question whether her actions were justified, or simply used as an abuse excuse.

The idea of "abuse excuse" originated in 1977 when Francine Hughes, a 29-year-old housewife, was charged with first-degree murder for the killing of her husband. Hughes experienced 13 years of abuse and tried on many occasions to leave her abuser or find assistance through the legal system, only to bring about further threats of harm to her or her children. One evening, while her husband was sleeping, Francine set the bed afire. Francine claimed that if she had not done anything, she would have surely met her death that evening. At the time, there had been no cases of non-confrontational situations where self-defense was used as a legal defense. Her lawyer decided to use a defense of "not guilty by reason of temporary insanity." An expert testified and Francine was found not guilty by reason of insanity. This case was a success for Francine Hughes; however, as a result, it perpetuated the assumption that battered women suffer from mental instability, when in fact most scholars now believe battered women are not mentally ill, but rather are acting as any reasonable person would in the same circumstance.

By contemporary standards, any lawyer in the same situation would likely use a justification defense (Mahoney, 1991). Gillespie (1989) argues that the law of self-defense was not equipped to handle non-confrontational situations. As the law states, the threat must be imminent, suggesting that a battered woman had to basically wait until her abuser was beating her so badly that she believed she was in imminent threat of death or bodily injury. Other scholars (e.g., Maguigan, 1991) believe existing definitions of the law of self-defense were already equipped to accommodate non-confrontational situations if the woman's circumstances were considered. Once circumstances of the situation are addressed, the jury could decide whether the perceived threat was imminent.

Since the Francine Hughes case, the law of self-defense has been greatly expanded. Now, cases include non-confrontation, duress and coercion, and contract killing, all falling under the umbrella of self-defense. Mental capacity is the root of the conflict between those who believe a battered woman's actions were justified and those who view battered syndrome as merely an excuse. The doctrine of self-defense can accommodate women who claim abuse in most contexts, including confrontational and non-confrontational killings. Yet, scholars (Coughlin, 1994; Downs, 1996) argue that when unique defenses are allowed for women because of their inability to control their own behaviors, traditional stereotypes of women and battered women as overly emotional, unable to control their behaviors, or generally unstable are perpetuated.

Some scholars (Roberts, 2003) wonder if it is possible for anyone claiming that they suffer from the battered woman (persons/partner) syndrome to kill their abuser at any time because they fear constant attack. While this defense might be effective in situations in which women claim to be battered by a male spouse, if heterosexual males or same-sex couples use the same defense, they may have a difficult time convincing juries. Moreover, the courts have yet to address the true definition of "battered." If there is no agreed-upon definition of the term, then is it possible that testimony of the battered woman syndrome can be abused.

The argument that women need special unique defenses (in this case, expert evidence) is contrary to building equality among genders (Downs, 1996; MacKinnon, 1982; Rapaport, 1991). As long as women claim to be victims in need of paternal assistance because a man coerced them, or were unable to resist a man's influence, they will always be victims and in need of special assistance. In this regard, women can never be equal. Coughlin stated, "Criminal law has been content to excuse women for criminal misconduct on the ground that they cannot be expected to, and indeed, should not, resist the influence exerted by their husbands" (p. 5). Under the paternal instincts of traditional gender roles, women are viewed as unable to take care of themselves and in need of sympathy. Therefore, their criminal behavior can be excused. Many feminists believe that women continue to be under the control of male domination. Others (Felson, 2002) suggest that when considering control and power differences, it should be considered that men and women are interdependent. Women may often be more dependent upon men financially and men may often be more emotionally dependent upon women, and therefore each gender has their own form of coercive power.

Men are assumed to resort to physical violence when other forms of coercion fail (Felson, 2002). Women also use coercive power to control men (Ward & Muldoon, 2007). While men are more likely to use coercive control in relationships compared to women, Felson (2002) believes motives of men's violence toward women are no different from violence toward men, and therefore violence toward women is not always sexually motivated. It should also be noted that that the use of force may not necessarily be an issue of morality, but rather the odds of success. A woman may be much less likely to use force against a man in much of the same way a man will think twice before picking a fight with someone much stronger and larger than he is.

If the syndrome is used to evoke sympathy and demonstrate why the defendant was not rational at the time of the crime, then it is used as an excuse from criminal liability. If women are portrayed as victims who have become psychologically impaired and unstable, then this depicts them as less able to take care of themselves and perpetuates the idea that women need protection. It is interesting to note that some studies have found that expert testimony of the battered woman syndrome led mock jurors to believe female defendants were more mentally unstable than those who did not receive expert testimony (Schuller & Hastings, 1996; Terrance & Matheson, 2003). Yet, expert testimony led to more lenient verdicts. However, more recent research (Russell et al., 2010) found that despite the existence of expert testimony, heterosexual women were perceived as less in control of their actions compared to heterosexual men or homosexual defendants. This suggests that perhaps the syndrome is perceived as justified for heterosexual women but not necessarily justified for men and homosexual women. While expert testimony might assist in mediating judgments of culpability for victims of abuse who strike back against their abusers, it should be noted that results may be gender-dependent. The stereotype that has been perpetuated appears to promote the syndrome as a woman's defense. When women need special protection or unique defenses, traditional gender stereotypes of women will continue to be perpetuated because of their "fragile state" and mental incapacity to be in control of their actions. Perhaps, as scholars fight to abdicate reference to pathology associated with the terminology of the syndrome, this might bring about much needed change. Yet, as some research suggests (Russell et al., 2010), stereotypes might continue to be perpetuated despite the use of expert testimony and its content because they are so deeply rooted in sex roles. However, in contrast, it could also be suggested that if the syndrome were used more often by both men and women of any sexual orientation, then perhaps the stereotype of a victim of battering and an individual in need of protection can be extended to include anyone. In this case, its use might eliminate the perception that it used as a special protection.

These are issues to consider when examining the use of the battered woman syndrome in cases of self-defense, as well as other cases explored in this book. There is no clear path that differentiates whether the use of the syndrome is a justification or an excuse, yet the interaction between the use of cognitive processing strategies and society's need for syndromes will continue to perpetuate the use of the syndromes in our courts. So what should the future of the syndrome be?

DISCUSSION QUESTIONS

1. Describe what is meant by the battered woman syndrome as a cultural compromise?
2. Can you recommend some ways we can move away from stereotyping victims of battering?
3. Do you think the shift toward effects of battering represent a compromise of equal treatment theory and post feminism?
4. Is it human nature for individuals to want to categorize others into groups? Why do we do this? Use some of the social psychological concepts learned in this book to explain.
5. Do you believe the syndrome should be used in the courtroom? Do you believe the syndrome is an excuse? If you were a defendant, would you use it? Explain why or why not.

CHAPTER 14

Redefining the Future of the Syndrome

It is clear that much more research on the topic of how prototypes associated with the syndrome—or battering and its effects—affect society and the legal decision-making process. Recent research has begun to examine some of the cognitive factors that individuals believe are important when evaluating battered women who kill their partners (Huss et al., 2006). In particular, such work focuses on determining which characteristics of defendants or cases drive legal decisions. One study investigated the most important factors used by mock jurors that lead to judgments of culpability of battered women who kill (Huss et al., 2006). The participants in this study read 16 summaries of real cases of battered women who killed their abusers. The findings revealed that the foremost considerations of participants were whether premeditation was involved, defendant blame and culpability, whether the force used was necessary, and the severity of abuse. Participants also made their judgments based on how well the defendant's story fit the evidence presented in the case. In essence, the researchers found that participants judged cases primarily on the law as it is presented, rather than their own moral judgments of what is right or wrong. From a legal standpoint, the results of this study suggest that jurors are doing their jobs by following legal instruction. Unfortunately, the study falls short of explaining possible interaction effects between moral judgments and inherent biases associated with defendant characteristics, and it fails to explain how expert testimony of battering might affect the cognitive processing of such cases. While this is promising new research investigating the cognitive structures of how legal decision making is used in cases in which battered women kill their abusers, researchers have much further to go to investigate how these additional factors affect legal decision making.

Why Courts Are Resistant to Change and What We Can Do About It

It is clear that that once expert testimony regarding the syndrome was allowed into the courts (*Ibn-Tamas v. U.S.*, 1983), it stayed, despite heated debate over the syndrome's reliability, validity, and unintended effects in the courtroom. Syndrome evidence has been expanded in the courtroom to include a wide range of situations (i.e., child custody, theft, drug running, child homicide, parole and clemency decisions, etc.). For the most part, when syndrome evidence is admitted, it is for four basic reasons. The first is to provide support for the battered woman's argument that she acted under duress or coercion; the second is to provide mitigating circumstances when the defendant pleads guilty; the third is to support a claim of diminished capacity during sentencing (Follingstad, 2003); and the fourth is to assist in demonstrating the defendant's actions were reasonable given the circumstances. Syndrome evidence is admitted in these cases despite a lack of general acceptance by scholars (Follingstad, 2003). Even though issues such as reliability, relevance, and probative value have been offered as a series of rules with which to evaluate admissibility of expert evidence, there is little scientific reliability that the battered woman syndrome even exists. Courts seem uninterested in acknowledging or revisiting issues of reliability and general acceptance. Once legal precedent is set, it is very difficult to undo. One reason why courts are reluctant to re-review whether expert testimony of the syndrome (or battering and its effects) should be admissible is because this would open the door to additional appeals in an already overburdened legal system, and it is difficult, costly, and time-consuming for courts to re-review previously accepted research methodologies. With that said, I should note that many courts have more recently embraced the use of "battering and its effects" in lieu of the battered woman syndrome. This might reflect the courts awareness of research and their sensitivity to the potential adverse effects of the use of the syndrome. While this seems to suggest a step in the right direction, the content of such testimony can vary dramatically and jurors will continue to compare their own stereotype of a victim of abuse to the defendant on trial.

Many courts within the United States and across the world continue to refer to the battered woman syndrome or battered spouse syndrome within their statutes. It is up to courts and legislators to re-evaluate the use of the syndrome; yet, this is asking for a great deal. Judges and lawyers have little training in evaluating what distinguishes good research from bad research. Research methods and design have increased in scientific rigor tremendously since the initial admission of the syndrome over 25 years ago. Consistent lack of reliability regarding syndrome theory and symptomology make it difficult to verify the existence of the syndrome. Furthermore, the research methodology used to substantiate the syndrome, which was condoned by the American Psychological Association in an amicus brief back in 1979 and 1981 (*Ibn v. Tamas*), would most likely not be considered reliable, valid, or generally accepted today. The field of science is constantly changing; it is a dynamic process that accommodates new research and technology. However, just as novel research is scrutinized for reliability, relevance, and general acceptance, perhaps more recent research regarding the battered woman syndrome and its use in the courts should be re-evaluated.

Despite no clear, testable, or reliable definition of a "syndrome," expert testimony continues to be admitted as the norm in the U.S. Experts who testify in cases where battered women kill their abusers can come from any domain that is associated with working with battered women. This most often includes psychiatric doctors and clinical psychologists. However, social workers, psychiatric nurses, and advocates may also testify. Experts can come from various disciplines and have a wide range of experience, degrees and expertise. Those working with battered women (i.e., advocates, shelter workers, etc.) may also be called to testify because of their experience with the defendant.

Now that many courts are moving toward the inclusion of testimony of battering and its effects, will this alleviate some of these problems? The use of social framework as expert evidence may be more helpful than a medical model of a "syndrome" or addressing whether or not a person exhibits characteristics of the syndrome, but social framework only speaks to the facts that research has confirmed. If experts provide social framework evidence pertinent to a particular case, the content of each expert's testimony can differ, making it impossible to measure the effectiveness of the testimony. When researchers conduct experiments to determine the effectiveness of testimony, they often use experimental control techniques to account for differences in the presentation of testimony. When examining the effect of testimony in real life, researchers lack the experimental control that would allow them to determine the actual effectiveness of the testimony. When the content of each expert's testimony differs, they cannot be compared.

With this in mind, the diversity of expert testimony on the battered woman syndrome should be considered. Each expert's approach may be different. Some may continue to use the medical model, while some may continue to adhere to identifying the characteristics of the battered woman syndrome by focusing on pathology or passivity, and others might provide social framework testimony. It is difficult to obtain a reasonable measure of the effects of testimony, as each takes a different approach. The call to shift from using the battered woman syndrome to providing social framework testimony is a step in the right direction, and avoids the issue of pathologizing the defendant, but research has demonstrated that testimony with or without reference to terminology associated with learned helplessness helps the defendant, yet adds pathological components (Schuller & Rzepa, 2002; Terrance & Matheson, 2003). Further research is needed to investigate whether the use of social framework is beneficial for all battered defendants accused of homicide, as well as child custody, tort cases, clemency, parole, or other situations where credibility and rationality create similar issues.

Additional research is also necessary to assist us in understanding which type of expert testimony is most successful in helping jurors evaluate the context of the situation. For instance, testimony referring to PTSD might be more successful in some situations than others, and it should be determined whether PTSD would be more effective for men who kill their abusive wives than for women. Scholars must also establish whether the content of some types of expert testimony reduces the potential for jurors to pathologize the defendant. Similarly, it is unclear whether trial outcomes might differ as a function of expert testimony using the battered woman syndrome versus social agency (explaining the effects of battering with no reference to learned helplessness or battered woman syndrome). Results of alternative forms of expert testimony have been mixed, and research needs to continue to investigate various avenues which decrease a focus on pathology of the defendant.

This book focused primarily on the use of the syndrome as it applies in situations of self-defense. However, there are many other situations in which the syndrome or battering and its effects are used. For instance, research has yet to examine the role of typicality and the syndrome (or battering and its effects) as it applies to civil cases, such as child custody or felony crimes like purchasing illegal firearms or assault. In this same regard, this book did not address issues associated with protection from abuse (PFA) orders. For instance, there is little to no research that examines whether victims of abuse are perceived differently when an order of protection is issued or if a victim of abuse chooses to withdraw an order of protection. Similarly, it is possible that cases will be evaluated differently when a PFA is in effect and the victim of abuse kills and claims self-defense. Research has also addressed how socio-economic status plays a role in the propensity for victimization of domestic violence, though scholars have yet to consider the possible interaction effects between socio-economic status and the ability to pay for an expert to testify on their behalf. It is more likely that women above the median income would be able to pay for an expert to testify on their behalves, yet, abuse tends to occur more often among those in the lower socio-economic stratum. It should be acknowledged that while it is clear the circumstances of each case will differ, which can ultimately affect verdict decisions, these are all concerns that relate to the outcome of self-defense cases, and further study of these issues could prove extremely beneficial.

Can the Standard Created by the Syndrome Be Circumvented Using Battering and Its Effects?

When considering what the content of expert testimony should include or exclude, one of the primary questions that should be asked is whether the standard created by the battered woman syndrome can be circumvented using evidence of battering and its effects. In other words, would testimony of battering and its effects curtail the tendency to fall back on prototypes? This would depend upon whether individuals could actually refrain from using stereotypes associated with the syndrome. Despite the fact that many experts now abstain from using terminology associated with the syndrome (i.e., learned helplessness, passivity) as an artifact of the standard created by the syndrome, jurors continue to assume that dominance of an abuser and passivity of a victim are key components to maintaining abusive relationships. If individuals do indeed fall back on stereotypes of abusive relationships, then it would be extremely difficult to refrain from comparing the defendant to one's own perception of a typical battered woman. Research has demonstrated that informing jurors of their potential biases can help mock jurors to recognize their biases and evaluate cases in a more objective manner. Perhaps it would be helpful to provide instructions to jurors informing them of their potential biases about victims of abuse (particularly in "atypical" situations). If experts acknowledge that individuals hold biases regarding victims of abuse, then jurors would be more aware of their own biases when making informed decisions about a case.

Another way to impart this information is through social framework testimony. Ironically, one of the reasons why the battered woman syndrome was allowed into the courts was to help dispel myths that jurors might embrace about battered women. Social framework testimony allows experts to discuss the status of research on domestic violence in layperson's terms to help jurors make more informed decisions. No one really knows exactly how often experts actually address some of the common misconceptions about battered women. In fact, some of the more recent research suggests many of these misconceptions may not be misconceptions at all, yet it is clear that many misperceptions remain. Perhaps one of the most important ideas to convey to jurors is one that will show them that they actually hold stereotypes about victims of battering. To look at the broader picture, an expert can ask jurors to imagine what comes to mind when they think of a victim of domestic abuse. This can then assist jurors in realizing they actually embrace stereotypes of victims of battering. If experts enlighten jurors that they (and the general public) have created a standard of a battered woman to which all other battered women are compared, experts can then address related topics such as how bias, stereotyping, stories, and norm theory can ultimately affect legal decision making. Conceivably, instructing jurors to be aware of their own potential biases should not only make jurors more informed, but, at the least, help make more objective legal decisions.

Just as jurors can be informed, it is essential that lawyers realize how syndrome evidence can affect their cases; ultimately, the burden of proof lies with the defense. The defendant's counsel must consider whether the battered woman syndrome (or evidence of battering and its effects) should be injected into the case. This is a difficult decision for defense lawyers, as lawyers can be caught in a catch-22. Not only should the characteristics of their client be considered when deciding to use expert testimony of the syndrome, but when testimony is used, lawyers must also be careful not to portray the defendant as pathological. Lawyers must realize that atypical defendants will have a more difficult time convincing jurors that their actions were in self-defense, and legal actors must walk a fine line between portraying their client as suffering from the syndrome and demonstrating that killing was a justified response to the situation.

There is general agreement that the battered woman syndrome no longer captures the current state of knowledge regarding battering. While testimony regarding battering and its effects may be a more effective vehicle to explain the context of the situation, particularly in cases where the defendant does not fit the stereotype of a battered woman, it may take some time to change the public's tendency to perceive the defendant as mentally unstable, even if testimony on battering and its effects refrains from focusing on pathology or learned helplessness.

As society shifts toward the inclusion of expert testimony of battering to include an increasing number of situations (i.e., fraud, theft, drug running, child homicide, child custody, tort cases, elderly abuse, coercion and duress, etc.), it is not clear what the impact of such testimony in these cases will be. While the use of expert testimony has expanded to include self-defense for homosexual abuse, elderly abuse, and duress and coercion, it is simply a matter of time before a heterosexual male who kills his wife will use expert testimony on battering for a plea of self-defense. After reading this book, it is hoped that legal actors would think twice before offering expert testimony for heterosexual male defendants and other individuals who do not fit the stereotype of a battered woman due to limited amount of data existing on the topic, and because of the fact that preliminary data suggests that if the defendant doesn't fit into the stereotype of a victim of abuse, expert evidence can have a backlash effect.

Assessing Tests of Reasonableness

It is widely believed that because the majority of homicide cases that appear in court are direct confrontational cases between the defendant and victim (Browne, 1987; Downs, 1996; Maguigan, 1991), it is likely that, in these cases, women who kill actually do so in self-defense, but one cannot assume that all battered women who kill do so in self-defense. Less common, yet just as important, is recognizing how non-confrontational cases are perceived. Many of the defendants in these cases also claim self-defense, yet their claims are less likely to be perceived as self-defense. Future research needs to determine whether the application of a subjective or objective test of reasonableness and imminence of danger affects pleas of a battered woman defendant claiming self-defense and whether imminence and subjective or objective tests of reasonableness would differ as a function of sexual orientation of the couple. Presumably, similar results would be found for imminence, yet tests of reasonableness might differ according to subjective or objective jury instructions.

It is difficult to grasp the concept of what constitutes a reasonable person or a reasonable battered woman (Roberts, 2003). Thought of as a continuum, one end of the scale would be the use of the subjective standard of reasonableness (what would a reasonable battered woman do?) to assess the battered woman's situation. On the other side of the continuum would be the objective standard of reasonableness (what would a reasonable person do?) to assess the battered woman's plight. Is there really a difference between these standards?

Some states have adopted the use of a "reasonable woman's standard" when evaluating cases of hostile work environment sexual harassment (*Ellison v. Brady*, 1991). Researchers (Wiener, Hurt, Russell, Mannen, & Gasper, 1997) examined whether the use of the different standards (i.e., reasonable person standard v. reasonable woman standard) influenced judgments of sexual harassment. Overall, the researchers found male participants were less receptive to the reasonable woman standard; however, legal standard results were mediated by sexism, whereby men high in benevolent sexism were more likely to recognize the reasonable woman standard. Furthermore, participants who recognized the reasonable person standard and were more benevolent (protective) toward women believed the defendants' harassing conduct was more severe than those low in sexism. Studies such as these can be extended to examine mediating and interaction effects of judgments of culpability in cases of self-defense, depending upon the legal standards used and the efficacy of expert testimony.

Additional research is also needed to investigate what happens when a battered woman's actions are at odds with the general concept of self-defense and battered woman syndrome. For instance, if women are just as likely to be perpetrators of assault toward men, then what happens when women who kill their abusers are the initial or primary aggressors? Would police be able to identify or pursue the initial aggressor? Syndrome evidence (or battering and its effects) can be used to explain why women may be the primary aggressor. There have been incidents in which the syndrome has been used to explain why a woman might actually initiate a violent act toward a man. Syndrome theory suggests that as the tension grows within the battering cycle, some women may initiate violence to get the impending violence over with (Walker, 1984). Others (Downs, 2005) believe that women who are abused are especially attuned to the special circumstances of captivity or violence and can recognize when their partner will become abusive. Women may react by initiating violence to protect themselves from what they perceive to be imminent danger. At this point, no research has been conducted on the topic of whether the victim of battering is the primary aggressor. Even more interesting to consider is whether being the primary aggressor in a situation would differ as a function of sexual orientation. For instance, could this distinctive ability to sense danger be extended to heterosexual men or homosexual couples?

Providing a Context for the Defendant's Behavior: Is the Testimony Helpful?

Some (Slobogin, 1998) believe it is very difficult for an expert to evaluate the mental state of an individual who claims to have been in imminent danger and saw the use of lethal force as necessary to defend themselves. An expert cannot know how or what the defendant believed during the crime; they can only provide a context for the woman's behavior and why it may have led to a mental state where the battered victim felt the need to use lethal force. The shift toward admitting social framework evidence as expert testimony does not take into consideration the specific individual, but rather addresses the state of the art of research in order to provide a context for a particular situation, which makes it difficult to address the state of mind of the individual.

Testimony should be helpful to jurors, but there is no research that has examined the helpfulness of a particular type of testimony; consequently, the question of whether the syndrome has probative value remains unanswered. Since it has been revealed that expert testimony offered in cases in which battered women kill seems to lead to more lenient verdicts (Schuller, 1992), one can assume that such evidence is helpful in assisting jurors to decide how the woman's actions were reasonable and justified. However, if someone is mentally unstable, can their acts be justified? That is one of the problems associated with the use of expert testimony in these cases.

Testimony often bolsters the credibility of the defendant (Follingstad, 2003). Courts tend to believe that jurors need information pertaining to effects of battering to provide a context for the defendant but also to correct any misconceptions that jurors may hold. While research has suggested that individuals have held stereotypes and misconceptions of battered women, more recent research suggests that perceptions of battered women have changed substantially over the last 10 years (Carlson & Worden, 2005; Reddy et al., 1997). Unfortunately, this means that it remains unclear whether admitting testimony based on the premise that the public holds misconceptions of battered women is necessarily warranted.

If It's Here to Stay, Then When Should It Be Used?

The crux of the issue is whether expert evidence on battering or the battered partner syndrome (battered woman syndrome, battered person syndrome) would be beneficial for the defendant. This depends on the characteristics of the defendant. It may, in fact, be detrimental to include any form of expert testimony on the battered woman syndrome in cases when the defendant does not fit the stereotype of a battered woman. Given what little is known at this point, using expert testimony for unusual or atypical female heterosexual defendants is questionable at best, and testimony also seems to have the potential to create a backlash effect for homosexual defendants or heterosexual male defendants.

Many scholars argue that expanding the use of the syndrome as evidence demonstrates society's acceptance and awareness of problems associated with battered women (Bradfield, 2002; Dutton, 2007), but others (Faigman, 1986; McMahon, 1999; Morse, 1998) believe that testimony should not be admitted until scientific evidence demonstrates that it does not have adverse effects on various populations and situations. Based on previous research, it is suggested that testimony should not be used (or at least should be evaluated carefully) in cases that do not fit neatly into the stereotypic standard created by the syndrome, until additional research explores the effects of the testimony in various cases and situations.

The difficulty in using the battered woman syndrome evidence to bolster an individual's defense is that the mere action of committing a crime or homicide conflicts with the characteristics of the syndrome. People have difficulty comprehending how a battered woman can suffer from distorted perceptions of the situation in some situations (inability to leave the abuser, perceive impending violence) yet such distortion does not affect her ability to react rationally and reasonably by defending herself (Follingstad, 2003). In order to rectify this situation, the battered woman must generally concede that her actions were "unreasonable" and hope that the syndrome evidence then excuses her from criminal liability if she can prove that she was a "passive, obedient wife whose choices were determined not by her own exercise of will, but by the superior will of her husband" (Coughlin, 1994, p. 50). The heart of the matter then becomes one's inability to refrain from such criminal behavior.

While this strategy may help to evoke sympathy for battered women who kill their abusers, the mere suggestion that a woman is mentally unstable and irrational can be counteractive in civil cases such as child custody and child abuse (Follingstad, 2003). There is the potential that once a woman proclaims she is a battered woman, she may have difficulty demonstrating she is a "fit" parent (Follingstad, 2003). When battering was established in a case where children were present, the courts stated that witness to such abuse was considered child neglect (*In re Heather,* 1996). Other cases found that a woman was an unfit mother based on the fact that she previously chose an abusive partner and was likely to do it again (*In re John V.,* 1992; *In re Ranker,* 1996). These cases suggest that the use of the syndrome can be detrimental in some situations. The time is right for empirical investigation to examine the implications for battered women that use the syndrome to bolster their defense.

Society seems to have created stereotypes attributable to sub-categories of men and women, in which heterosexual females and homosexual males are believed to share feminine traits, while homosexual females and heterosexual males may be perceived as sharing more masculine traits. These beliefs and biases create a norm from which exceptional situations are excluded, and this affects juror judgments when defendants in the court systems react contrary to expectations. Judgments may be affected in exceptional cases when the woman's characteristics deviate from the norm or "prototypical" battered woman. It is likely that the same processes are used when evaluating same-sex couples or heterosexual men. Contemporaneously, to do this prevents the jury from answering objectively and, at best, leaves the juror to ask, "What would a reasonable person suffering from battered woman's syndrome believe?"

In conclusion, there has been a great deal of societal insight and research on intimate partner violence, yet violence among intimate partners continues, and some (Straus, 2005) suggest will continue to rise. While there is zero tolerance for bullying, harassment, or violence in schools, it is necessary to educate young adults that violence of any kind should not be tolerated.

The battered woman syndrome was effective in the quest for human liberation and freedom from oppression. Despite the fact that the syndrome can be considered outmoded, outdated, and arguably non-existent, remnants of it remain because of the natural inclination to use stereotypes and prototypes. When information is processed, it is much easier to fit various groups of individuals into categories in order to explain and predict behavior. It will take time for society and, specifically, the legal system to shift away from the syndrome mentality. In the meantime, there is much to be learned about how the use of the syndrome affects legal decision making. There is much work to be done to evaluate the effects of the battered woman syndrome before using it.

The syndrome that was first used to enlighten the public and the courtrooms has now led to an intense controversy. Not only has it led to debates among scholars, but the use of special (or unique) defenses might actually work against women (and minority populations) in general. This book has demonstrated that women that deviate from the traditional gender role, or from a prescribed symptomology, will often receive more harsh sentences. In fact, when women do not fit the stereotype of a battered woman, their actions are more likely to be perceived as an excuse rather than a reasonable response. Unless the defendant fits the narrow definition of the stereotype associated with battered women, it appears inadvisable to use the syndrome as evidence in a trial until more of the effects of its use are understood.

Traditional gender roles and stereotypes of race or ethnicity dictate perceptions of ourselves and others. The goal of this book was to provide an overview of the battered woman syndrome and its use in the courts but also to shed some insight into how prototypes and stereotypes affect legal decision making, and how race, gender, and societal norms color perceptions of others and create a societal need for syndromes. When the stereotype that women are victims who are in need of special assistance is perpetuated, this can only generate further inequality.

DISCUSSION QUESTIONS

1. Do you think the syndrome will re-examine the content of the battered woman syndrome testimony based on the Daubert trilogy? Explain why the courts are resistant to change. Name at least three reasons why courts are reluctant to re-review the syndrome.

2. Do you think that if jurors were informed about their own biases and stereotypes of victims of battering, this would change their decision making process? If so how? Would female defendants still be perceived as pathological? Would gender differences still exist?

3. Name at least three types of cases (civil and criminal) that research has not examined, and explain how typicality might affect the outcome of the cases.

4. If you were not a typical victim of battering, would you use expert testimony of the syndrome? Explain your answer.

5. Even if expert testimony refrained from using terminology associated with pathology and learned helplessness, do you think that female defendants would still be perceived as more pathological and helpless compared to male defendants?

References

Adams, D. 1988. "Treatment models of men who batter: A profeminist analysis." In *Feminist perspectives on wife abuse*, eds. K. Yllo and M. Bograd, 176–199. Newbury Park, CA: Sage.

Adams, S. R., and D. R. Freeman. 2002. "Women who are violent: Attitudes and beliefs of professionals working in the field of domestic violence." *Military Medicine* 167 (6): 445–450.

Aguirre, B. E. 1985. "Why do they return? Abused wives in shelters." *Social Work* 30: 350–354.

Allard, S. A. 2005. "Rethinking battered woman syndrome: A black feminist perspective." In *Domestic violence at the margins: Readings on race, class, gender, and culture*, eds. N. J. Sokoloff and C. Pratt, 194–205. New Brunswick, NJ: Rutgers University Press.

Allen, C. T., S. C. Swan, and C. Raghavan. 2009. "Gender symmetry, sexism, and intimate partner violence." *Journal of Interpersonal Violence* 24 (1): 1816–1834.

Alsdurf, J. M. 1985. "Wife abuse and the church: The response of pastors." *Response* 8 (1): 9–11.

Amato, P. 2000. "The consequences of divorce for adults and children." *Journal of Marriage and the Family* 62: 1269–1287.

American Psychiatric Association. 1994. *Diagnostic and statistical manual of mental disorders*. 4th ed. Washington, D.C.: Author.

Anderson, C. A., M. R. Lepper, and L. Ross. 1980. "Perseverance of social theories: The role of explanation in the persistence of discredited information." *Journal of Personality and Social Psychology* 39: 1037–1049.

Anderson, K. 2002. "Perpetrator or victim? Relationships between intimate partner violence and well-being." *Journal of Marriage and Family* 64 (4): 851–863.

Archer, J. 2000. "Sex differences in aggression between heterosexual partners: A meta-analytic review." *Psychological Bulletin* 126: 651–680.

Archer, N. H. 1989. "Battered women and the legal system: Past, present and future." *Law and Psychology Review* 13: 145–163.

Arias, I., and K. D. O'Leary. 1984. Factors moderating the intergenerational transmission of marital aggression. Paper presented at the 18th Annual Meeting of the Association for Advancement of Behavior Therapy, Philadelphia.

_____, and K. Pape. 1999. "Psychological abuse: Implications for adjustment and commitment to leave violence partners." *Violence and Victims* 14 (1): 55–67.

Armstrong, G. 1977. "Females under the law: Protected but unequal." *Crime and Delinquency* 23: 109–120.

Aron, C. J. 1993. "In defense of battered women: Is justice blind"? *Human Rights* (Fall): 14–17.

Astin, M. C., S. M. Ogland-Hand, E. M. Coleman, and D. W. Foy. 1995. "Posttraumatic stress disorder and childhood abuse in battered women: Comparisons with maritally distressed women." *Journal of Consulting and Clinical Psychology* 63 (2): 308–312.

Aubrey, M., and C. P. Ewing. 1989. "Student and voter subjects: Differences in attitudes towards battered women." *Journal of Interpersonal Violence* 4: 289–297.

Babcock, J. C., C. E. Green, and C. Robie. 2004.

"Does batterers' treatment work? A meta-analytic review of domestic violence treatment." *Clinical Psychology Review* 23: 1023–1053.

Balistreri v. Pacifica Police Dept., 855 F. 2d 1421 (9th Cir. Ct. 1988).

Balsam, K., and D. Szymanski. 2005. "relationship quality and domestic violence in women's same-sex relationships: The role of minority stress." *Psychology of Women Quarterly* 29 (3): 258–269.

Bard, M., and D. Sangrey. 1986. *The crime victim's book*. 2d ed. New York: Brunner/Mazel.

Barlow, D. H., and V. M. Durand. 1999. *Abnormal psychology*. 2d ed. Pacific Grove, CA: Brooks/Cole.

Barnett, O. W., and R. W. Fagan. 1993. "Alcohol use in male spouse abusers and their female partners." *Journal of Family Violence* 8: 1–25.

Bartol, C. R., and A. M. Bartol. 2004. *Introduction to forensic psychology*. Thousand Oaks, CA: Sage.

Belknap, J., R. E. Fleury, H. C. Melton, C. Sullivan, and A. Leisenring. 2001. "To go or not to go? Preliminary findings on battered women's decisions regarding court cases." In *Women battering in the United States: Till death do us part,* ed. H. Eigenberg, 39–326. Prospect Heights, IL: Waveland.

Bent-Goodley, T. 2001. "Eradicating domestic violence in the African American community: A literature review and action agenda." *Trauma, Violence & Abuse: A Review Journal* 2: 316–330.

Berk, S. F., and D. R. Loseke. 1980–1981. "'Handling' family violence: Situational determinants of police arrests in domestic disturbances." *Law and Society Review* 15: 317–346.

Biden, J. R., Jr. 1993. "Violence against women: The congressional response." *American Psychologist* 48: 1058–1060.

Biggers, J. R. 2005. "The utility of diagnostic language as expert testimony: Should syndrome terminology be used in battering cases?" *Journal of Forensic Psychology Practice* 5 (1): 43–61.

Bitney, C. 2001, Spring. "Have a heart: Help prevent hate crimes." *National NOW Times.* www.now.org/nnt/spring-2001/hatecrimes. html (accessed August 1, 2006).

Black, D. 1980. *The manners and customs of the police*. New York: Academic Press.

Blackman, J. 1989. *Intimate violence: A study of injustice*. New York: Columbia University Press.

_____. 1990. "Emerging images of severely battered women and the criminal justice system." *Behavioral Sciences and the Law* 8 (2): 121–130.

Blowers, A. N., and B. Bjerregaard. 1994. "The admissibility of expert testimony on the battered woman syndrome in homicide cases." *Journal of Psychiatry & Law* 22 (4): 527–560.

Boninger, D., F. Gleicher, and A. Strathman. 1994. "Counterfactual thinking: From what might have been to what may be." *Journal of Personality and Social Psychology* 67 (2): 297–307.

Bookwala, J., I. Frieze, C. Smith, and K. Ryan. 1992. "Predictions of dating violence: A multivariate analysis." *Violence and Victims* 7: 297–311.

Bornstein, R. 2006. "The complex relationship between dependency and domestic violence: converging psychological factors and social forces." *American Psychologist* 61 (6): 595–606.

Bowker, L. H. 1983. "Battered wives, lawyers, and district attorneys: An examination of law in action." *Journal of Criminal Justice* 11 (5): 403–412.

_____. 1993. "A battered woman's problems are social, not psychological." In *Current controversies on family violence,* eds. R. J. Gelles, and D. R. Loseke. Newbury Park, CA: Sage.

Bradfield, R. 2002. "Understanding the battered woman who kills her violent partner—the admissibility of expert evidence of domestic violence." *Psychiatry, Psychology and Law* 9 (2): 177–190.

Branscombe, N. R., and J. Coleman. 1991. *Judgment consequences of mentally simulating alternative victim or rapist behaviors and outcomes.* Paper presented at the Annual Meeting of the Mid-western Psychological Association, Chicago.

_____, and J. A. Weir. 1992. "Resistance as stereotype-inconsistency: Consequences for judgments of rape victims." *Journal of Social and Clinical Psychology* 11: 80–102.

Brewer, K. R. 1988. "Missouri's new law on 'battered spouse syndrome': A moral victory, a partial solution." *Saint Louis University Law Journal* 33 (1): 227–255.

Brody, D. C., J. R. Acker, and W. A. Logan. 2008. *Criminal law.* Sudbury, MA: Jones and Bartlett Publishers.

Brookoff, D. 1997. "Drugs, alcohol, and domestic violence in Memphis. National Institute of Justice Research Preview." Washington, D.C.: U.S. Department of Justice.

Browne, A. 1987. *When battered women kill.* New York: Free Press.

_____. 1993. "Violence against women by male partners: Prevalence, outcomes and policy implications." *American Psychologist* 48: 1077–1087.

_____, and S. S. Bassuk. 1997. "Intimate violence in the lives of homeless and poor housed women: Prevalence and patterns in an ethnically diverse sample." *American Journal of Orthopsychiatry* 67: 261–278.

_____, A. Salomon, and S. S. Bassuk. 1999. "The impact of recent partner violence on poor women's capacity to maintain work." *Violence Against Women* 5: 393–426.

_____, and K. R. Williams. 1989. "Exploring the effect of resource availability and the likelihood of female-perpetrated homicides." *Law and Society Review, 23(1)*, 75–94.

_____, and K. R. Williams. 1993. "Gender, intimacy and lethal violence: Trends from 1976–1987." *Gender and Society* 7: 78–98.

Brownmiller, S. 1975. *Against our will: Men, women and rape.* New York: Simon & Schuster.

Buhrle v. State, 627 P.2d 1374 (Wyo. 1981).

Bureau of Justice Statistics. 1992, December. *Criminal victimization in the U.S., 1991.* Washington, D.C.: U.S. Department of Justice.

_____. 1993, March. *Survey of state prison inmates, 1991.* NCJ-136949: 9.

_____. 2005. U.S. Department of Justice, Office of Justice Programs. Retrieved December 27, 2007 from http://bjs.ojp.usdoj.gov/content/homicide/gender.cfm.

Burgess, A. W., and L. L. Holmstrom. 1974. "Rape trauma syndrome." *American Journal of Psychiatry* 131 (9): 981–986.

Burris, C.T., and N. R. Branscombe. 1993. "Racism, counterfactual thinking and judgment severity." *Journal of Applied Social Psychology* 23 (12): 980–995.

Bushway, S., and A. Piehl. 2001. "Judging judicial discretion: Legal factors and racial discrimination in sentencing." *Law and Society Review* 35: 733–764.

Buzawa, E.S., and C.G. Buzawa. 2003. *Domestic violence: The criminal justice response.* 3d ed. New York: Sage.

_____, and G. Hotaling. 2000, September. *The police response to domestic violence calls for assistance in three Massachusetts towns: Final report.* Washington, D.C.: National Institute for Justice.

Campbell, J., J. Kub, R. Belknap, and T. Templin. 1997. "Predictors of depression in battered women." *Violence Against Women* 3 (3): 271–293.

_____, P. Miller, M. Cardwell, and R. Belknap. 1994. "Relationship status of battered women over time." *Journal of Family Violence* 9 (2): 99–111.

Campbell, J. C. 1986. "Nursing assessment for risk of homicide with battered women." *Advances in Nursing Science* 8 (4): 36–51.

Cantos, A. L., P. H. Neidig, and K. D. O'Leary. 1994. "Injuries in women and men in a treatment program for domestic violence." *Journal of Family Violence* 9: 113–124.

Carlson, B. E., and A. P. Worden. 2005. "Attitudes and beliefs about domestic violence: Results of a public opinion survey: I. Definitions of domestic violence, criminal domestic violence, and prevalence." *Journal of Interpersonal Violence* 20 (10): 1197–1218.

Carter v. State, 469 So. 2d 194 (Fla. Dist. Ct. App. 1985).

Casanave, N., and M. Zahn. 1986. *Women, murder and male domination: Police reports of domestic homicide in Chicago and Philadelphia.* Paper presented at the annual meeting of the American Society of Criminology, Atlanta, GA.

Cascardi, M., and K. D. O'Leary. 1992. "Depressive symptomatology, self-esteem, and self-blame in battered women." *Journal of Family Violence* 7 (4): 249–259.

Casey, P. J. 1992. "A reexamination of the roles of typicality and category dominance in verifying category membership." *Journal of Experimental Psychology: Learning, Memory, and Cognition* 18 (4): 823–834.

Castel, J. R. 1990. "Discerning justice for battered women who kill." *University of Toronto Faculty Law Review* 48: 229–258.

Catalano, S. M. 2005. An examination of the convergence between police recording and victim reporting of serious violent crime, 1973–2002. *Dissertation Abstracts International, A: The Humanities and Social Sciences,* vol. 65, no. 9: 3577.

Chimbos, P. D. 1978. *Marital violence: A study of interspouse homicide.* Oxford, England: R & E Research Associates.

Cimino, J. J., and M. A. Dutton. 1991. Factors influencing the development of PTSD in battered women. Paper presented at the 99th Annual Convention of the American Psychological Association, San Francisco, CA.

Coffee, C. L. 1986–87. "A trend emerges: A state survey on the admissibility of expert testimony concerning the battered woman syndrome." *Journal of Family Law* 25 (2): 373–396.

Coker, D. 2000. "Shifting power for battered women: Law, material resources, and poor women of color." *U.C. Davis Law Review* 33: 1009–1055.

Commonwealth v. Beeler, 428 Pa. Super. 633, 627 A.2d 199 (1993).

Commonwealth v. Jones, 92-CR-00006 (Ky. 1993).

Commonwealth v. Miller, 430 Pa. Super. 297, 634 A.2d 614 (1993).

Commonwealth v. Raposo, 413 Mass. 182, 595 N.E.2d 773 (1992).

Commonwealth v. Rodriguez, SJC-6245 (Mass 1994).

Commonwealth v. Scott, 072980, Super. Ct. (MA. 1989).

Commonwealth v. Stonehouse, 521 Pa. 41, 555 A.2d 772 (1989).

Cook, P. W. 1997. *Abused men: The hidden side of domestic violence.* Westport, CT: Praeger Publishers/Greenwood Publishing Group, Inc.

Cook, S., and S. C. Swan. 2006. "Guest editor's introduction to the special issue on gender symmetry." *Violence Against Women* 12: 995–996.

Coughlin, A.M. 1994. "Excusing Women." *California Law Review* 82 (1): 93p.

Crawford v. Washington, 541 U.S. 36 (2004).

Crocker, L. 1985. "The meaning of equality for battered women who kill men in self-defense." *Harvard Women's Law Journal* 8: 121–139.

Curry, T. R., G. Lee, and S. F. Rodriquez. 2004. "Does victim gender increase sentence severity: Explorations of gender dynamics and sentencing outcomes." *Crime and Delinquency* 50 (3): 319–343.

Dalton, C., and E. M. Schneider 2001. "Dimensions of the battering experience." In *Battered women and the law*, eds. R. C. Clark, D. A. Farber, and O. M. Fiss, 132–152. New York: Foundation Press.

Dane, F. C. 1992. "Applying social psychology in the courtroom: Understanding stereotypes in jury decision making." *Contemporary Social Psychology* 16 (3): 33–36.

_____, and L. S. Wrightsman. 1982. "Effects of defendants' and victims' characteristics on jurors' verdicts." In *The psychology of the courtroom*, eds. N. L. Kerr and R. M. Bray, 83–115. New York: Academic Press.

Darley, J. M., and P. H. Gross. 1983. "A hypothesis-confirming bias in labeling effects." *Journal of Personality and Social Psychology* 4: 20–33.

Das Dasgupta, S. 2002. "A framework for understanding women's use of nonlethal violence in intimate heterosexual relationships." *Violence Against Women* 8: 1364–1389.

Daubert v. Merrell Dow Pharm., Inc., 113 S. Ct. 2786 (1993).

Davis v. Washington, 126 S. Ct. 2266, 165 L. Ed. 2d 224 (2006).

DeKeseredy, W. S., and Dragiewicz, M. (2007). Understanding the complexities of feminist perspectives on woman abuse. *Violence Against Women*, 13 (8), 874–884.

Dershowitz, A. M. 1994. *The abuse excuse and other cop-outs, sob stories, and evasions of responsibility.* Boston: Back Bay Books, Little, Brown.

Devine, P. G. 1989. "Stereotypes and prejudice: Their automatic and controlled components." *Journal of Personality and Social Psychology* 56: 5–18.

Dion, K. L., and R. A. Schuller. 1991. "The Ms. stereotype: Its generality and its relation to managerial and marital status stereotypes." *Canadian Journal of Behavioural Science/Revue* 23 (1): 25–40.

District of Columbia Coalition Against Domestic Violence Center (DCCADV). http://www.dccadv.org/statistics.htm (accessed October 03, 2005).

Dobash, R. E., and R. P. Dobash. 1979. *Violence against wives: a case against the patriarchy.* New York: Free Press.

Dodge, M., and E. Greene. 1991. "Jurors and expert conceptions of battered women." *Violence and Victims* 6: 271–282.

Doe v. Commissioner of Internal Revenue, 91–1678, U.S. Ct. App. (3d Cir. Ct. 1991).

Douglas, E. M. 2006. "Familial violence socialization in childhood and later life approval of corporal punishment: a cross-cultural perspective." *American Journal of Orthopsychiatry* 76 (1): 23–30.

Douglas, M. A. 1987. "The battered woman syndrome." In Sonkin, D. J. (Ed.), *Domestic Violence on Trial*, New York: Springer.

Dowd, M. 1992. "Dispelling the myths about the battered woman's defense: Towards a new understanding." *Fordham Urban Law Journal* 14: 567–583.

Downs, D. A. 1996. *More than victims: Battered women, the syndrome society, and the law.* Chicago: University of Chicago Press.

_____, and J. Fisher. 2005. "Battered woman syndrome: Tool of justice or false hope in self-defense cases"? In *Current controversies on family violence*, eds. D. R. Loseke, R. J. Gelles, and M. M. Cavanaugh. Thousand Oaks, CA: Sage.

Dunn v. Roberts, 963 F.2d 308 (Kan. 10th Cir. Ct. 1992).

Dutton, D. G. 1994. "Patriarchy and wife assault. The ecological fallacy." *Violence and Victims* 9: 167–182.

_____. 2007. "The complexities of domestic violence." *American Psychologist* 62 (7): 708–709.

_____, and M. Bodnarchuk. 2003. "Through a psychological lens: Personality disorder and spouse assault." In *Current controversies on family violence*, eds. D. R. Loseke, R. J. Gelles, and M. M. Cavanaugh. Thousand Oaks, CA: Sage.

_____, and S. L. Painter. 1981. "Traumatic bonding: The development of emotional attachments in battered women and other relationships of intermittent abuse." *Victimology* 6: 139–155.

Dutton, M. A. 1992. "Assessment of treatment of PTSD among battered women." In *Treating PTSD: Procedure for combat veterans, battered women, adult and child sexual assaults,* ed. D. Foy. New York: Guilford Press.

———. 1993. "Understanding women's responses to domestic violence: A redefinition of battered woman syndrome." *Hofstra Law Review* 21: 1191–1242.

———. 1996. "Battered women's strategic response to violence: The role of context." In J. Edelson & Z. Eiskovitz (Eds.). *Future interventions with battered women and their families* (pp. 105–124). Thousand Oaks, CA: Sage.

———, L. C. Hohnecker, P. M. Halle, and K. J. Burghardt. 1994. "Traumatic responses among battered women who kill." *Journal of Traumatic Stress* 7 (4): 549–564.

Dutton-Douglas, M.A. 1992. "Treating battered women in the aftermath stage." *Psychotherapy in Private Practice* 10: 93–98.

Dyas v. U. S., 376 A.2d. 827 (D.C. 1977).

Eagly, A. H., and S. Chaiken. 1993. *The psychology of attitudes.* San Diego, CA: Harcourt Brace Janovich.

———, M. G. Makhijani, and B. G. Klonsky. 1992. "Gender and the evaluation of leaders: A meta-analysis." *Psychological Bulletin* 111 (1): 3–22.

Easteal, P. W. 1992. "Battered woman syndrome: Misunderstood?" *Current Issues in Criminal Justice* 3 (3): 356–359.

Easterling v. U. S., 267 P.2d 185, 187 (Okla. Crim. Ct. App. 1954).

Eaton, S., and A. Hyman. 1992. "Domestic violence component of the New York task force report on women in the courts: An evaluation and assessment of New York City courts." *Fordham Urban Law Journal* 19: 391–534.

Echols v. State, 503 U.S. 912; 112 S. Ct. 1280; 117 L. Ed. 2d 505 (1991).

Edelson, J. L., A. Eisikovits, and E. Guttman. 1985. "Men who batter women: A critical review of the evidence." *Journal of Family Issues* 6 (2): 229–247.

Ehrensaft, M. K., T. E. Moffitt, and A. Caspi. 2004. "Clinically abusive relationships in an unselected birth cohort: Men's and women's participation and developmental antecedents." *Journal of Abnormal Psychology* 113 (2): 258–270.

Ellison v. Brady, 924 F.2d 872 (9th Cir. Ct.1991).

Eng, P. 1995. "Domestic violence in Asian/Pacific island communities." *Health Issues for Women of Color.* Thousand Oaks, CA: Sage.

English, B. 2007. "Fatal Cape shooting reveals a secret: In hindsight, doctor's family says it now sees abuse." *The Boston Globe.* http://www.boston.com/news/local/articles/2007/04/29/fatal_cape_shooting_reveals_a_secret/ (accessed November 27, 2008).

Everett, R. and R. Wojtkiewicz. 2002. "Difference, disparity, and race/ethnic bias in federal sentencing." *Journal of Quantitative Criminology* 18: 189–211.

Ewing, C. P. 1987. *Battered women who kill: Psychological self defense as legal justification.* Lexington, MA: DC Heath.

———. 1990. "Psychological self defense: A proposed justification for battered women who kill." *Law and Human Behavior* 14 (6): 579–593.

———, and M. Aubrey. 1987. "Battered women and public opinions: Some realities about the myths." *Journal of Family Violence* 2 (3): 257–265.

"Factsheet: Incarcerated women," National Women's Law Center, Washington, D.C., 1993.

Faigman, D. L. 1986. "The battered woman syndrome and self defense: A legal and empirical dissent." *Virginia Law Review* 72: 619–647.

———. 1987. "Discerning justice when battered women kill." *Hastings Law Journal* 39 (1): 207–227.

Family Violence Prevention Fund (FVPF). http://endabuse.org/resources/facts/ (accessed May 14, 2007).

Farrell, R. A., and M. D. Holmes. 1991. "The social and cognitive structure of legal decision making." *The Sociological Quarterly* 32 (4): 529–542.

FBI. 1989. *Uniform crime reports for the United States.* Washington, D.C.: Government Printing Office.

———. 1990, 1997, 2004, 2006. *Uniform crime reports.* Washington, D.C.: U. S. Department of Justice.

Feather, N. T. 1996. "Domestic violence, gender, and perceptions of justice." *Sex Roles* 35 (7–8): 507–519.

Feigenson, N. R. 1995. "The rhetoric of torts." *Hastings Law Journal* 47 (1): 1–165.

Felson, R. B. 2002. "Violence and gender reexamined." American Psychological Association, Washington, D.C.

———, and S. F. Messner. 1998. "Disentangling the effects of gender and intimacy on victim precipitation in homicide." *Criminology* 36: 405–423.

———, and M. C. Outlaw. 2007. "The control motive and marital violence." *Violence and Victims* 22 (4): 387–403.

Ferguson, C. J., and C. Negy. 2004. "The influence of gender and ethnicity on judgment of culpability in a domestic violence scenario." *Violence and Victims* 19: 203–220.

Fergusson, D. M., L. J. Horwood, and E. M. Ridder. 2005. "Partner violence and mental health outcomes in a New Zealand birth cohort." *Journal of Marriage and Family* 67 (5): 1103–1119.

Ferraro, K. J. 2003 "The words change, but the melody lingers." *Violence Against Women* 9 (1): 110–129.

_____, and S. M. Johnson. 1983. "How women experience battering: The process of victimization." *Social Problems* 30 (3): 325–339.

Fiebert, M. S., and D. M. Gonzalez. 1997. "College women who initiate assaults on their male partners and the reasons offered for such behavior." *Psychological Reports* 80: 583–590.

Final report of the California Judicial Council Advisory Committee on Racial & Ethnic Bias in the Courts. 1997. http://www.courtinfo.ca.gov/reference/documents/rebias.pdf (accessed June 2007).

Finkel, N. J., K. H. Meister, and D. M. Lightfoot. 1991. "The self-defense and community sentiment." *Law and Human Behavior* 15 (6): 585–602.

Finklehor, D., and K. Yllo. 1985. *License to rape: Sexual abuse of wives.* New York: Free Press.

Finn, J. 1985. "The stresses and coping behavior of battered women." *Social Casework* 66 (6): 341–349.

Fiske, S. T., and S. E. Taylor. 1991. *Social cognition.* 2d ed. New York: McGraw-Hill.

Fleury, R., C. Sullivan, and D. Bybee. 2000. "When ending the relationship does not end the violence: Women's experiences of violence by former partners." *Violence Against Women* 6 (12): 1363–1383.

Follingstad, D. R. 2003. "Battered woman syndrome in the courts." In *Handbook of psychology: forensic psychology,* vol. 1, ed. A. M. Goldstein, 485–507. Hoboken, NJ: John Wiley & Sons, Inc.

_____, R. G. Bradley, C. M. Helff, and J. E. Laughlin. 2002. "A model for predicting dating violence: Anxious attachment, angry temperament, and need for relationship control." *Violence and Victims* 17: 35–47.

_____, A. F. Brennan, E. S. Hause, D. S. Polek, and L. L. Turledge. 1991. "Factors moderating physical and psychological symptoms of battered women." *Journal of Family Violence* 6 (1): 81–96.

_____, A. P. Neckerman, and J. Vormbrock. 1988. "Reactions to victimization and coping strategies of battered women: The ties that bind." *Clinical Psychology Review* 8: 373–390.

_____, D. S. Polek, E. S. Hause, L. H. Deaton, M. W. Bulger, and Z. D. Conway. 1989. "Factors predicting verdicts in cases where battered women kill their husbands." *Law and Human Behavior* 13: 253–269.

_____, R. D. Shilinglaw, and D. D. Dehart. 1997. "The Impact of elements of self-defense and objective versus subjective instructions on jurors' verdicts for battered women defendants." *Journal of Interpersonal Violence* 12 (5): 729–747.

Franklin, C. A., and N. E. Fearn. 2008. "Gender, race, and formal court decision-making outcomes: Chivalry/paternalism, conflict theory, or gender conflict?" *Journal of Criminal Justice* 36: 279–290.

Frieze, I. H. 2005a. "Female violence against intimate partners: An introduction." *Psychology of Women Quarterly* 29: 229–237.

_____. 2005b. *Hurting the one you love.* Belmont, CA: Thomson Wadsworth.

Frye v. U. S., 293 F. 1013 (D.C. Cir. Ct. 1923).

Gagne, P. 1998. *Battered women's justice: The movement for clemency and the politics of self-defense,* ed. R. D. Benford. New York: Twayne.

Gauthier, D.K., and W.B. Brankston. 2004. "'Who kills whom' revisited: A sociological study of variation in the sex ratio of spouse killings." *Homicide Studies* 8 (2): 96–122.

Gavanski, I., and G. L. Wells. 1989. "Counterfactual processing of normal and exceptional events." *Journal of Experimental Social Psychology* 25: 314–325.

Gelles, R. J. 1976. "Abused wives: Why do they stay?" *Journal of Marriage and the Family* 38: 659–668.

_____. 1987. *Family violence.* Newbury Park, CA: Sage.

_____. 1993. "Through a sociological lens: Social structure and family violence." In *Current controversies on family violence,* ed. R. J. Gelles. Newbury Park, CA: Sage.

_____. 1999. "The missing persons of domestic violence: Battered men." *The Women's Quarterly,* Autumn: 18–22.

_____, and C. P. Cornell. 1990. *Intimate violence in families.* Newbury Park, CA: Sage.

_____, and J. W. Harrop. 1989. "Violence, battering and psychological distress among women." *Journal of Interpersonal Violence* 4: 400–420.

_____, and L. Loseke. 1993. *Current controversies on family violence.* Newbury Park, CA: Sage.

General Electric Co. v. Joiner, 522 U.S. 136, 118 S. Ct. 512 (1997).

George, M. J. 1994. "Riding the donkey backwards: Men as the unacceptable victims of marital violence." *Journal of Men's Studies* 3 (2): 137–159.

Giles-Sims, J. 1983. *Wife battering: A systems theory approach.* The Guilford Press, New York.

Gillespie, C. K. 1989. *Justifiable homicide: Battered women, self defense and the law.* Columbus: Ohio State University Press.

Gilligan, C. 1982. *In a different voice: Psychological theory and women's development.* Cambridge, MA: Harvard University Press.

Gleason, W. J. 1993. "Mental disorders in battered women: An empirical study." *Violence and Victims* 8 (1): 53–68.

Gleicher, F., K. A. Kost, S. M. Baker, A. Strathman, S. A. Richman, and S. J. Sherman. 1990. "The role of counterfactual thinking in judgments of affect." *Personality and Social Psychology Bulletin* 16: 284–295.

Goetting, A. 1989. "Patterns of marital homicide: A comparison of husbands and wives." *Journal of Comparative Family Studies* 20: 231–354.

Gondolf, E. W. 1988. "The effect of batterer counseling on shelter outcome." *Journal of Interpersonal Violence* 3: 275–289.

_____. 1999. "Characteristics of court-mandated batterers in four cities: Diversity and dichotomies." *Violence Against Women* 5: 1277–1293.

_____, and E. Fisher. 1988. *Battered women as survivors: An alternative to treating learned helplessness.* Lexington, MA: Lexington Books.

_____, _____, and J. R. McFerron. 1991. "Racial differences among shelter residents: A comparison of Anglo, Black, and Hispanic battered women." *Journal of Family Violence* 3: 39–51.

Goodman, L. A., and D. Epstein. 2008. "Listening to battered women: A survivor-centered approach to advocacy, mental health, and justice." *Psychology of women.* Washington, D.C.: American Psychological Association.

Goodmark, L. 2007. "The punishment of Dixie Shanahan: Is there justice for battered women who kill?" *Kansas Law Review, Inc.* 55 L Rev 269.

Gordon, K., S. Burton, and L. Porter. 2004. "Predicting the intentions of women in domestic violence shelters to return to partners: Does forgiveness play a role?" *Journal of Family Psychology* 18 (2): 331–338.

Gordon, R.A. 1993. "Effect of strong versus weak evidence on the assessment of race stereotypic and race nonstereotypic crimes." *Journal of Applied Social Psychology* 23 (9): 734–749.

Graham-Kevan, N. and J. Archer. 2003. "Intimate terrorism and common couple violence. A test of Johnson's predictions in four British samples." *Journal of Interpersonal Violence* 18 (11): 1247–1259.

_____. 2005. "Investigating three explanations of women's relationship aggression." *Psychology of Women Quarterly* 29: 270–277.

Grant, C. A. (1995). Women who kill: The impact of abuse. *Issue in Mental Health Nursing,* 16, 315–326.

Greene, E., A. Raitz, and H. Linblad. 1989. "Jurors' knowledge of battered women." *Journal of Family Violence* 4 (2): 105–125.

Greven, P. 1996. "Christian beliefs foster family violence." In *Family Violence.* San Diego, CA: Greenhaven Press.

Grove, W. M., and C. R. Barden. 1999. "Protecting the integrity of the legal system: The admissibility of testimony from mental health experts under Daubert/Kuhmo analyses." *Psychology, Public Policy, and Law* 5 (1): 224–242.

Haley, J. 1992. A study of women imprisoned for homicide. Georgia Department of Corrections: 16.

Hamberger, L. K., and J. E. Hastings. 1986. "Personality correlates of men who abuse their partners: A cross-validation study." *Journal of Family Violence* 1: 37–49.

_____, J. M. Lohr, D. Bonge, and D. F. Tolin. 1996. "A large empirical typology of male spouse abusers and its relationship to dimensions of abuse." *Violence and Victims* 11: 277–292.

Hamel, M., S. Gallagher, and C. Soares. 2001. "The Rorschach: Here we go again." *Journal of Forensic Psychology Practice* 1 (3): 79–88.

_____, N. Graham-Kevan, and M. Prospero. 2008. Controlling and abusive tactics: Preliminary findings of a gender-inclusive questionnaire.

Hammon v. State, 52S02–0412-CR-510 (2005).

Hansen, J. O. 1992. "Is justice taking a beating?" *The Atlanta Constitution* (April 26): A1–A7.

Harrison, L. A., and C. W. Esqueda. 1999. "Myths and stereotypes of actors involved in domestic violence: Implications for domestic violence culpability attributions." *Aggression and Violent Behavior* 4 (2): 129–138.

Hassouneh, D. and N. Glass. 2008. "The influence of gender role stereotyping on women's experiences of female same-sex intimate partner violence." *Violence Against Women* 14: 310–325.

Heath, L., R. S. Tindale, J. Edwards, E. J. Posavac, and F. B. Bryant. 1994. "Applications of heuristics and biases to social issues." *Social psychological applications to social issues,* vol. 3, 91–115. New York: Plenum Press.

Heck v. Heck (1986).

Henderson, M., C. Mason, and D. Jeans. 2000.

"Australia's CEO challenge: Partnerships addressing domestic violence." *Australia's CEO Challenge*. http://www.engagingcommunities 2005.org/abstracts/Mason-Carolyn-final.pdf.

Henning, K., and L. Feder. 2005. "Criminal prosecution of domestic violence offenses: An investigation of factors predictive of court outcomes." *Criminal Justice and Behavior* 32 (6): 612–642.

Herman, J. 1997. *Trauma and recovery: The aftermath of violence- from domestic abuse to political terror*. New York: Basic Books.

Hilberman, E., and K. Munson. 1977–78. "Sixty battered women." *Victimology* 2: 460–470.

Hill, J. 2000. "The effects of sexual orientation in the courtroom: A double standard." *Journal of Homosexuality* 39: 93–111.

Hines, D. A., and K. Malley-Morrison. 2001. "Psychological effects of partner abuse against men: A neglected research area." *Psychology of Men & Masculinity* 2 (2): 75–85.

Hoff-Summers, C. 1996. *Who stole feminism: How women have betrayed women*. New York: Simon and Schuster. Inc.

Holmes, R. M. 1992, August. "Partner homicide: America's shame." *Law and Order*: 85–88.

Holtzworth-Munroe, A. 2005. "Male versus female intimate partner violence: Putting controversial findings into context." *Journal of Marriage and Family* 67 (5): 1120–1125.

_____, and K. Anglin. 1991. "The competency of responses given by maritally violent versus nonviolent men to problematic marital situations." *Violence and Victims* 6: 257–269.

_____, and G. Hutchinson. 1993. "Attributing negative intent to wife behavior: The attributions of martially violent versus non violent men." *Journal of Abnormal Psychology* 102: 206–211.

_____, N. Smutzler, and E. Sandin. 1997. "A brief review of the research on husband violence." *Aggression and Violent Behavior* 2 (2): 179–213.

Hotaling, G. T., M. A. Straus, A. J. and Lincoln. 1989. "Intrafamily violence and crime and violence outside the family." In *Physical violence in American families: Risk factors and adaptations to violence in 8,145 families*, eds. M. A. Straus and R. J. Gelles, 431–470. New Brunswick, CT: Transaction.

_____, and D. B. Sugarman. 1986. "An analysis of risk markers in husband to wife violence: The current state of knowledge." *Violence and Victims* 1: 101–124.

Hotton, T. 2001. "Spousal violence after marital separation." *Juristat* 21: 1–19.

Huntley, J. E., and M. Costanzo. 2003. "Sexual harassment stories: Testing a story-mediated model of juror decision-making in civil litigation." *Law and Human Behavior* 27 (1): 29–51.

Huss, M. T., A. J. Tomkins, C. P. Garbin, R. F. Schopp, and A. Kilian. 2006. "Battered women who kill their abusers: An examination of commonsense notions, cognitions, and judgments." *Journal of Interpersonal Violence* 21 (8): 1063–1080.

Ibn-Tamas v. U. S., 407 A.2d 626 (D.C. Ct. App. 1979).

Ibn-Tamas v. U. S., 455 A.2d 893 (D.C. Cir. Ct. 1983).

In re Heather, A., 60 Cal. Rptr 2d 315 (Ct. App. 1996).

In re John V., 5 Cal. App. 4th 1201, 1211 (1992).

In re Ranker, WL 761159 (Ohio Ct. App. 1996) (unpublished).

Innes, C., and L. Greenfield. 1990. *Violent state prisoners and their victims*. Washington, D.C.: U.S. Department of Justice.

Jacob's Institute of Women's Health. 1996. "Violence against women is under reported." *Family violence*. San Diego, CA: Greenhaven Press.

Jacobson, C., K. Mizga, and L. D'Orio. 2007, Winter. "Battered women homicide convictions and sentencing: The case for clemency." *Hastings Women's Law Journal* 18 (1): 31–66.

Jacobson, N., J. Gottman, E. Gortner, S. Burns, and J. Shortt. 1996. "Psychological factors in the longitudinal course of battering: When do the couples split up? When does the abuse decrease?" *Violence and Victims* 11 (4): 371–392.

Janoff-Bulman, R. 1979. "Characterological versus behavioral self-blame: Inquiries into depression and rape." *Journal of Personality and Social Psychology* 37: 1798–1809.

Jenkins, P., and B. Davidson. 1990. "Battered women in the criminal justice system: An analysis of gender stereotypes." *Behavioral Sciences and the Law* 8 (2): 171–180.

Johnson, H. 1996. "Professional women are often victims of domestic violence." In *Family Violence*. San Diego, CA: Greenhaven Press.

_____. 2000. "The role of alcohol in male partners' assault on wives." *Journal of Drug Issues* 30: 725–741.

Johnson, M. P. 1995. "Patriarchal terrorism and common couple violence: Two forms of violence against women." *Journal of Marriage and the Family* 57: 283–294.

_____. 2000. "Conflict and control: Images of symmetry and asymmetry in domestic violence." In *Couples in conflict*, eds. A. Booth, A. C. Crouter, and M. Clements. Hillsdale, NJ: Erlbaum.

_____, and K. J. Ferrero. 2000. "Research on domestic violence in the 1990's: Making distinctions." *Journal of Marriage and Family* 62: 948–963.

Jones, C. S., and M. F. Kaplan. 2003. "The effects of racially stereotypical crimes on juror decision-making and information processing strategies." *Basic and Applied Social Psychology* 25 (1): 1–13.

Joseph, J. 1997. "Women battering: A comparative analysis of Black and White women." In *Out of darkness: Contemporary perspectives on family violence*, eds. G.K. Kantor and J. L. Jasinski, 161–169. Thousand Oaks, CA.

Jurik, N. C., and P. Gregware. 1989. *A method for murder: An interactionist analysis of homicides by women*. School of Justice Studies. Tempe: Arizona State University.

_____, and D. T. Miller. 1986. "Norm theory: Comparing reality to its alternatives." *Psychological Review* 93: 136–153.

_____, and R. Winn. 1990. "Gender and homicide: A comparison of men and women who kill." *Violence and Victims* 5 (4): 227–242.

Kahneman, D., and A. Tversky. 1982. "The simulation heuristic." In *Judgment under uncertainty: Heuristics and biases*, eds. D. Kahneman, P. Slovic and A. Tversky, 201–208. New York: Cambridge University Press.

Kaliher v. Kaliher, 24796, Cir. Ct. Montgomery Co. (MD 1990).

Kantor, G. K., and M. Straus. 1989. "Response of victims and the police to assaults on wives." In *Physical violence in American families: Risk factors and adaptations to violence in 8,145 families*, eds. M. A. Straus and R. J. Gelles, 473–486. New Brunswick, NJ: Transaction.

Kasian, M., N.P. Spanos, C. A. Terrance, and S. Peebles. 1993. "Battered women who kill: Jury simulation and legal defenses." *Law and Human Behavior* 17 (3): 289–312.

Kaufman, J., and E. Zigler. 1987. "Do abused children become abusive parents?" *American Journal of Orthopsychiatry* 57 (2): 186–192.

Kellermann, A. 1992. "Men, women and murder." *The Journal of Trauma* 2.

Kemp, A., B. L. Green, C. Hovanitz, and E. I. Rawlings. 1995. "Incidence and correlates of posttraumatic stress disorder in battered women: Shelter and community samples." *Journal of Interpersonal Violence* 10 (1): 43–55.

_____, E. I. Rawlings, and B. L. Green. 1991. "Post traumatic stress syndrome in battered women: A shelter sample." *Journal of Traumatic Stress* 4: 137–148.

Kemp, C. H., F. N. Silverman, B. F. Steele, W. Druegenmuller, and H. Silver. 1962. "The battered child syndrome." *Journal of the American Medical Association* 181: 17–24.

Kernsmith, P. 2006. "Gender differences in the impact of family of origin violence on perpetrators of domestic violence." *Journal of Family Violence* 21 (2): 163–171.

Kershner, M., D. Long, and J. Anderson. 1998. "Abuse against women in rural Minnesota." *Public Health Nursing* 15 (6): 422–431.

Kessler, R., and S. Zhao. 1999. "The prevalence of mental illness." In *A handbook for the study of mental health*, eds. A. Horwitz and T. Scheid, 58–78. New York: Cambridge University Press.

Kilpatrick, D. G., R. Acierno, H. Resnick, B. E. Saunders, and C. L. Best. 1997. "A 2-year longitudinal analysis of the relationship between violence assault and substance use in women." *Journal of Counseling and Clinical Psychology* 65: 834–847.

Kinports, K. 1988. "Defending battered women's self-defense claims." *Oregon Law Review* 61 (1): 393–465.

Kocot, T., and L. Goodman. 2003. "The roles of coping and social support in battered women's mental health." *Violence Against Women* 9: 322–346.

Koepsell, J., M. Kernic, and V. Holt. 2006. "Factors that influence battered women to leave their abusive relationships." *Violence and Victims* 21 (2): 131–147.

Korlath, M. J. 1979. "Alcoholism in battered women: A report of advocacy services to clients in a detoxification facility." *Victimology: An International Journal* 4: 292–299.

Koss, M. P. 1996. "The measurement of rape victimization in crime surveys." *Criminal Justice and Behavior* 23 (1): 55–69.

_____, L. A. Goodman, A. Browne, L. F. Fitzgerald, G. P. Keita, and N. F. Russo. 1994. *No safe haven: Male violence against women at home, at work, and in the community*. American Psychological Association: Washington, D.C.

Kovera, M. B., M. B. Russano, and B. D. McAuliff. 2002. "Assessment of the commonsense psychology underlying Daubert: Legal decision makers' abilities to evaluate expert evidence in hostile work environment cases." *Psychology, Public Policy, and Law* 8 (2): 180–200.

Kruttschnitt, C. 2001. "Gender and violence." In *Women, crime, and criminal justice: Original feminist readings*, eds. C. M. Renzetti and L. Goodstein. Los Angeles, CA: Roxbury Publishing Company.

_____, and D. E. Green. 1984. "The sex-sanctioning issue: Is it history?" *America Sociological Review* 49: 541–551.

Kumho Tire Co. v. Carmichael, 526 U.S. 137, 119 S. Ct 1167 (1999).

Kwong, M. J., K. Bartholomew, and D. G. Dutton. 1999. "Gender differences in patterns of relationship violence in Alberta." *Canadian Journal of Behavioural Science* 13 (3): 150–160.

Labastida v. State, 112 Nev. 1502, 931 P.2d 1334 (1996).

LaFave, W., and A. Scott. 1972. *Handbook of criminal law.* St. Paul, MN: West Publishing Co.

_____, and _____. 1986. *Handbook of criminal law.* 2d ed. St. Paul, MN: West Publishing Co.

Lafferty, G. P. 1990. "Criminal law: Battered women and self defense; Pennsylvania allows expert evidence on battered woman syndrome as a basis for proving justification in the use of deadly force when evidence indicates defendant is victim of abuse: *Commonwealth v Stonehouse,* 521, Pa 41, 555 A.2d 772 (1989)." *Dickinson Law Review* 94: 553–560.

Lambert, A. J., and R. S. Wyer, Jr. 1990. "Stereotypes and social judgment: The effects of typicality and group heterogeneity." *Journal of Personality and Social Psychology* 59 (4): 676–691.

Lambert, L., and J. Firestone. 2000. "Economic context and multiple abuse techniques." *Violence Against Women* 6 (1): 49–67.

Landman, J. 1988. "Regret and elation following action and inaction." *Personality and Social Psychology Bulletin* 13: 524–536.

LaRoche, D. 2005. "Aspects of context and consequences of domestic violence-situational couple violence and intimate terrorism in Canada in 1999." Government of Quebec: Instit de la Statistique du Quebec, Quebec.

LaViolette, A.D. and O. W. Barnett. 1993. *It could happen to anyone: Why battered women stay.* New York: Sage.

Lempert, R. O., and S. A. Saltzburg. 1982. *A modern approach to evidence.* 2d ed. St. Paul, MN: West.

Lentz, S. 1999. "Revisiting the rule of thumb: An overview of history of wife abuse." In *Women and domestic violence: An interdisciplinary approach,* ed. L. Feder, 9–27. Binghampton, NY: Haworth.

Letellier, P. 1996. "Gays are often victims of domestic violence." In *Family violence.* San Diego, CA: Greenhaven Press.

Levinson, D. 1988. "Family violence in cross cultural perspective." In *Handbook of family violence,* eds. V. B. Van Hasselt, R. L. Morrison, A. S. Bellack, and M. Hersen, 435–456. New York: Plenum.

_____. 1989. *Family violence in a cross-cultural perspective.* Newbury Park, CA: Sage.

Levit, H. I. 1991. "Battered women: Syndrome versus self defense." *American Journal of Forensic Psychology* 9 (1): 29–35.

Levit, N. and R. Verchick. 2006. *Feminist legal theory: A primer.* New York: New York University Press.

Lewis v. State, S 95 A. 0250 (Ga. 1995).

Lindhorst, T., and E. Tajima. 2008. "Reconceptualizing and operationalizing context in survey research on intimate partner violence." *Journal of Interpersonal Violence* 23 (3): 362–388.

Lippman, L. G., and D. J. Selder. 1992. "Mental practice: Some observations and speculations." *Revista de Psicologia del Deporte* 1: 17–25.

Loftus, G. R., and E. F. Loftus. 1976. *Human memory: The processing of information.* Hillsdale, NJ: Lawrence Erlbaum.

Lombroso, C., and W. Ferrero. 1895. *The female offender.* London: T. Fisher Unwin.

Lord, C. G., D. M. Desforges, S. Fein, M. A. Pugh, and M. A. Lepper. 1994. "Typicality effects in attitudes toward social policies: A concept-mapping approach." *Journal of Personality and Social Psychology* 66 (4): 658–673.

_____, _____, S. L. Ramsey, G. R. Trezza, and M. R. Lepper. 1991. "Typicality effects in attitude-behavior consistency: Effects of category discrimination and category knowledge." *Journal of Experimental Social Psychology* 27: 550–575.

Loseke, D. R. 1992a. *The battered woman and shelters.* Albany: State University of New York Press.

_____. 1992b. *The battered woman and shelters: The social construction of wife abuse.* New York: State University of New York Press.

_____, R. J. Gelles, and M. M. Cavanaugh. 2005. "Introduction: Understanding controversies on family violence." In *Current controversies on family violence,* 2d ed., eds. D. R. Loseke, R. J. Gelles, and M. M. Cavanaugh. Thousand Oaks, CA: Sage.

_____, and D. Kurtz. 2003. "Men's violence toward women is the serious social problem." In *Current controversies on family violence,* eds. D. R. Loseke, R. J. Gelles, and M. M. Cavanaugh. Thousand Oaks, CA: Sage.

Lurigio, A. J., J. S. Carroll, and L. J. Stalans. 1994. "Understanding judges' sentencing decisions: Attributions of responsibility and story construction." In *Applications of heuristics and biases to social issues,* eds. L. Heath, et al., 91–115. New York: Plenum.

Macchietto, J. G. 1992. "Aspects of male victimization and female aggression: Implications for counseling men." *Journal of Mental Health Counseling* 14 (3): 372–392.

MacCorquodale, P., and G. Jensen. 1993. "Women in the law: Partners or tokens?" *Gender and Society* 7: 582–593.

MacDonald, L. 1989. "Helping with the termination of an assaultive relationship." In *Intervening with assaulted women: Current theory, research, and practice*, eds. B. Pressman and G. C. Rothery, 93–110. Hillsdale, NJ: Lawrence Erlbaum.

MacKinnon, C. 1979. *Sexual harassment of working women: A case of sex discrimination*. Connecticut: Emerson.

_____. 1982. "Feminism, Marxism, method, and the state: An agenda for theory." *Signs* 7 (3): 515–544.

_____. 2001. *Sex equality: On difference and dominance*. Colorado: Westview Press.

MacKinnon, C. A. 1982. "Toward feminist jurisprudence." *Stanford Law Review* 34: 724–725.

_____. 1989. *Toward a feminist theory of the state*. Cambridge, MA: Harvard University Press.

MacRae, C. N., and A. B. Milne. 1992. "A curry for your thoughts: Empathetic effects on counterfactual thinking." *Personality and Social Psychology Bulletin* 18: 625–630.

_____, _____, and R. J. Griffiths. 1993. "Counterfactual thinking and the perception of criminal behavior." *British Journal of Psychology* 84: 221–226.

Maguigan, H. 1991. "Battered women and self-defense: Myths and misconceptions in current reform proposals." *University of Pennsylvania Law Review* 140 (2): 379–460.

Mahoney, M. 1991. "Legal images of battered women: Redefining the issue of separation." *Michigan Law Review* 90.

Malley-Morrison, K., and D. A. Hines. 2004. *Family violence in a cultural perspective. Defining, understanding, and combating abuse*. Thousand Oaks, CA: Sage.

Malloy, K. A., K. McCoskey, N. Grigsby, and D. Gardner. 2003. "Women's use of violence within intimate relationships." *Journal of Aggression, Maltreatment, & Trauma* 6: 37–59.

Malone, J., K. D. O'Leary, and A. Tyree. 1989. "Generalizations and containment: Difference effects of past aggression for husbands and wives." *Journal of Marriage and the Family* 51: 687–697.

Mann, C. R. 1990. "Black female homicide in the United States." *Journal of Interpersonal Violence* 5: 176–201.

_____. 1996. *When women kill*. Albany: State University of New York Press.

Marley v. State, 49S02-0009-CR-521 (Ind. Ct. App. 1996).

Martin, M. E. 1997. "Double your trouble: Dual arrest in family violence." *Journal of Family Violence* 12: 139–157.

Martinson, D., M. MacCrimmon, I. Grants, and C. Boyle. 1991. "A forum on *LaVallee v. R*: Women and self defense." *University of British Columbia Law Review* 25: 23–68.

Maryland Special Joint Committee 1989. *Gender Bias in the Courts* 20: 127.

Mather, V. M. 1988. "The skeleton in the closet: The battered woman syndrome, self defense and expert testimony." *Mercer Law Review* 39 (2): 545–589.

McCarthy, C. 1991, July 23. "Countering violence at home." *Washington Post*: D13.

McClennen, J.C. 2005. "Domestic violence between same-gender partners." *Journal of Interpersonal Violence* 20 (2): 149–154.

_____, A. B. Summers, and C. Vaughan. 2002 "Gay men's domestic violence: Dynamics, help-seeking behaviors, and correlates." *Journal of Gay and Lesbian Social Service* 14 (1): 23–49.

McCormick, J. S., A. Maric, M. C. Seto, and H. E. Barbaree. 1998. "Relationship to victim predicts sentence length in sexual assault cases." *Journal of Interpersonal Violence* 13 (3): 413–420.

McCue, M. L. 1995. *Domestic violence*. Santa Barbara, CA: ABC-CLIO.

McElroy, W. 1996. "Women are not victims more often than men." In *Family violence*. San Diego, CA: Greenhaven Press.

McKeever, M., and N. Wolfinger. 2001. "Reexamining the economic costs of marital disruption for women." *Social Science Quarterly* 82 (1): 202–217.

McMahon, M. 1999. "Battered women and bad science: The limited validity and utility of battered woman syndrome." *Psychiatry, Psychology and Law* 6 (1): 23–49.

Meier, J. 1997. "Domestic violence, character, and social change in the welfare reform debate." *Law and Policy* 19 (2): 205–263.

Melior Group, V. Kramer & Associates. 2001. "Final report on perceptions and occurrences of gender bias in the courtroom." http://www.friendsfw.org/PA_Courts/Race_Gender_Link.pdf (accessed June 2008).

Merrill, G. S., and V. A. Wolfe. 2000. "Battered gay men: An explanation of abuse, help seeking, and why they stay." *Journal of Homosexuality* 39 (2): 1–30.

Miller, D. T., and C. McFarland. 1986. "Counterfactual thinking and victim compensation: A test of norm theory." *Personality and Social Psychology Bulletin* 12: 513–519.

_____, W. Turnbull, and C. McFarland. 1990. "Counterfactual thinking and social perception: Thinking about what might have been." In *Advances in experimental social psychology*, vol. 23, ed. M. P. Zanna, 305–331. Orlando, FL: Academic Press.

Miller, T., M. Cohen, and B. Wiersema. 1996. *The extent and costs of crime victimization: A new look (*NCJ 155281).Washington, D.C.: U.S. Department of Justice, National Institute of Justice.

Mills, J. F., and D. Kroner. 2003. "Antisocial constructs in predicting institutional violence among violent offenders and child molesters." *International Journal of Offender Therapy and Comparative Criminology* 47 (3): 324–334.

Mills, L. G. 2003. *Insult to injury: Rethinking our responses to intimate abuse.* Princeton: Princeton University Press.

Moewe, M. C. 1992. "The hidden violence: For richer and for poorer." *Fort Worth Star-Telegram.*

Moffitt, T., R. Robins, and A. Caspi. 2001. "A couples analysis of partner abuse with implications for abuse prevention policy." *Criminology & Public Policy* 1: 5–36.

_____, A. Caspi, M. Rutter, and P. A. Silva. 2001. *Sex differences in antisocial behavior.* Cambridge, England: Cambridge University Press.

Monahan, J., and L. Walker. 1993. *Social science in law: Cases and materials.* New York: Foundation Press.

_____, and _____. 2002. *Social science in law: Cases and materials,* 5th ed. New York: Foundation Press.

Münsterberg, H. 1908. *On the Witness Stand.* New York: Doubleday, Page and Co.

National Clearinghouse for the Defense of Battered Women (NCDBW). (1997). Philadelphia: Legislative Update.

"National Clearinghouse on Marital Rape and Date Rape." 2005. http://members.aol.com/ncmdr/state_law_chart.html R (accessed April 21, 2008).

National Institute of Mental Health. 2000. Depression research (Report No. 00-4501). Bethesda, MD: Author.

National Judicial Education Program. 2008. Philadelphia: Legislative Update.

National Organization for Women. 2001. Violence Against Women in the United States. Retrieved November 25, 2001 from http://www.org/issues/violence/stats.html.

Ninth Circuit Task Force on Gender Bias. 1993. "Executive summary of the preliminary report of the ninth circuit task force on gender bias." *Stanford Law Review* 45: 2171–2172.

Novello, A., M. Rosenberg, L. Saltzman, and J. Shosky. 1992. "From the surgeon general, U.S. Public Health Service." *The Journal of the American Medical Association* 267 (23): 3132.

Ohio Rev. Code Ann. Stat. Sec 2901–06 (A) (1990).

Okun, L. 1988. "Termination or resumption of cohabitation in women battering relationships: A statistical study." In *Coping with family violence: Research and policy perspectives,* eds. G. T. Hotaling, D. Finkelhor, J. T. Kirkpatrick, and M. A. Straus, 107–119. Thousand Oaks, CA: Sage.

O'Leary, R. D. 1993. "Through a psychological lens: Personality traits, personality disorders and levels of violence." In *Current controversies on family violence,* ed. R. J. Gelles. Newbury Park, CA: Sage.

O'Shea, K. A. 1993. "Women on death row." In *Women prisoners: A forgotten population,* eds. B. R. Fletcher, L. D. Shaver, and D. G. Moon, 75–91. Westport, CT: Praeger Publishers/Greenwood Publishing Group, Inc.

Osthoff, S. 2001. "When victims become defendants: Battered women charged with crimes." In *Women, crime, and criminal justice,* eds. C. M. Renzetti and L. Goodstein. Los Angeles: Roxbury.

_____, and H. Maguigan. 2004. "Explaining without pathologizing: Testimony on battering and its effects." In *Current controversies on family violence,* eds. D. R. Loseke, R. J. Gelles, and M. M. Cavanaugh. Thousand Oaks: Sage.

PA Stat. Ann. Tit. 18, 505.1(b), 1991

Pagelow, M.D. 1981. *Woman-battering: Victims and their experiences.* Beverly Hills, CA: Sage.

_____. 1984. *Family violence.* New York: Praeger.

_____. 1992. "Adult victims of domestic abuse." *Journal of Interpersonal Violence, 7* (1), 87–120.

Panchanadeswaran, S., and L. McCloskey. 2007. "Predicting the timing of women's departure from abusive relationships." *Journal of Interpersonal Violence* 22 (1): 50–65.

Parry, J., and E. Y. Drogan. 2000. *Criminal law handbook on psychiatric and psychological evidence and testimony.* Washington, D.C.: American Bar Association.

Parsons, D. 1996, Summer. "Insurance companies sock it to battered women." *On the Issues:* 14–15.

Pease, K., and G. Laycock. 1996. Revictimization: Reducing the heat on hot victims. Research in action. Washington, D. C: National Institute of Justice.

Pence, E., and M. Paymar. 1993. *Education groups for men who batter: The Duluth model.* New York: Springer Publishing Co.

Pennington, N., and R. Hastie. 1986. "Evidence evaluation in complex decision making." *Journal of Personality and Social Psychology* 51: 242–258.

People v. Bazzetta, 444 Mich. 887; 511 N.W.2d 688 (1990).

People v. Bush, 84 3d 294 148 (Cal. Ct. App. 1978).

People v. Callahan, 124 4th 198 (Cal. Ct. App. 2004).

People v. Colberg, 182 Misc. 2d 798, 701 N.Y. S.2d 608 (1999).

People v. Emick, 103 A.D.2d 643, 481 N.Y.S.2d 552 (1984).

People v. Giacalone, 242 Mich. 16, 217 N.W. 758 (1928).

People v. Hernandez, 2d Crim. B120703 (Cal. 2000).

People v. Wilkinson, A094008 (Cal. 2002).

People v. Yaklich, 744 P.2d 504 (Colo. 1988).

People v. Yaklich, 833 P.2d 758 (Colo. Ct. App. 1991).

Pierce, G., S. Spaar, and B. Briggs. 1988, November. Character of calls for police work. NIJ Report. Washington, D.C.: Department of Justice.

Pizzey, E. 1974. *Scream quietly or the neighbors will hear.* London: If Books.

Plass, P. S. 1993. "African American family homicide: Patterns in partner, parent, and child victimization, 1985–1987." *Journal of Black Studies* 23 (4): 515–538.

Pleck, E. 1987. *Domestic tyranny.* Oxford, UK: Oxford University Press.

———. 1989. "Criminal approaches to family violence 1640–1980." In *Crime and justice: A review of research,* vol. 11, eds. L. Ohlin and M. Tonry, 19–58. Chicago: University of Chicago Press.

Plumm, K. M., and C. A. Terrance. 2009. "Battered women who kill: The impact of expert testimony and empathy induction in the courtroom." *Violence Against Women* 15 (2): 186–205.

Potoczniak, M. J., J. E. Mourot, M. Crosbie-Burnett, and D. J. Potoczniak. 2003. "Legal and psychological perspectives on same-sex domestic violence: A multisystematic approach." *Journal of Family Violence* 17 (2): 252–259.

Prospero, M. 2008. "The effect of coercion on aggression and mental health among reciprocally violence couples." *Journal of Family Violence* 23 (3): 195–202.

Ptacek, J. 1988. "Why do men batter their wives?" In *Feminist perspectives on wife abuse,* eds. K. YIlo and M. Bograd, 133–157. Newbury Park, CA: Sage.

Ragatz, L., and B. F. Russell. "Decisions of guilt depending on sexual orientation and the role of benevolent sexism," *Journal of Social Psychology.*

Rand, M. R. 1997. *Violence-related injuries treated in hospital emergency departments.* Washington, D.C.: U.S. Department of Justice, Bureau of Justice Statistics.

Rapaport, E. 1991. "The death penalty and gender discrimination." *Law and Society Review* 25: 67.

Raphael, J. 1995. "Domestic violence and welfare receipt: The unexplored barrier to employment." *Georgetown Journal on Fighting Poverty III:* 29–34.

———. 1996. "Prisoners of abuse: Policy implications of the relationship between domestic violence and welfare receipt." *Clearinghouse Review* 30: 186–194.

———, and R. M. Tolman. 1997. "Trapped by poverty, trapped by abuse: New evidence documenting the relationship between domestic violence and welfare." http://www.ssw.umich.edu/trapped /pubs_trapped.pdf.

Rasche, C. E. 1990. "Early models for contemporary thought on domestic violence and women who kill their mates: A review of the literature from 1895 to 1970." *Women and Criminal Justice* 1 (2): 31–53.

———. 1993. "Given reason for violence in intimate relationships." In *Homicide: The victim offender connection,* ed. A. Wilson, 88. Cincinnati, OH: Anderson.

Rauma, D. 1984. "Post-prison experiences of released offenders: The impact of income on crime." *Dissertation Abstracts International* 45 (5-A): 1536–1537.

Reddy, P., A. Knowles, J. Mulvany, M. McMahon, and I. Freckelton. 1997. "Attributions about domestic violence: A study of community attitudes." *Psychiatry, Psychology, and Law* 4 (2): 125–145.

Regina v. LaVallee, 65 C.R.3d 387 (1988).

Rennison, C. M. 2001, June. *Criminal victimization 2000: Changes 1999–2000 with trends 1993–2000.* Washington D.C.: Bureau of Justice Statistics.

———, and S. Welchans. 2000. *Intimate partner violence.* Washington, D.C.: Bureau of Justice Statistics.

Renzetti, C. 1992. *Violent betrayal: Partner abuse in lesbian relationships.* Newbury Park, CA: Sage.

"Report of the Oregon Supreme Court/Oregon State Bar Task Force on Gender Fairness, 1998." https://scholarsbank.uoregon.edu/xmlui/bitstream/handle/1794/1026/GENDERpercent20Judgepercent20Fullpercent20Report.pdf?sequence=3 (accessed June, 2007).

"Report of the Third Circuit Task Force on Equal Treatment in the Courts." 1997. *Villanova Law Review* 42: 1355–1539.

Resnick, H., D. Kilpatrick, B. Dansky, B. Saunders, and C. Best. 1993. "Prevalence of civilian trauma and posttraumatic stress disorder in a representative national sample of women." *Journal of Consulting and Clinical Psychology* 61 (6): 984–991.

Resnik, J. 1991. "Naturally without gender: Women, jurisdiction, and the federal courts." *New York University Law Review* 66: 1682–1684.

Revised Missouri Statutes. 563.026 to 563.033 (1988).

_____. 563.026 to 563.033 (1996).

Rhatigan, D., and A. Street. 2005. "The impact of intimate partner violence on decisions to leave dating relationships: a test of the investment model." *Journal of Interpersonal Violence* 20 (12): 1580–1597

Richardson, J. T. 1998. *A case law survey of social and behavioral science evidence after Daubert*. Unpublished manuscript.

Richey-Mann, C. 1996. *When women kill*. New York: New York Press.

_____. 1989. *Representing ... battered women who kill*. Springfield, IL: Charles C Thomas.

Rigakos, G. S. 1995. "Constructing the symbolic complainant: Police subculture and the non-enforcement of protection orders for battered women." *Violence and Victims* 10 (3): 227–246.

Riger, S., P. Foster-Fishman, J. Nelson-Kuna, and B. Curran. 1995. "Gender bias in courtroom dynamics." *Law and Human Behavior* 19 (5): 465–480.

Riggs, D. S., and K.D. O'Leary. 1992. *Violence between dating partners: Background and situational correlates of courtship aggression*. Manuscript submitted for publication.

Roberts, J. W. 2003. "Between the heat of passion and cold blood: Battered woman's syndrome as an excuse for self-defense in non-confrontational homicides." *Law and Psychology Review* (27): 135–156.

Roesch, R., S. D. Hart, and J. R. P. Ogloff. 1999. *Psychology and law: The state of the discipline*. Dordrecht, Netherlands: Kluwer Academic Publishers.

Romero, D., W. Chavkin, P. H. Wise, and L. A. Smith. 2003. "Domestic violence and poverty." *Violence Against Women*, special issue 9 (10): 1231–1244.

Rosenbaum, A., and R. Maiuro. 1990. "Perpetrators of spouse abuse." In *Treatment of family violence*, eds. R. T. Ammerman and M. Hersen, 280–389. New York: John Wiley.

_____, and K. D. O'Leary. 1981. "Marital violence: Characteristics of abusive couples." *Journal of Consulting and Clinical Psychology* 49: 63–71.

Rosewater, L.B. 1985. "Schizophrenic, borderline, or battered?" In *Handbook of feminist therapy: Women's issues on psychotherapy*, eds. L.B. Rosewater and L. E. A. Walker, 215–225. New York: Springer.

Rothenberg, B. 2002. "The success of the battered woman syndrome: An analysis of how cultural arguments succeed." *Sociological Forum* 17 (1): 81–103.

_____. 2003. "'We don't have time for social change.' Cultural compromise and the battered woman syndrome." *Gender & Society* 17 (5): 771–787.

Roy, M. 1977. *Battered women*. New York: Van Nostrand Reinhold Company.

Rucker v. Davis, 237 F.3d 1113, 1129 (9th Cir. Ct. 2001).

Rusbult, C. E., and J. M. Martz. 1995. "Remaining in an abusive relationship: An investment model analysis of nonvoluntary dependence." *Personality and Social Psychology Bulletin* 21 (6): 558–571.

Russell, B. L. 1999. Attitudes towards battered women who kill: Prototypes and counterfactual thinking in judgments of culpability. Unpublished doctoral diss., St. Louis Univ.

_____, and L. S. Melillo. 2006. "Attitudes toward battered women who kill: Defendants typicality and judgments of culpability." *Criminal Justice and Behavior* 33: 219–241.

_____, L. Messerli, and S. W. Kraus. 2009, April. "Does expert testimony of the battered person syndrome affect attitudes towards abused? An examination of sexual orientation and gender. Perceptions of self-defense as a function of participant gender, expert testimony, sexual orientation of the couple and perpetrator gender." Midwestern Psychological Association, Chicago, IL.

_____, and D. L. Oswald. 2002. "Sexual coercion and victimization among college men: The role of lovestyles." *Journal of Interpersonal Violence* 17 (3): 273–285.

_____, L. Ragatz, and S. W. Kraus. 2009. "Does ambivalent sexism influence verdicts for heterosexual and homosexual defendants in a self-defense case?" *Journal of Family Violence* 24: 145–157.

_____, _____, and _____. 2010. "Self-defense and legal decision making: The role of defendant and victim gender and gender neutral expert testimony of the battered partner's syndrome." *Partner Abuse*.

Saathoff, A., and E. Stoffel. 1999. "Community-based domestic violence services." *The future of children: Domestic violence and children* 9 (3): 97–110.

Saltzman, L., J. Fanslow, P. McMahon, and G. Shelley. 1999. "Intimate partner violence surveillance: Uniform definitions and recommended data elements." Atlanta, GA: Centers for Disease Control and Prevention.

Sarre, R. 1994. "Uncertainties & possibilities: A discussion of selected criminal justice issues in contemporary Australia." *Alternative Law Journal* 20 (5): 252–257.

Saunders, D. G. 1995. "The tendency to arrest victims of domestic violence: A preliminary analysis of officer characteristics." *Journal of Interpersonal Violence* 10 (2): 147–158.

_____. 2002. "Are physical assaults by wives and girlfriends a major social problem?" *Violence Against Women* 8 (12): 1424–1448.

Schaffer, M. 1990. "*R. v. LaVallee*: A review essay." *Ottawa Law Review* 22: 607–624.

Schechter, S. 1982. *Women and male violence: The visions and struggles of the battered woman's movement.* Boston: South End Press.

Schneider, E. M. 1980. "Equal rights to trial for women: Sex bias in the law of self defense." *Harvard Civil Rights and Civil Liberties Law Review* 115: 623–641.

_____. 1986. "Describing and changing: Women's self defense work and the problem of expert testimony on battering." *Women's Rights Law Reporter* 9: 195–225.

_____. 2000. *Battered women and feminist lawmaking.* New Haven, CT: Yale University Press.

_____, and S. B. Jordan. 1981. "Representation of women who defend themselves in response to physical or sexual assault." In *Self-defense cases: Theory and practice,* ed. E. Bochnak, Charlottesville, VA: Michie Law.

Schrager, A. 2008. "Does one abused woman = 100 abused puppies?" *More Intelligent Life.* http://www.moreintelligentlife.com/story/does-one-abused-woman-100-abused-puppies.

Schuller, R. A. 1992. "The impact of battered woman syndrome evidence on jury decision processes." *Law and Human Behavior* 16: 597–620.

_____. 1994. "Applications of battered woman syndrome in the courtroom." In *Violence and the law,* eds. M. Costanzo and S. Oskamp. Thousand Oaks, CA: Sage.

_____, and J. Cripps. 1998. "Expert evidence pertaining to battered women: The impact of gender of expert and timing of testimony." *Law and Human Behavior* 22 (1): 17–31.

_____, and P. A. Hastings. 1996. "Trials of battered women who kill: The impact of alternative forms of expert evidence." *Law and Human Behavior* 20 (2): 131–146.

_____, and S. Rzepa. 2002. "Expert testimony pertaining to battered woman syndrome: Its impact on jurors' decisions." *Law and Human Behavior* 26 (6): 655–673.

_____, V. L. Smith, and J. M. Olson. 1994. "Ju-

rors' decisions in trials of battered women who kill: The role of prior beliefs and expert testimony." *Journal of Applied Social Psychology* 24 (4): 316–337.

_____, D. Terry, and B. McKimmie. 2001. "The impact of an expert's gender on jurors' decisions." *Law & Psychology Review* 25: 59–79.

_____, and N. Vidmar. 1992. "Battered woman syndrome evidence in the courtroom: A review of the literature." *Law and Human Behavior* 16: 273–291.

_____, E. Wells, S. Rzepa, and M. A. Klippenstine. 2004. "Rethinking battered woman syndrome evidence: The impact of alternative forms of expert testimony on mock jurors' decisions." *Canadian Journal of Behavioural Science* 36 (2), 12–136.

Seligman, M. E. P. 1975. *Helplessness: On depression, development, and death.* San Francisco: Freeman.

Shaffer, M. 1997. "The battered woman syndrome revisited: Some complicating thoughts five years after *R. v. LaVallee*." *The University of Toronto Law Journal* 47 (1): 1–33.

Shainess, N. 1977. "Psychological aspects of wifebeating." In *Battered women,* ed. M. Roy. New York: Van Nostrand Reinhold Company.

Sheehy, E. A., J. Stubbs, and J. Tolmie. 1992. "Defending the battered women on trial: The battered woman syndrome and its limitations." *Criminal Law Journal* 16: 369–394.

Shepard, M. F., and E. L. Pence, eds. 1999. *Coordination community responses to domestic violence: Lessons from Duluth and beyond.* Thousand Oaks, CA: Sage.

Simon, T., and C. Perkins. 2001. *Injuries from violent crime, 1992–1998: Special Report.* U. S. Department of Justice, Bureau of Justice Statistics.

Slobogin, C. 1998. "Psychiatric evidence in criminal trials: To junk or not to junk?" *William and Mary Law Review* 40 (1).

Smith, S. M., K. H. Rosen, K. A. Middleton, A. L. Busch, K. Lundberg, and R. P. Carlton. 2000. "The intergenerational transmission of spouse abuse: A meta-analysis." *Journal of Marriage and the Family* 62: 640–654.

Smith, V. L. 1991. "Prototypes in the courtroom: Lay representations of legal concepts." *Journal of Personality and Social Psychology* 61 (6): 857–872.

_____. 1993. "When prior knowledge and law collide: Helping jurors use the law." *Law and Human Behavior* 17: 507–536.

Smith v. State, 247 Ga. 612, 277 S.E.2d 678 (1981).

Snell, T. L. 1991. 1994, March. *Women in prison, survey of state prison inmates.* Bureau of Statistics: 3–6.

Snow, D., T. Sullivan, S. Swan, D. Tate, and I. Klein. 2006. "The Role of Coping and Problem Drinking in Men's Abuse of Female Partners: Test of a Path Model." *Violence and Victims* 21 (3): 267–285.

Snyder, D. K., and I. A. Fruchtman. 1981. "Differential patterns of wife abuse: A data-based typology." *Journal of Consulting and Clinical Psychology* 49: 878–885.

_____, and N. S. Scheer. 1981. "Predicting disposition following brief residence at a shelter for battered women." *American Journal of Community Psychology* 9: 559–566.

Sokoloff, N. J., and I. Dupont. 2005a. "Domestic violence at the intersection of race, class, and gender: Challenges and contribution to understanding violence against marginalized women in diverse communities." *Violence Against Women* 11: 38–64.

_____, and _____. 2005b. "Domestic violence: Examining the intersections of race, class, and gender: An introduction." In *Domestic violence at the margins*, eds. N. Sokoloff and C. Pratt, 1–14. New Brunswick, NJ: Rutgers University Press.

Sorenson, C. A., and S. B. Taylor. 2005. "Female aggression toward male intimate partners: An examination of social norms in a community based sample." *Psychology of Women Quarterly* 29 (1): 78–86.

Sorenson, S. B., and C.A. Telles. 1991. "Self-reports of spousal violence in Mexican- American and non–Hispanic white population." *Violence and Victims* 6: 3–15.

Spohn, C. 2000. "Thirty years of sentencing reform: The quest for racially neutral sentencing process." In *Criminal justice 2000: Volume 3. Policies, processes, and decisions of the criminal justice system*, ed. J. Horney, 427–501. Washington D.C.: U.S. Department of Justice, National Institute of Justice.

_____, and D. Holleran. 2004. "Prosecuting sexual assault: A comparison of charging decisions in sexual assault cases involving strangers, acquaintances, and intimate partners, final report." National Institute of Justice. *http://www.ncjrs.gov/pdffiles1/nij/199720. pdf*.

Stangor, C., and M. Schaller. 1996. "Stereotypes as individual and collective representations." In *Foundations of stereotypes and stereotyping*, eds. C. N. Macrae, M. Hewstone, and C. Stangor, 3–37. New York: Guilford Press.

Star, B., C. G. Clark, K. M. Goetz, and L. O'-Malia. 1979. "Psychosocial aspects of wife battering." *Social Casework* 60: 479–487.

Stark, E. 1992. "Framing and reframing battered women." In *Domestic violence: The changing criminal justice responses*, eds. E. Buzawa and C. Buzawa, 271–292. Westwood, CT: Auburn House.

_____. 2006. "Commentary on Johnson's 'Conflict and control: Gender symmetry and asymmetry in domestic violence.'" *Violence Against Women, 12 (11)*, 1019–1025.

_____, and A. Flitcraft. 1983. "Social knowledge, social policy, and the abuse of women: The case against patriarchal benevolence." In *The dark side of families: Current family violence research*, eds. D. Finkelhor, R. J. Gelles, G. T. Hotaling, and M. A. Straus, 330–348. Thousand Oaks, CA: Sage.

Starplus.com. 2007. http://www.starpulse.com/news/index.php/2007/06/12/amywinehouse_ (accessed April 15, 2008).

State v. Allery, 101 Wash. 2d 591, 682 P.2d 312 (1984).

State v. Allison, 845 S.W.2d 642 (Mo. Ct. App. W.D. 1992).

State v. Anaya, 456 A.2d 1255 (Me. 1983).

State. v. Bailey, 733, 601 S.E.2d 861 (N.C. Ct. App. 2004).

State v. Blackman, 875 S.W.2d 122 (Mo. Ct. App. E.D. 1994).

State v. Bobbitt, 415 So.2d 724 (Fla. 1982).

State v. Ciskie, Wash. 2d 263, 751 P.2d 1165 (1988).

State v. Corujo, 744 S.W.2d 66 (Mo. Ct. App. S.D. 1982).

State v. Dozier, 225 S.E.2d W.Va. (1979).

State v. Dunn, 5ct. 85-CR-59T (Kan. 1992).

State v. Felton, 110 Wis. 2d 485 (1983).

State v. Fincher, 655 S.W.2d 54, 58 (Mo. Ct. App. W. D. 1983).

State v. Frazier, 30 Kan. Ct. App. 2d 398 (2002).

State v. Gallegos, 104 N.M. 247, 250, 719 P.2d 1268, 1271 (N.M. Ct. App.1986).

State v. Gardner, 606 S.W.2d 236 (Mo. Ct. App.1980).

State v. Goforth, 721 S.W.2d 756 (Mo. Ct. App.1986).

State v. Green, Cir. Ct. (AR 1994).

State v. Hundley, 693 P2.d 475, 480 (Kan. 1985).

State v. Isom, 660 S.W.2d 739 (Mo. Ct. App. E.D. 1983).

State v. Janes, 121 Wash. 2d 220, 850 P.2d 495 (1992, 1993).

State v. Kelly, 478 A.2d 364, 97 N.J. 178 (1984).

State v. Lambert, 312 S.E. 2d 31 W. Va. (1984).

State v. Leidholm, 33 N.W. 2d 811 N.D. (1983).

State v. Long, 192 Wis. Ct. App. 2d 762, 532 N.W.29 468 (1995).

State v. Lundgren, 90-CR-019 (1994).

State v. Maupin, 1991 WL 197420 (Tenn. Crim. Ct. App.1991).

State v. McBride, IK 80-05-0058 (Del. 1982).

State v. McGowan, 621 S.W.2d 557 (Mo. Ct. App. 1981).

State v. Norman, 384 366 S.E. 2d586 (N.C. Ct. App.1988).

State v. Nunn, 356 N. W. 2d 601 (Iowa Ct. App.1984).

State v. Sales, 285 S.C. 113, 328 S.E.2d. 619 (1985).

State v. Shaw, 185, Conn. 372, 441 A.2d 561 (1981).

State v. Stewart, 243 Kan. 639 (1988).

State v. Thomas, 423 N.E. 2d 137; 66 Ohio St.2d 518 (1981).

State v. Wanrow, 88 Wash. 2d 221, 559 P.2d 548 (1977).

State v. Williams, 787 S.W.2d 308 (Mo. Ct. App. E.D. 1990).

State v. Wyatt, 482 S.E.2d 147 (W.Va. 1996).

Steinmetz, S. K. 1980. "Women and violence: Victims and perpetrators." *American Journal of Psychotherapy* 34 (3): 334–350.

Stets, J. E., and M. A. Straus. 1990. "Gender differences in reporting of marital violence and its medical and psychological consequences." In *Physical violence in American families: Risk factors and adaptations to violence in 8,145 families,* eds. M. A. Straus and R. J. Gelles, 151–165. New Brunswick, NJ: Transaction.

Stith, S. M., and S. C. Farley. 1993. "A predictive model of spousal violence." *Journal of Family Violence* 8: 183–201.

_____, K. Rosen, K. Middleton, A. Busch, K. Lundeberg, and R. Carlton. 2000. "The intergenerational transmission of spouse abuse: A meta-analysis." *Journal of Marriage and the Family* 62 (3): 640–654.

Straus, M. A. 1973. "A general systems approach to a theory of violence between family members." *Social Science Information* 12: 105–125.

_____. 1979. "Measuring intrafamily conflict and violence: The conflict tactics (CT) scale." *Journal of Marriage and the Family, 41,* 75–88.

_____. 1993. "Identifying offenders in criminal justice research on domestic assault." *American Behavioral Scientist,* 36 (5): 587–600.

_____. 1994. *Beating the devil out of them: Corporal punishment in American families.* San Francisco: Jossey-Bass/Lexington Books.

_____. 1999. "The controversy over domestic violence by women: A methodological, theoretical, and sociology of science analysis." In *Violence in intimate relationships,* eds. X Arriaga and S. Oskamp, 17–44. Thousand Oaks, CA: Sage.

_____. 2000. "Corporal punishment and primary prevention of physical abuse." *Child Abuse and Neglect* 24 (9): 1109–1114.

_____. 2005. "Women's violence toward men is a serious social problem." In *Current contro-*

versies on family violence, 2d ed., eds. D. R. Loseke, R. J. Gelles, and M. M. Cavanaugh, 55–77. Newbury Park, CA: Sage.

_____. 2006. "Future research on gender symmetry in physical assaults on partners." *Violence Against Women* 12 (11): 1086–1097.

_____, and R. J. Gelles. 1990. *Physical violence in American families: Risk factors and adaptations to violence in 8,145 families.* New Brunswick NJ: Transaction.

_____, _____, and S. Steinmetz. 1980. *Behind closed doors: Violence in the American family.* Garden City, NJ: Anchor Press.

_____, G. Kaufman Kantor, and D. W. Moore. 1997. "Change in cultural norms approving marital violence: From 1968 to 1994." In *Out of the darkness: Contemporary perspectives on family violence,* eds. G. Kaufman Kantor and J. L, Jasinski. Thousand Oaks, CA: Sage.

Street, A. E., and I. Arias. 2001. "Psychological abuse and posttraumatic stress disorder in battered women: Examining the roles of shame and guilt." *Violence and Victims* 16 (1): 65–78.

Strube, M. J. 1988. "The decision to leave an abusive relationship: Empirical evidence and theoretical issues." *Psychological Bulletin* 104: 236–250.

_____, and L. S. Barbour. 1983. "The decision to leave an abusive relationship: Economic dependence and psychological commitment." *Journal of Marriage and the Family* 45: 785–793.

_____, and _____. 1984. "Factors related to the decision to leave an abusive relationship." *Journal of Marriage and the Family* 46: 837–844.

Stubbs, J. 1992. "The (un)reasonable battered woman? A response to Easteal." *Current Issues in Criminal Justice* 3 (3): 359–361.

_____, and J. Tolmie. 1999. "Falling short of the challenge? A comparative assessment of the Australian use of expert evidence on the battered woman syndrome." *Melbourne University Law Review* 23 (709).

Sugarman, D. B., and S. L. Frankel. 1996. "Patriarchal ideology and wife-assault: A meta-analytic review." *Journal of Family Violence,* 11 (1): 13–39.

_____, and G. T. Hotaling. 1989. "Dating violence: Prevalence, context, and risk markers." In *Violence in dating relationships: Emerging social issues,* eds. M. Pirog-Good, and J. E. Stets. New York: Praeger.

Sunnafrank, M., and N.E. Fontes. 1983. "General and crime related stereotypes and influence on juridic decisions." *Cornell Journal of Social Relations* 17: 1–15.

Swan, S., L. Gambone, A. Fields, T. Sullivan, and D. Snow. 2005. "Women who use violence in intimate relationships: The role of anger, victimization, and symptoms of post-traumatic stress and depression." Women's and men's use of interpersonal violence. *Violence and Victims*, special issue 20 (3): 267–285.

_____, and D. L. Snow. 2003. "Behavioral and psychological differences among abused women who use violence in intimate relationships." *Violence Against Women* 9: 75–109.

_____, and _____. 2006. "The development of a theory of women's use of violence in intimate relationships." *Violence Against Women* 12 (11): 1026–1045.

Swanberg, J., and T. Logan. 2005. "The effects of intimate partner violence on women's labor force attachment: Experiences of women living in rural and urban Kentucky." *Journal of Occupational Health Psychology* 10, 1: 3–17.

_____, T. K. Logan, and C. Macke. 2006. "Intimate partner violence, women, and work: coping on the job." *Violence and Victims* 21 (5): 561–578.

Tabachnick, B. G., and L. S. Fidell. 1989. *Using multivariate statistics*, 2d ed. CA: Harper College Publishers.

Terrance, C., and K. Matheson. 2003. "Undermining reasonableness: Expert testimony in a case involving a battered woman who kills." *Psychology of Women Quarterly* 27: 37–45.

_____, _____, and N. P. Spanos. 2000. "Effects of judicial instructions and case characteristics in a mock jury trial of battered women who kill." *Law and Human Behavior* 24 (2): 207–229.

Thurman v. City of Torrington, 595 F. Supp. 1521 (Dist. Ct. Conn. 1984).

Thyfault, R. K. 1984. "Self-defense: Battered women syndrome on trial." *California Western Law Review* 20: 319–334.

Tifft, L. L. 1993. *Battering of women: The failure of intervention and the case for prevention*. Boulder: Westview Press.

Tjaden, P., and N. Thoennes. 1998. *Prevalence, incidence and consequences of violence against women: Findings from the National Violence Against Women Survey*. Washington, D.C. National Institute of Justice.

_____, and _____. 2000. *Extent, nature, and consequences of intimate partner violence: Findings from the National Violence against Women Survey*. Washington, D.C.: Bureau of Justice Statistics.

Tolman, R. M. and J. Raphael. 2000. "A review of research on welfare and domestic violence." *Journal of Social Issues* 56: 655–682.

Town of Castle Rock v. Gonzales, 125 S. Ct. 2796, 162 L. Ed. 2d 658 (Colo. 2005).

Turell, S. C. 2000. "A descriptive analysis of same-sex relationship violence for a diverse same." *Journal of Family Violence* 15: 281–293.

Turley, K. J., L. J. Sanna, and R. L. Reiter. 1995. "Counterfactual thinking and perceptions of rape." *Basic and Applied Social Psychology* 17 (3): 285–303.

Tversky, A., and D. Kahneman. 1974. "Judgment under uncertainty: Heuristics and biases." *Science* 185: 1124–1130.

"Understanding Intimate Partner Violence Fact Sheet" 2006. Atlanta, GA: Center for Disease Control (CDC), *http://www.cdc.gov/ncipc/dvp /ipv.faactsheet.pdf* (accessed February, 20, 2008).

Uniform crime reports. See FBI.

U.S. Bureau of Justice Statistics. 1991. *Criminal victimization in the United States, 1989.* Washington, D.C.: U.S. Department of Justice.

U.S. Crime Survey. 1990. *Report.* Washington, D.C: U.S. Department of Justice.

U.S. Department of Justice. 1983. *Report to the nation on crime and justice: The data.* Washington, D.C.: U. S. Department of Justice.

U.S. Judicial Conference. 1995, Summer. *Report of the proceedings of the judicial conference of the United States, 23–24.*

U.S. v. Dixon, 04–10250 5th Cir. (2005)

U.S. v. Gaviria, 804 F. Supp 476 (E.D.N.Y. 1992).

Vogel, L. C. M., and L. L. Marshall. 2001. "PTSD symptoms and partner abuser: Low income women at risk." *Journal of Traumatic Stress* 14 (3): 569–584.

Walker, L. 1979. *The battered woman.* New York: Harper and Row.

_____. 1984. *The battered woman syndrome.* New York: Springer.

_____. 1987. "Inadequacies of the masochistic personality disorder diagnosis for women." *Journal of Personality Disorders* 1 (2): 183–189.

_____, and J. Monahan. 1987. "Social frameworks: A new use of social science in law." *Virginia Law Review* 73: 559–598.

Walker, L. E. 1993. "The battered woman syndrome is a psychological consequence of abuse." In *Current controversies on family violence*, 1st ed., eds. R. J. Gelles, and D. R. Loseke, 133–153. Newbury Park, CA: Sage.

_____, R. K. Thyfault, and A. Browne. 1982. "Beyond the juror's ken: Battered women." *Vermont Law Review* 7: 1–14.

Walker, L. E. A. 1995. "Current perspectives on men who batter women—implications for intervention and treatment to stop violence against women: Comment on Gottman et al." *Journal of Family Psychology* 9 (3): 264–271.

Walker, R., T. K. Logan, C. Jordan, and J. Campbell. 2004. "An integrative review of separation in the context of victimization: Consequences and implications for women." *Trauma, Violence, & Abuse* 5 (2): 143–193.

Ward, R., Jr., and J. Muldoon. 2007. "Female tactics and strategies of intimate partner violence: A study of incident reports." *Sociological Spectrum* 27 (4): 337–364.

Warren, J., and W. Lanning. 1992. "Sex role beliefs, control, and social isolation of battered women." *Journal of Family Violence* 7 (1): 1–8.

Washington v. Wanrow. See *State v. Wanrow.*

Watt, A. 2004. "Jury hoodwinked or husband really battered?" Washington State Minority and Justice Commission, Annual Report, 2001. http://www.courts.wa.gov/committee/pdf/MJCAnnual2001.pdf#xml=http://206.194.185.202/texis/search/pdfhi.txt?query=Washington+State+minority+and+justice+commission+2001&pr=www&prox=page&rorder=500&rprox=500&rdfreq=500&rwfreq=500&rlead=500&rdepth=0&sufs=0&order=r&cq=&id=475518b31b (accessed July, 2007).

Wells, G. L., and I. Gavanski. 1989. "Mental simulation of causality." *Journal of Personality and Social Psychology* 56: 161–169.

_____, B. R. Taylor, and J. W. Turtle. 1987. "The undoing of scenarios." *Journal of Personality and Social Psychology* 53: 421–430.

West, C. M. 2002. "Black battered women: New directions for research and black feminist theory." In *Charting a new course for feminist psychology*, eds. L. H. Collins, M. R. Dunlap, and J. C. Chrisler, 216–237. Westport, CT: Praeger Publishers/Greenwood Publishing Group, Inc.

"Where the injured fly for justice." A Ten-Year Retrospect on the Report and Recommendations of the Florida Supreme Court Racial and Ethnic Bias Study Commission, 2000. http://www.flcourts.org/gen_public/family/diversity/bin/bias_study2.pdf (accessed June 2007).

Whitaker, D. J., T. Haileyesus, M. Swahn, and L. S. Saltzman. 2007. "Differences in the frequency of violence and reported injury between relationships with reciprocal and nonreciprocal interpersonal violence." *American Journal of Public Health* 97 (5): 941–947.

Wiener, R.L. 1995. "Social analytic jurisprudence in sexual harassment litigation: The role of social framework and social fact." *Journal of Social Issues* 61 (1): 167–180.

_____, M. Gaborit, C. C. Pritchard, E. M. McDonough, C. R. Staebler, D. C. Wiley, and K. S. Goldkamp. 1994. "Counterfactual thinking in mock juror assessments of negligence: A preliminary investigation." *Behavioral Sciences and the Law* 12: 89–102.

_____, K. Habert, G. Shkodriani, and C. Staebler. 1991. "The social psychology of jury nullification: Predicting when jurors disobey the law." *Journal of Applied Social Psychology* 21: 1379–1401.

_____, L. Hurt, B. L. Russell, K. Mannen, and C. Gasper. 1997. "Perceptions of sexual harassment: The effects of gender, legal standard, and ambivalent sexism." *Law and Human Behavior* 21 (1): 71–93.

_____, and C. C. Pritchard. 1994. "Negligence law and mental mutation: A social inference model of apportioning fault." *Social psychological applications to social issues.* In *Applications of heuristics and biases to social issues*, vol. 3, eds. L. Heath, R. S. Tindale, J. Edwards, E. J. Posavac, F. B. Bryant, E. Henderson-King, Y. Suarez-Balcazar, and J. Meyers. New York: Plenum Press.

Williams, C. W., P. R. Lees-Haley, and R. S. Brown. 1993. "Human response to traumatic events: An integration of counterfactual thinking, hindsight bias, and attribution theory." *Psychological Reports* 72: 483–494.

Williams, S., and I. Frieze. 2005. "Courtship behaviors, relationship violence, and breakup persistence in college men and women." *Female violence against intimate partners. Psychology of Women Quarterly,* special issue 29 (3): 248–257.

Willis, C. E. 1992. "The effect of sex role stereotype, victim and defendant race, and prior relationship on rape culpability attributions." *Sex Roles* 26 (5–6): 213–227.

Willson, P., J. McFarlane, A. Malecha, K. Watson, D. Lemmey, P. Schultz, J. Gist, and N. Fredland. 2000. "Severity of violence against women by intimate partners and associated use of alcohol and/or illicit drugs by the perpetrator." *Journal of Interpersonal Violence* 15: 996–1008.

Wilson, M., and M. Daley. 1992. "Who kills whom in spouse killings? On the exceptional sex ratio of spousal homicides in the United States." *Criminology* 20: 189–215.

Winn, R.G., L. M. Haugen, and N. C. Jurik. 1988. "A comparison of the situational determinants of males and females convicted of murder." Presented at the annual meeting of the Academy of Criminal Justice Sciences.

Wisner, C., T. Gilmer, L. Saltzman, and T. Zink. 1999, June. "Intimate partner violence against women: Do victims cost health plans more?" *Journal of Family Practice.*

Woffordt, S., D. E. Mihalic, and S. Menard. 1994. "Continuities in marital Violence." *Journal of Family Violence* 9: 195–225.

Wolak, J., and D. Finkelhor. 1998. "Children exposed to partner violence." In *Partner violence: A comprehensive review of 20 years of research*, eds. J. L. Jasinski and L. M. Williams, 73–112. Thousand Oaks, CA: Sage.

Wolfgang, M., and F. Feracutti. 1982. *The subculture of violence*. 2d ed. London: Tavistock.

Worden, A. P., and B. E. Carlson. 2005. "Attitudes and beliefs about domestic violence: Results of a public opinion survey: II. Beliefs about causes." *Journal of Interpersonal Violence* 20 (10): 1219–1243.

Yarmey, A. D., and S. Kruschenske. 1995. "Facial stereotypes of battered women and battered women who kill." *Journal of Applied Social Psychology* 25: 338–352.

Yllo, K. A. 1993. "Through a feminist lens: Gender, power and violence." In *Current controversies on family violence*, ed. R. J. Gelles. Newbury Park: Sage.

_____. 2005. "Through a feminist lens: Gender, diversity, and violence: Extending the feminist framework." In *Current controversies on family violence*, eds. D. R. Loseke, R. J. Gelles, and M. M. Cavanaugh. Thousand Oaks: Sage.

_____, L. Gary, E. H. Newberger, J. Pandolfino, and S. Schechter. 1992. *Pregnant women abuse and adverse birth outcomes*. Paper presented at the annual meeting of the Society for Applied Sociology, Cleveland, OH.

Zlotnick, C., R. Kohn, J. Peterson, and T. Pearlstein. 1998. "Partners physical victimization in a national sample of American families: Relationship to psychological functioning, psychosocial factors, and gender." *Journal of Interpersonal Violence* 13: 156–166.

Index